Eliza M. Lavin, John Q Reed

Needle-Craft

Artistic and practical

Eliza M. Lavin, John Q Reed

Needle-Craft
Artistic and practical

ISBN/EAN: 9783337373740

Printed in Europe, USA, Canada, Australia, Japan

Cover: Foto ©Andreas Hilbeck / pixelio.de

More available books at **www.hansebooks.com**

METROPOLITAN ART SERIES.

NEEDLE-CRAFT:

ARTISTIC AND PRACTICAL.

NEW YORK:
THE BUTTERICK PUBLISHING COMPANY, (Limited).
1889.

INTRODUCTION.

THERE is no subject which receives a greater share of attention than that of home decoration, and among the many books devoted to the consideration of various interests, none is more carefully read or more fairly condemned or approved, than those which are published for the aid and instruction of home-makers who are constantly looking about for helpful hints and suggestions. Much that is artistic is often impracticable, because it does not come within the possibilities of busy women, whose time must be carefully apportioned. Again, a great many of the beautiful designs furnished for home decoration are compatible only with certain modern styles of architecture and special furnishings. Pretty things that are not too capricious in style nor too extravagant in their requirements of material and labor are the most adaptable to the majority of homes, which owe their attractiveness to the busy fingers of wives and daughters.

The actual value of decoration depends on its relation to surrounding objects, and designs which can be adapted to simple as well as to elaborately furnished rooms are the best aids to the woman whose efforts to make her home beautiful may make her acquainted with many implements beside palette and brush.

This book is the first in a series devoted to home art. In it are included many of the numberless objects of use and beauty which deft fingers and artistic tastes enable a lady to provide at trifling or moderate expense, according to her means and inclination, for the adornment of her home. In the remainder of the series a still greater number of fancy and practical articles will be illustrated and described. Upon its merits as a help to those who desire the aid of such a book, the initial volume is offered to home artists.

THE BUTTERICK PUBLISHING COMPANY,

(LIMITED).

CONTENTS.

NEEDLE-CRAFT.

CONTENTS.

CONTENTS.

CONTENTS.

✳ NEEDLE ✳ CRAFT. ✳

CHAPTER I.

WHAT IS ARTISTIC NEEDLE-WORK?

"Man to the field, and woman to the hearth,
Man with the sword, *and with the needle she* ;
Man with the head, and woman with the heart ;
Man to command, and woman to obey."

AFTER reading the lines quoted, no one would expect a man to answer the question, "What is artistic needle-work?" But curiously enough the qualities which earn for needle-work the adjective "artistic" are those which men as well as women are quick to perceive and admire. Nowadays the value of beauty is gauged largely by its relation to utility, and any product of the needle which not only serves a useful purpose, but adds a touch of beauty to an otherwise plain object is rightfully considered artistic. With both head and heart womankind essays to render her needle useful in imparting attractiveness to the numerous belongings of home, and the results are often beautiful, and rarely unworthy of commendation.

More than eight centuries ago was wrought the famous Bayeux tapestry, which is to-day a highly prized relic of ancient needle-work.

It is only about half a yard wide, but is nearly seventy-five yards in length, and upon it Matilda, the pious Norman Princess, and her ladies wrought a scenic history of the invasion and conquest of Britain by Duke William. As a relic and as a monument of industry and patience it is most valuable, and its merits appreciate in proportion to its faults ; for certainly such an accomplishment must reflect credit upon those who encompassed it at a time when the materials for such work were none of the best and the highest approval accorded it could not be termed an incentive toward artistic results. But it remains as a monument of woman's ingenuity, and we who gazed upon it when it was unrolled in this city, could not but ponder upon its weird and intricate history, apart from its association with events which all the civilized world may now read of around the evening lamp ; and we willingly forgave the observer who stated that "even a casual observation of the Bayeux tapestry quite reconciled any one to living in an age which decorated its whisk-broom handles," for the happy mistress of the tiniest cottage would not care to accept this specimen of ancient needle-work, if she were obliged to look at it constantly. As a result achieved under unfavorable circumstances and conditions, it however teaches a valuable lesson.

Nowadays all the aids which taste and ingenuity can devise are supplied to those who desire to use the needle in the cause of home decoration, and those who take delight in making their homes beautiful are eager to seize each opportunity for varying or increasing their efforts. The *Delineator* has long been highly prized for the help it has afforded in this respect alone, and new subscribers in large numbers have written to us, asking for instructions regarding fancy-work illustrated previous to the time when their subscriptions began. Whenever practicable, information on the subject has been afforded them, but the rapid and steady increase in the circulation of the magazine has often made it impossible to furnish back numbers. Appreciating the desire of our patrons for a complete and connected book possessing the same practical and artistic value that has always characterized the specimens of fancy-work illustrated in the *Delineator*, we have collected within the pages of NEEDLE-CRAFT the choicest illustrations of such articles of use and beauty as are most in demand at the present time, and likely to remain permanent favorites with people of cultured tastes.

Our selections have been made from the lists of those which have been published from month to month in the *Delineator*, and supplemented by many that have not been published in the magazine. We have been aided by the suggestions and requests of new subscribers who have written us for information, and we feel confident that this book will fully meet the wants of those busy homemakers and housekeepers who are constantly seeking something new in the line of decoration for their homes and belongings. Every illustration is accompanied by an accurate description of the method to be followed and the purpose which the article it represents or is intended to serve; and the book is replete with suggestions of especial value to those who are often in doubt about the best way of obtaining certain decorative effects, in producing which the needle is woman's implement.

The practicality and also the beauty of the designs illustrated are quite evident, for not a single fancy stitch, however simple or complex, is illustrated that its special application to prevailing decorative purposes is not fully explained; not a design for embroidery is illustrated that may not be transferred to paper and reproduced without difficulty on the article to which it is adapted. Indeed, the book might appropriately have been named "a complete guide to all kinds of household decoration," for it covers a range of subjects extending from the simplest towel-working to the making of the various decorative adjuncts which impart an air of refinement, and without which the most sumptuously furnished apartment is never quite satisfying.

The value of the aid to be obtained from this book is not gauged by large expenditures of money; its contents include suggestions and illustrations which the possessor of a large income will find valuable, but they are in the main intended to meet the wants of those who freely aver that they have more time than money to spend on their belongings.

We are sure that our patrons will consider themselves fully compensated for the time devoted to a perusal of the book, and that they will accept it as a convincing explanation of what artistic needle-work really is.

CHAPTER II.

MATERIALS FOR ARTISTIC NEEDLE-WORK.

" To gild refined gold, to paint the lily,
To throw a perfume on the violet,
To smooth the ice, or add another hue
Unto the rainbow, or with taper-light
To seek the beauteous eye of heaven to garnish,
Is wasteful and ridiculous excess."

THUS wrote the bard of Avon, and how truly! He, at least, understood the charm of perfection and in inimitable similes presented facts which are, alas, in principle still unheeded by wordy desecrators of much that is perfect both in ideal and reality. The charm of a golden sunset, to a real admirer, is not complete without silence. A voice dispels it, even though that voice be as sweet as the silvery note of a forest-bird—a charm in itself, but inharmonious with that entrancing the vision.

So in Art. Although we are obliged to dally with the practical to reach the ideal, no words can add to the enchantments of artistic productions. They surround the worker with an influence that is like a dream, and in it he lives, with Genius for his master and Silence for his companion.

Although ranking below the scale of high Art, the subject under discussion is one which justly receives much attention, and regarding which many inquiries have been made. Aided by our personal knowledge and all the information obtainable, we have gathered together such facts in regard to materials and stitches, with illustrations of designs, as will enable our readers to indulge, to the fullest extent of their fancy, in "artistic needlework" of every description. Its fascinations we shall not attempt to describe; the worker will discover them herself, once her design is before her and her needle threaded to begin.

Foundation Fabrics.

In commerce the word "canvas" embraces certain varieties of fabric, each with the same predominating characteristic of permitting regular cross or single stitches to be made upon it in every direction. One which is extremely desirable on account of its texture and width, is

Plain Worsted Canvas.

This canvas is woven of thick wool threads in the ordinary manner, two threads of warp and two of woof forming each square required for a cross stitch. It is generally worked in silk, crewel or *filoselle*, and is used for all the ordinary canvas work, and sometimes for furniture or piano spreads. It comes in all shades of red, blue, buff, etc., as well as in black, and occasionally in white. Its widths, like nearly every variety of canvas, are half a-yard, three-quarters, one yard, and a yard and a-half.

Silk Canvas.

This canvas is always used for fine work, which is for inspection rather than for service. It is generally embroidered in floss and beads or in either alone, and is used for glove and kerchief boxes, cases for spectacles, covers for fancy toilette cushions and boxes, and especially for bracket-lambrequins. It comes in black, white and various tints, and requires no "filling in" after the design is worked, being a sufficiently handsome fabric in itself.

Java Canvas.

This variety comes in cotton and linen, and includes the worsted canvas before mentioned. As the threads are finer, two are woven together so that four of the warp and four of the woof make the square or block marking out the stitch. It comes in all the desirable shades, colors and widths, and is used for tidies, mats, sofa-pillows, slippers, covers for stools, bags for brushes, shoes, etc.

Panama Canvas.

This fabric is straw-colored and straw-like in texture, and forms beautiful fancy articles for the table, such as baskets, mats, card-cases, etc. It is generally worked in crewel, split zephyr or silk.

Honey-Comb Canvas.

This is a cotton canvas familiar to almost every one, from the resemblance its surface bears to honey-comb, except that the mesh is square instead of hexagonal. It is worked on the surface with long stitches of single worsted run under the threads forming the squares or meshes. The worsted run in for the border is cut off or looped at some distance from the edge, to form a fringe. It is used principally for toilette-sets for bureaus and wash-stands.

Railroad or Net Canvas.

This is a stiff linen and cotton fabric in black or white, and woven in a large, open mesh. It requires double worsted to work with, and may be filled in for a background or lined. Cross and star stitches are principally used for it, but it may be worked in the same way as honey-comb canvas. It is often used for tidies and sofa-pillows.

Mummy Canvas.

This is a variety presenting the same surface as regular mummy cloth, except that it is woven in close, irregular-looking meshes. Even for experts, counting threads will be necessary for regular work on this canvas, and therefore it is not advisable for beginners. It is handsome, however, and will require no grounding or filling-in. The color is the natural linen tint, and the fabric may be worked with crewel, silk or zephyr. It is used for chair backs and seats, fancy camp-stools, cushion-covers, sofa-pillows and any article requiring a strong foundation.

Ida Canvas.

This is a new, unbleached linen canvas, which is woven in loose meshes that look as if they had once been embroidered and then had the work picked out again. It is just the thing for beginners, and is also preferred to the Java for some purposes. It is worked with single zephyr and silk floss.

Congress Canvas.

For delicate tidies, covers, etc., to be done in fine crewel, floss or *filoselle*, this canvas is especially liked. Although it is really very strong, being made of hard, twisted linen threads, it looks like coarse or heavy tarlatan, without the stiffness of and with the transparency natural to the latter fabric. It is ornamented in stripes as follows: The length required is cut, and a satin ribbon, about No. 12, is basted through the middle, and one of another color at each side, so as to leave four spaces of canvas. The ribbon is fastened down at each edge, and at the center if desired, with fancy stitches in gay flosses. A floral pattern is then stamped between the ribbons, and is embroidered in one of the South Kensington stitches in natural colors with silk floss or *filoselle*. Tassels and the fringed ends of the ribbon finish the ends, and the sides are hemmed in a fancy stitch with bright flosses. It comes in white, black and all the fancy tints, and is very dainty.

Fancy Canvases.

Ida canvas, having its surface blocked off in two-and-a-half-inch diamond squares by a Grecian pattern that is woven in, constitutes a pretty background for several varieties of decoration. The squares are decorated in any fancy design in cross or back stitch, or with appliquéed classics, the Grecian effect being left either undecorated or otherwise, as the taste directs. This canvas is suitable for tidies, toilette sets, cushion-covers, chair-backs, etc., and is seen in unbleached and cream-white.

Another fancy canvas is of worsted, and its squares are one inch and a-half in size, and are separated or marked out by inch-wide weavings in honey-comb pattern. The squares are worked in either cross-stitch or back-stitch, and in any colors harmonious with the color of the canvas. For cushions and spreads it is very handsome.

Cloth Fabrics.

Upon regular fabrics all embroidery designs have to be stamped, and are generally worked in over-and-over or back stitch with crewel or silk, or with both combined. There are several varieties, such as broadcloth, mummy cloth, felt, and French flannel; which latter is only an "artistic" rendering of the old-fashioned Canton or cotton flannel. Stand, table and piano covers, lambrequins, upholstery and wall-hangings are all made from these materials, which are soft in texture, rich in falling folds and eminently suitable for any purpose for which they are chosen. All the olives, old gold, æsthetic reds and antique blues and pinks are fashionable in embroidery materials for such fabrics.

Rug Materials.

Sackcloth—better known as coffee-bagging—burlaps and a thick, coarse, unbleached canvas are generally selected for rugs. Berlin or Germantown wools and double zephyr are the embroidering materials. The bordering may be purchased and then embroidered along its heading and sewed on, or one may be crochetted along the edge. Cross and star stitches are frequently used for rugs.

Miscellaneous Fabrics.

Scrim, a strainer-like fabric for curtains; crash, which is made into chair-backs, cushions, rugs, spreads and towels, with crewel work for the decoration; heavy linen and Bolton sheeting, and also any linen not having a glazed finish, are worked with crewels and silks. Then there are sail-cloth and fancy bed-ticking, Turkish towelling and cricketing flannel, all of which find a place on the list of fabrics for artistic needle-work, and are used for any purpose seeming appropriate.

Fine Fabrics.

The silk and velvet and plush textures used for decorative work are especially beautiful. Embroidery or floss silk, *filoselle*, chenille, beads, gold and silver threads and fancy metal ornaments are adapted to their embellishment.

Implements and Working Materials.

The proper kind of needle is one of the first considerations upon the list of

Implements.

Whether intended for silk or worsted, it should have an eye sufficiently large to allow the strand to pass through easily and without fraying, and yet not so large as to crowd the threads of the fabric. For all canvas embroidery, choose a needle with a blunt or rounded point ; but for embroidery upon close fabrics, a sharp-pointed needle must be used. A silver thimble, worn nearly smooth, or a plain ivory one, is considered best for embroidery. In embroidery upon satin or silk, two thimbles are used, one upon each hand.

In large pieces of work, and in some small ones also, it will be found necessary to use a frame. A frame like that of a slate, made of the desired size, is nice. Two hoops are often used, one large enough to slip on over the other after the latter is covered with the fabric.

The scissors should be small, very sharp and finely pointed. For cutting skeins of silk or wool into proper lengths, round-pointed shears are best.

In some of the finer designs it will be necessary to pierce small holes, and for this a bodkin is needed.

Just at present there is no material so popular among wools as the kind called

Crewel.

Away back in our childhood crewel was simply penny skeins of what we now call single zephyr, and though it worked softly and shaded beautifully, it is not so well adapted to artistic work as English crewel, which looks like coarse but even Shetland wool. It is composed of two closely-twisted strands of a soft and glossy, yet slightly wiry wool. This luster acts as an agent in shading, so that a leaf or petal done flatly and in but one tint changes its shadows or shades with every reflection of the light. This quality is considered one of its chief charms. It works in as easily and as prettily as silk, and is always used for satin stitch or a long back stitch. It comes in all tints of every shade, and is sold by the skein in small quantities and by weight in the larger ones.

Zephyr.

There are three kinds of this familiar wool —double, single and split, containing respectively eight, four and two threads. The double and single are very slightly twisted together, so that the strands can be divided for embroidery. The two strands of split zephyr are twisted as closely as crewel, and this wool is used principally for crochetting.

Germantown and Berlin Wools.

There is very little difference between these two varieties, each consisting of four strands of wiry wool twisted together a little more firmly than zephyr, but having more of the crewel finish. They are used principally for embroidering burlaps and canvas rugs, and for knitting spreads, house-sacks and shawls.

Shetland floss, which resembles these wools but is softer than either, and Shetland wool, with which every one is familiar, may also be included under this head, as both are used for knitting shawls.

Saxony Yarn.

There are two kinds of this yarn, the "two-thread" and the "three-thread," each twisted very closely. It comes in all shades, and while it is sometimes used for cross-stitch on canvas tidies, etc., it is principally used for crochetting lace, shawls, sacks, etc.

Fancy Wools.

Pompadour wool comes in all shades and is like split zephyr very loosely over-wound with fine-strand *filoselle* silk or floss.

A pretty novelty is "frosted" wool, which is extremely handsome, and comes not only in all the delicate tints but also in the *cachemire* or metal effect. The latter, of which we have a sample before us, consists of three very fine strands of black wool, each wound with a minute crimped wire of metal, two of the wires being gilt and one copper color. The effect is that of a string of very fine rainbow beads. The pale tints of blue, rose, cream, etc., are wound with silver tinsel, and the yellows with gilt. Care must be exercised in working it, as it will not pass through any but large-meshed canvas. It can be laid on the surface with the same effect as satin stitch, and fastened down with silk stitches.

Silk Materials.

Saddler's silk, embroidery silk, which comprises several kinds, floss and *filoselle* are the varieties in use. The first is used a great deal on flannels and for chain-stitch embroidery. The second is used for the main portion of any design and may be intermingled with floss to soften the edges of leaves and petals. *Filoselle* is a coarse, untwisted silk, composed of several strands of very slightly twisted threads. It is sometimes used in place of embroidery silk, especially in designs where large blossoms predominate. It shades prettily and makes a satiny surface that is very handsome. It comes in skeins like the other varieties.

Tinsel Threads.

Metallic threads and cords in gold, silver, copper and various tinsel effects are much used in artistic needle-work. They are sometimes employed separately, but more frequently they are associated with silk, chenille and crewel.

Chenille and Arasene.

These two materials are quite similar in effect, chenille being however round, while arasene is flat in strand. Both are employed for elegant embroidery, though work done with them is less durable than that developed with silk and crewels.

Embroidery Cotton.

Not only in white and the well-known Turkey-red, but also in pale blue and pink and in seal, black and navy, is good working cotton obtainable.

Crochet Thread.

For crochetting many varieties of worsted are used, and in addition there are cotton and linen threads in white and fast colors which make beautiful laces.

Linen Embroidery Thread.

The high cost of elaborate silk embroidery has led to the production of linen embroidery thread which possesses the gloss of silk, insures durability and permits of frequent laundering without danger of fading or fraying. Some of it is in very fine strands, suitable for the elaboration of fine napery, etc., while other brands are woven in the thick strands adapted to the development of strong bold designs.

Purlette Work.

Purlette is a novel and beautiful decorative material, which may be applied with most effective results upon any smooth surface. It is a fine cord, and is applied with button-hole stitches separated by regular spaces. It may be associated with any variety of Kensington stitch, and is one of the most beautifying varieties of ornamentation for table linen, cushion covers, etc. It is illustrated in another chapter.

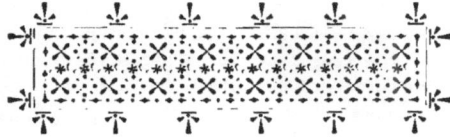

CHAPTER III.

SOUTH-KENSINGTON NEEDLE-WORK STITCHES.

South-Kensington Stitches.

T South-Kensington, some ladies of the nobility have es-
tablished an art school, in
which all styles of needle-
work, antique and modern,
are taught. One or two of
these stitches have taken
quite a hold upon the af
fections of the embroi-
dery-loving woman, and for
the want of a better name each is called
"South-Kensington stitch." It will thus be
seen that the article "a" is the appropriate
one to use, and not "the," since there is more
than one stitch belonging to the South-Kensington school. The stitch, however, which
has gone abroad in printer's ink as the South-
Kensington, is designated by this name in this
chapter.

South-Kensington Stitch.

FIGURE No. 1.—It will be seen by referring
to the engraving that it is nothing more than
a back stitch, the stitches being made to fit in
between one another with no special regularity
except to produce perfect shading. The outline of the design is stamped, and must be
perfectly even when worked; but the interior
of the petal or leaf is to be filled in according

to the shape, and shaded to the taste, or the
pattern—if there be one to copy. English
crewel is the usual working worsted for this
stitch.

South-Kensington Outline Stitch.

FIGURE No. 2.—Another stitch, known in the
school mentioned above as the "stem-stitch,"
is here called the South-Kensington outline-
stitch. It cannot be clearly explained in
words, but may be comprehended at once by
an inspection of the engraving. It forms an
unbroken outline, which appears like a finely-
twisted silk cord. It is very effective on satin,
and is used for such designs as statuary with
flowing draperies, Cupids, game, etc., looking
when finished like a fine pen-and-ink drawing.
One panel, done on old-gold satin with dark
olive embroidery silk, is exquisite. There is
no filling-in or shading—it is simply the outline that is followed, and also the strokes
which would be made with a pen to represent
drapery, or any of the other details of an
unshaded sketch. It is very effective in
foliage, butterflies, animals, etc., and may be
made upon almost any article of fancy-work,
as well as used for marking linen.

Cross Stitch.

FIGURE No. 3.—This is the first to be
learned in doing canvas-work. It is made by

a back-stitch movement, with the needle always pointing toward the left, as will be observed in the illustration, except sometimes in changing the direction of the design. Of Java or ordinary canvas two threads each way is the limit for the stitch, one-half of which crosses diagonally from left to right, and the other half in just the opposite direction. Each stitch is completed before the next is commenced, although in some instances a line of half-stitches may be made from left to right, and the other halves finished in the opposite direction.

Star Stitch.

FIGURE No. 4.—There are four varieties of this stitch, which is seldom used to delineate a design, unless upon coarse net or railroad canvas, for which the ordinary cross-stitch is not heavy enough. The illustrations delineate it very plainly, making it unnecessary to give a special description of it.

Borders in Ordinary Button-hole Stitch.

FIGURES Nos. 5, 6, 7 and 8.—These four samples show as many different methods of setting button-hole stitches along the edge of flannel, canvas, linen or whatever fabric or article requires a border of this style. The effects are produced by changing the direction of the needle when making the stitches. Silk floss, crewel, zephyr or any of the Saxony or German wools may be used for the purpose. In doing fancy-work or bordering any useful article that needs to be gay, shaded silk will be very effective in the leaf style illustrated.

Herring-bone Stitch.

FIGURE No. 9.—This is a stitch used for joining the seams of flannel in a flat manner, instead of by the usual way, thus doing away with the ridge a fell makes. Being ornamental as well as useful, it is also used for decorative purposes, and is seen upon tidies,

towels, and bands of applied ribbons or fabrics. While the work is done from left to right, the needle is set in the usual way in a sort of back-stitch, as will be seen by referring to the engraving.

Janina Stitch.

FIGURE No. 10.—This stitch has recently appeared, and is worked wholly on the surface, except where the short back-stitch occurs along the outline, in making the stitches. A back-stitch is taken at each side, inserting the point at the next to the last thread and pushing it through to the outside again below the last thread. An examination of the picture will make this clear to the reader, as the needle is set for one of the back-stitches described. The embroidery is suitable for toilette articles, small mats, and stand or table covers, and, in fact, for any purpose for which satin or any other surface stitch is used. Silk floss or English crewel is used in this embroidery.

Embossed Button-hole or Tongue Stitch.

FIGURE No. 11.—This style of stitch is much used in making borders on canvas or other materials when fringe is to be the completion for the edge, and also in embroidering monograms and initials. Two rows of running stitches are made wherever the border is to be located, and over them the button-hole stitch is made. The engraving fully explains the method of formation and further suggests the peculiar adaptability of the stitch to the purposes mentioned.

Satin Stitch.

FIGURE No. 12.—Although from time to time designs in this stitch have appeared in the *Delineator*, special instructions have not always accompanied them regarding the manner of making, as it is an old and familiar stitch. It is done in all sorts of flosses, embroidery silks, zephyrs and crewels, and

FIGURE NO. 1.—SOUTH-KENSINGTON
STITCH.

FIGURE NO. 3.—CROSS
STITCH.

FIGURE NO. 2.—SOUTH-KENSINGTON
OUTLINE STITCH.

FIGURE NO. 4.—
STAR STITCH.

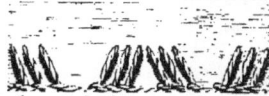

FIGURES NOS. 5, 6, 7 AND 8.—BORDERS IN ORDINARY BUTTON-HOLE
STITCH.

FIGURE NO. 9.—
HERRING-BONE
STITCH.

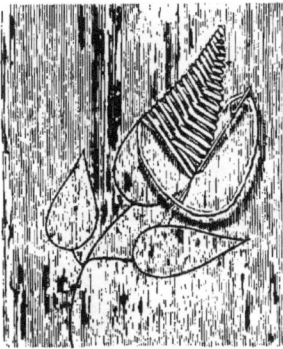

FIGURE NO. 11.—EMBOSSED
BUTTON-HOLE OR TONGUE
STITCH.

FIGURE NO. 12.—SATIN STITCH.

FIGURE NO. 10.—JANINA STITCH.

FIGURE NO. 13.—COVERED
KNOT-STITCH.

FIGURE NO. 14.—PERSIAN
CROSS-STITCH.

FIGURE NO. 15.—TAPESTRY STITCH.

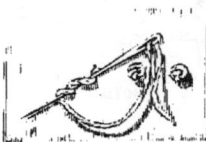

FIGURE NO. 16.—WOUND
KNOT-STITCH.

FIGURE NO. 17.—IRISH STITCH.

FIGURE NO. 18.—TENT STITCH.

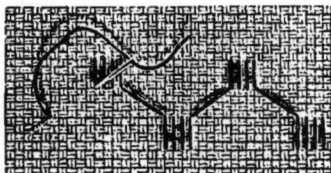

FIGURE NO. 19.—ORNAMENTAL STITCHES FOR
FLANNEL OR CANVAS.

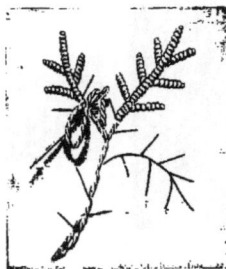

FIGURE NO. 20.—STEM STITCH.

FIGURE NO. 21.—WOUND
STITCH.

FIGURE NO. 22.—PLAIN
CHAIN-STITCH.

FIGURE NO. 23.—TWISTED
CHAIN-STITCH.

FIGURE NO. 24.—VINE
CHAIN-STITCH.

upon silk, satin, velvet, cloth and canvas. The pattern must be stamped and then "run" along all the lines with silk or worsted, and each leaf and petal, if of good size, must be crossed and recrossed with the same, all before the real embroidery begins. There must be no break in the edge of a leaf or petal, and consequently each must be carefully and evenly set. In leaves, such as the one shown in the illustration, the center is defined by the meeting of the stitches, which must be exactly even. Satin stitch is simply an over-and-over stitch, and generally both sides of the work look almost equally well.

Covered Knot-Stitch.

FIGURE No. 13.—Knot-stitches are much used in embroidering upon linen and cambric, and are usually done in linen and Moravian flosses. The engraving of Figure No.13 represents one style of knot-stitch made by taking an ordinary back-stitch, winding the floss twice about the needle and then drawing the latter through, with the left thumb held closely over the coil. The needle point is then thrust to the other side almost exactly where it came to the surface, so as to locate another knot. This stitch is frequently adopted in making initials, handkerchief-corners or any fine embroidery of that kind.

Persian Cross-Stitch.

FIGURE No. 14.—It is said that in the irregularity of this stitch, and the Oriental colors selected for it, consists its beauty when it covers a design. By varying the length of the stitch, almost any design can be copied. The silk or worsted is carried across two threads of the ground for the first half of the stitch, and is then brought up between the two threads, and the cross is made over the upper half of the long stitch. The illustration will clearly explain the method and effect.

Tapestry Stitch.

FIGURE No. 15.—It is in this stitch that the old hangings and pictures, now so valued from their antiquity, were made. Although very simple, only those having some knowledge of the art of painting should attempt anything in this stitch, as the shading must depend upon the eye and not upon a counting of the stitches. Many of the old designs were painted upon the foundation canvas, which was of great assistance to the worker; and we presume that some of the decorative art societies who are making a revival of Gobelin tapestry a specialty, will be able to furnish the same style of design. An artist in tapestry work can copy accurately from an oil-painted picture, with only the eye directing the coloring and shading. As we have before mentioned, four threads of canvas—two each way—mark out the space for one ordinary cross-stitch, and in this space two tapestry stitches are made. They are worked from left to right, crossing four threads in height and one in width with a back-stitch movement, bringing the needle out toward the worker at the bottom of the line upon which she is working. The picture illustrates clearly the effect and the method of making tapestry stitch.

Wound Knot-Stitch.

FIGURE No. 16.—This is used for the same purposes as the covered knot-stitch described, and is made as follows : The needle is set, wound and drawn through, the same as in the first stitch, and is then thrust through the outside at the place indicated by the dot above the needle. This draws the wound thread into the knot illustrated, which is just as pretty as its predecessor. This style of stitch appears universally in all fine French embroidery.

Irish Stitch.

FIGURE No. 17.—This is a "filling in" or "grounding" stitch, and is made with alternate long and short back-stitches, the short stitches of one row commencing at the ends of the long ones on the row above. It is generally done with zephyr, which is not too thick, as every perpendicular thread of the canvas is not overworked—only the spaces between. The engraving gives the idea of the effect and the manner of working. The German Stitch is done in precisely the same way as the Irish, except that the stitch crosses the canvas diagonally. By exercising a little judgment and ingenuity, it will be seen that the worsted need only cover the surface. In doing it in the regular way, the under side, as well as the upper, is covered with the zephyr, a method which many condemn.

Tent Stitch.

FIGURE No. 18.—This is simply a short stitch made over a single crossing of the canvas threads and all slanting from right to left, four tent stitches occupying the space of an ordinary cross-stitch. It produces a very fine grounding, and must be carefully and evenly done. The movement is the same as in the tapestry stitch, as will be seen by referring to the engraving, which illustrates "tent" stitch perfectly.

Ornamental Stitches for Flannel or Canvas.

FIGURE No. 19.—Although this stitch is illustrated upon canvas, where it is sometimes used in a decorative manner, it is especially adapted to flannels which require a neat finish and will not permit of an elaborate one. It can be done in white silk or floss, or in colored worsteds, as preferred, and is very pretty above a hem.

Stem Stitch.

FIGURE No. 20.—This engraving shows a style of stitch largely used in making over-wrought vines. The design is first run with floss, and then the work is done with a regular over-and-over stitch, which is clearly explained by the engraving. It is suitable for either white or colored embroidery, and is useful in vine patterns.

Wound Stitch.

FIGURE No. 21.—This is a pretty stitch for embroidering grain, small leaves, or flowers having small petals. The accompanying design shows the method by which the cord is formed. After the needle is wound, the thumb of the left hand is held firmly over it until the needle is pulled through and the coil is firmly drawn in place. Two stitches only are necessary to form each kernel. The tiny stitches seen at the ends of the kernels may be lengthened to represent the barbs on real grain, if desired. Linen or silk floss may be used in this style of embroidery.

Plain Chain-Stitch.

FIGURE No. 22.—The engraving represents the old-fashioned, plain chain-stitch, which is still used for many purposes, such as fastening the edges of appliqué work, embroidering slippers, mats, stand-covers, etc. Each stitch is made in the same way as the one for which the needle is set. The engraving explains the method better than any description can.

Twisted Chain-Stitch.

FIGURE No. 23.—This stitch is made on the same principle as the plain stitch, except that the needle, instead of being set back *into* the preceding stitch, is set at the *left* side of it. The engraving does not do full justice to the beauty of the stitch, as will be seen by making a few stitches for a trial with single zephyr. It is used along edges as headings to fringe, and sometimes to outline a design in Grecian or scroll work. Hems and tucks in flannel skirts may be stitched in this way in preference to machine or plain hand-sewing.

FIGURE NO. 25.—FANCY STITCHES AND PURLETTE WORK.

Vine Chain-Stitch.

FIGURE No. 24.—This stitch is often used upon hems, as are both the other styles, and sometimes above bindings of ribbon. It is often used to complete plain blankets, flannel petticoats, little undershirts or any article for which it seems a suitable finish. The stitches are made to the right and left alternately, and are longer and more open than the other varieties.

Fancy Stitches and Purlette Work.

FIGURE No. 25.—The fancy stitches represented in this design are developed by artistically varying and combining many of those illustrated and described on preceding pages. The exact method of their development is clearly pictured by the engraving, which also includes a very effective exposition of the work called "purlette." This is shown along the edges of the appliquéed plush sections upon the right of the engraving and in the scroll between these darker portions. It is done with a cord which is sold expressly for the purpose, and is applied with silk, Bargarran cotton, embroidery, flax, chenille or any variety of working material that can be carried with a needle. The stitch employed is a button-hole stitch made at rather long intervals. The process is clearly revealed in the engraving, and the work is effective on napery, sofa cushions, toilet towels and all articles which are commonly beautified by needle-work. A little ingenuity will enable any lady to develop this design into a size adapted to articles as large as a sofa cushion, and to separate it into sections suited to doilies or napkins. The fancy stitches may be worked inside any embroidery design done in outline stitch, with very pleasing results.

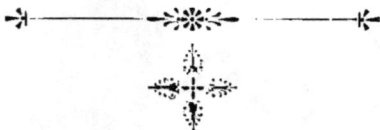

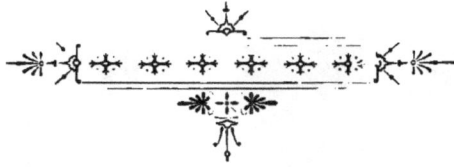

CHAPTER IV.

Embroidered Doily, and Embroidery Designs for Set of Doilies.

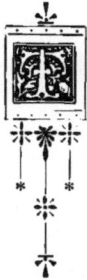

HE housewife who can embroider and do drawn-work finds much to be thankful for. The pretty doilies for tea-trays and cloths upon her table are evidences of her ability, while the dressing-tables and stand covers in the bedrooms also bear traces of her handiwork. The outline stitch is the one most favored for this work, and it is suggested that unless the worker is quite skilful it will be best to confine herself to one color in the material she selects to work with, as there is then no possibility of the so-called realistic errors being made. Scarlet is always a reliable shade, dark blue is almost as certain, and the browns and bronzes are to be commended. In doing the drawnwork much care should be taken that the threads are not pulled unevenly, as a little carelessness will result in making the doily a complete failure.

Embroidered Doily.

FIGURE No. 1.—A doily in miniature is here shown. It is embroidered in Kensington or outline stitch on linen; the border is formed of drawnwork carefully caught and the edges are fringed for a finish. The color used is a bright red and the work is very evenly done. Such doilies are in use for fingerbowls, plates and for all platters upon which fruits or small biscuits are placed.

FIGURE NO. 1.—EMBROIDERED DOILY.

Design in Embroidery for Doily.

FIGURE No. 2.—For the blossoms upon this doily a bright crimson would seem appropriate, and if chosen will, of course, also form the conventional design. For etchings, the blossoms alone will be very pretty.

FIGURE No. 4.

FIGURE No. 5

Figure No. 6.

Figure No. 7.

Design in Embroidery for Doily.

FIGURE No. 3.—This engraving, as well as the others in this department, shows the exact size the doily is to be to the first thread drawn in the border, the style of which is shown in the miniature doily. It may be made as much wider beyond this line as is desired, but the center portion should be no larger than shown. This design of carnations and blossoms is pretty done in crimson.

Design in Embroidery for Doily.

FIGURE No. 4.—This design is wrought out in dark blue, the principle probably being that in Nature grasses and leaves are so seldom blue that art should create them. If preferred, the entire set of doilies may be embroidered in the same colors, but suggestions of different shades are given, in order that individual preference may have sway.

Design in Embroidery for Doily.

FIGURE No. 5.—A dull shade of orange is used to evolve this rather Japanese-like design, which is, by-the-bye, one of the quaintest in the entire set. If preferred, brown may be substituted for the orange.

Design in Embroidery for Doily.

FIGURE No. 6.—The design here pictured may, like that showing carnations, be done in many shades of red. Dark green or blue crewel may also be effectively used for this design.

Design in Embroidery for Doily.

FIGURE No. 7.—Brown is the color of the needlework on this doily, a brown, however, with just a suggestion of gold about it and without the sombreness usually associated with the brown shades.

A Pretty Fancy.

THIS is how it was developed. A short piece of white sash-ribbon, having brocaded upon it a design of roses and their foliage, was left over from a sash. It was utilized by an ingenious young woman for the decorative portion of a chair cushion as follows :

The foliage she outlined in various shades of green representing the gamut of tints seen in the natural leaves, and some of them she rendered heavier in effect by working in considerable side-stitching, regulating its disposal to accord with the amount of shade that would fall upon leaves turned as they were. The roses were outlined with rose color and slightly shaded with side-stitching, and the plain portion of the ribbon was made the background for a lattice of gold thread, upon which the roses were apparently trained. It was then arranged diagonally across the corner of a rather flat cushion covered with electric-blue satin, and tied upon the back of a gilded chair, which illuminated as well as furnished a corner where a heavier and darker piece of furniture would have appeared sombre.

CHAPTER V.

TRAY-COVER, AND EMBROIDERY DESIGNS FOR ITS CORNERS.

IGURE No. 1.—This dainty tray-cover is made of white linen and is broadly hemmed at all its edges, the hems being generally hemstitched. A simple design is traced with narrow braid on the hems, and inside the hems square of the same fabric embroidered with white. These pieces are usually applied with hemstitching. In the corners, free from this border decoration, are embroidered designs, the correct sizes of which are given at Figures Nos. 2, 3, 4 and 5. The designs are all sprays, one showing blackberries, another a pear, another grapes, and the other cherries, all with their nat-

FIGURE No. 1.—TRAY-COVER.

are two rows of applied pieces of porcelain-blue linen in small diamond shapes, the rows being separated at each corner by a larger applied ural foliage. They are worked in Kensington outline stitch, the leaves and stems in greens and browns, and fruits in their natural colors.

A frill of the white material is the edge finish for the tray-cover and may be plainly hemmed,

FIGURE No. 2.

FIGURE No. 3.

may be chosen for the squares, old-blue, pink, terra-cotta, sage-green, vermilion, gold,

or button-hole, feather or briar stitched at the edge. Medici, torchon, antique or any

FIGURE No. 4.

FIGURE No. 5.

Nile-green, rose, crimson, etc., being desirable. The colors displayed in the china

preferred lace may be used instead of the material for the frill, and any preferred color

may be seen in the squares, with unique effect.

CHAPTER VI.

Ornamental Doily, and Embroidery Designs for a Set of Twelve.

HE designs illustrating this chapter will be appreciated very highly by ladies who take pride in the style of their table linen and toilet mats. It is now fashionable to e m b r o i d e r doilies or napkins in colored cotton, linen and wash-silks with floral designs, for use with finger bowls or under dishes of fruit or cake, following as nearly as possible the natural colors of blossoms, fruits and leaves.

Figure No. 1 on this page represents a doily all finished, and designs adapted to the embellishment of twelve doilies are included in the chapter. After a square of the desired size is cut, the center is worked as shown by the engravings numbered 2, 3, 4, etc. A few threads are then drawn from each side a short distance

FIGURE NO. 1.—FANCY DOILY.

from the edge, and the remaining threads are caught by a stout linen thread of the same color, in a hem-stitch design. A first glance at the representation of this part of the work would no doubt impress the observer with what would seem an impossible arrangement at the corners; but the effect is the result of study to overcome a difficulty experienced in washing doilies in which the threads have been fully drawn, and an open space left at each corner. The threads are clipped before being drawn, so that they will pull out only the length of the hem-stitched border at each side as illustrated. The threads that would pull out at the corners if left unsecured are firmly overcast by a linen thread of the same color, or with their own ends, which may be drawn for the purpose, from one corner to the other at the same side before they are clipped at the opposite corner. In making napkins or doilies it would be well to experiment on a piece of old material in the manner of drawing and fastening the threads.

White napery embroidered in gold silk is effective and beautiful, and many ladies will select from these engravings designs for the

FIGURE No. 2.

each corner is a floral design embroidered in the same color. The napkins are ornamented with drawn-work, and in the corner of each a floral design is worked. Linen embroidery thread, which may be obtained in a

FIGURE No. 3.

corners of table-cloths, tray-covers, tea-cloths, etc. A set of luncheon napery which is worthy of admiration comprises a cloth and twelve napkins. The cloth has the damask border along its edges, followed by chain stitching done in gold-colored silk, and in

variety of colors, is also used for the embellishment of napery. In the performance of work of this variety incongruous colors are of course avoided, but the good effect does not depend upon the choice of only those tints which are seen in the natural flowers.

Helps for Fancy Workers.

Appliquéed flowers and foliage, which may be easily attached to the surface that is to be decorated, are much valued by ladies who cannot afford the time to embroider lambrequins, scarfs, etc., and yet like to exercise their own taste in the selection of materials, tints, and style of ornamentation. Birds and

other ornamental objects adapted to a variety of uses are also obtainable, and so are plaited ribbons suitable for borderings and drop ornaments in silk and in lamb's-wool, which may be made into beautiful fringes or used to finish the ends of cords. Personal ingenuity will suggest their especial purposes.

FIGURE No. 4

FIGURE No. 5.

FIGURE No. 6.

FIGURE No. 7.

FIGURE No. 8.

FIGURE No. 9.   FIGURE No. 10.

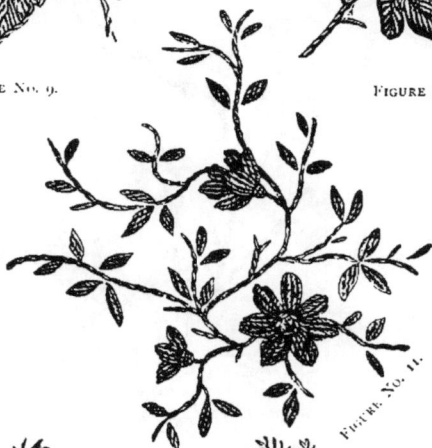

FIGURE No. 11.

FIGURE No. 12.   FIGURE No. 13.

CHAPTER VII.

OUTLINE EMBROIDERY DESIGNS.

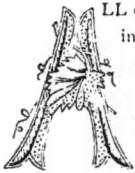

LL of the figure designs included in the present chapter, from the little darky dandy and the charming maiden making hay, to the music-master of the birds and the mischievous school-boy, are suitable for embellishing tidies, screens, fans, mats, cushions, and table and other house linen of all descriptions. The outlines wrought in short back-stitch or fine chainstitch. Cotton or linen embroidery thread

FIGURE No. 2.

in fast colors, crewels and etching silks are suitable working materials. The darky faces are imitated with indelible ink, so that they will wash nicely; but if a sable face be desired, it must be cut from a bit of black flannel or cloth and arranged as represented. The floral designs cover a still broader range in this application, and may be effectively reproduced in decorating table scarfs, lambrequins and other draperies.

FIGURE No. 1.

are generally followed in the Kensington outline stitch, but may also be

FIGURE No. 3.

FIGURE No. 1.

FIGURE No. 5.

FIGURE No. 6.

FIGURE No. 7.

FIGURE No. 8.

FIGURE No. 9.

FIGURE No. 10.

FIGURE No. 11.

FIGURE No. 12.

CHAPTER VIII.

SPRAYS OF PINKS IN CORRECT SIZES FOR EMBROIDERING.

THE flower which forms the subject of this design is one dear to the heart of the worker in decorative materials, because it is effective upon all sorts of fabrics and does not require elaborate outlay to make it seem realistic. The designs may be simply outlined as illustrated by Figure No. 2, or they may be done in South-Kensington stitch as shown by Figures No. 1 and No. 3. The leaves are in natural shades of green, and the flowers and buds of pink, red, white, or any of the tints in which the flowers appear. These designs may be appropriately used to decorate lambrequins, table scarfs, handkerchief-cases, etc.; and they may be painted or embroidered, as preferred. The sizes illustrated are in correct proportion for working and may be easily transferred.

Transferring and Stamping.

Any design for embroidering or painting illustrated in this book may be transferred to paper, and a perforated pattern made, which may be stamped upon material, ready for working. Parchment paper is the best upon which to trace the design, because it is transparent without being too thin to be perforated closely, and it does not tear easily. Lay the paper over the design to be transferred and with a lead pencil reproduce all its outlines. With a tracing wheel follow these outlines upon the paper, using care in turning curves and corners to keep to the original outlines. The next step is to lay the perforated paper upon the material that is to be decorated, with the rough side up, and rub the perforated lines lightly with any good stamping powder, taking up enough of the powder upon a bit of chamois or flannel tied over a cork to leave a clear impression along the perforations. Now remove the stamping pattern, lay a piece of tissue paper over the goods, and pass a warm iron slowly over it. If these directions are carefully followed, the design will be accurately reproduced upon the material when the tissue paper is lifted.

A blue powder is best for light materials, and upon smooth black goods a white powder may be successfully used, though if it is liable to become indistinct, it is wise to outline the principal points of the design after it is transferred to the material, with cotton.

A liquid preparation which will not run and is indelible is essential for stamping long-pile plushes and velvets. An ingenious method which may be followed without difficulty, is as follows: After the design has been traced upon parchment paper, lay the latter upon the material with the *smooth* side up and then should be thin enough to go through the perforations readily, but not so thin as to spread

FIGURE NO. 1.—SPRAY OF PINKS IN SOUTH-KENSINGTON STITCH.

with a rather stiff brush, dipped in tube paint, go over the perforations slowly. The paint upon the material, and it should be of a lighter shade than the goods, in order to produce a distinct impression. When it has dried, the pattern will be ready for working.

paper used several times. If rather heavy paper be used for designs that are reproduced

FIGURE No. 2.—SPRAYS OF PINKS
IN SOUTH-KENSINGTON
OUTLINE-STITCH.

The powder that adheres to the paper tracing may be easily brushed out and the same

with the aid of a liquid preparation or tube paint, it may be cleansed for future use by the aid of a little naphtha or turpentine. Pour either over the perforations and wipe them dry and evaporation will do the rest.

In using a tracing wheel, great care should be exercised in following circles or curves, because wherever perforations are made by the wheel, the powder or paint is very liable to sift through: hence the necessity for following the pencilled lines accurately.

FIGURE NO. 3.—SPRAYS OF PINKS IN SOUTH-KENSINGTON STITCH.

CHAPTER IX.

DESIGNS SHOWING VARIOUS EMBROIDERY STITCHES.

Open-Work Embroidery.

FIGURE No. 1.—This engraving is intended to illustrate the plan followed in making open embroidery, etc., and the stitch employed. The design is first marked or stamped, and then run with floss. Each leaf or petal is then slashed with a sharp scissors, and the material drawn back to the running with an over-and-over stitch done with coarse linen floss.

FIGURE NO. 1.—OPEN-WORK EMBROIDERY.

The style and stitch are much used in French embroidery and make light, pretty work.

Filling for Embroidered Scollops.

FIGURE No. 2.—The method illustrated for "filling in" scollops before the embroidery is done, is very successful in giving a rounded effect to the work when finished. The outlines are run, and then an under-filling,

formed of chain-stitching, is made in two rows between the outlining stitches. After this,

FIGURE NO. 2.—FILLING FOR EMBROIDERED SCOLLOPS.

the usual button-hole stitch is employed to cover the filling and complete the embroidery.

Design for Embroidery.

FIGURE No. 3.—This design will be found

FIGURE NO. 3.—DESIGN FOR EMBROIDERY.

very pretty to darn along a strip of net to form regular Breton edging.

Embroidered Bee.

FIGURE No. 4.—The Kensington stitch is used in forming the body, head and legs of the bee, and the Kensington outline-stitch in forming the wings. The colors may be selected to form a very realistic-looking bee, or may be of any preferred commingling. To embroider in connection with a spray of

FIGURE No. 4.—EMBROIDERED BEE.

flowers, etc., in positions suggesting several bees in search of honey, the design is very pretty.

Design for Bordering.

FIGURE No. 5.—This bordering is done in embossed or plain satin stitch. The latter is among the list of stitches described and illustrated on other pages, but perhaps it will not be amiss to state that it is simply an over-and-over stitch, which on the wrong side looks nearly as well as on the right. In regular designs a running is first made to give a roundness to the work, but in borders it is not required. After the border is worked in one shade, a fancy stitching is done with another shade as represented, being woven in and out through the other stitches in regular splint style. The border may be

FIGURE No. 5.—DESIGN FOR BORDERING.

worked on tidies, mats, sofa-pillows or any article requiring a finish of this description.

Butterfly for Embroidering.

FIGURE No. 6.—This represents the exact size of a butterfly for embroidering in silk or *filoselle*. A person skilled in the combination of colors may make the delineation realistic, but it will often be worked in one color alone. On silk handkerchiefs, the colors used should

FIGURE No. 6.—BUTTERFLY FOR EMBROIDERING.

accord with the ground shade, or the effect will be *bizarre*.

Blue Jay, in South-Kensington Stitch.

FIGURE No. 7.—This design, worked in blue crewel in the South-Kensington stitch, is especially suitable for scarfs, towels, tea-cloths, or *serviettes*. The stem is in brown and the leaves are in dark green, while much artistic taste may be shown in the blue shades used for the saucy bird himself. Silk, cotton or linen floss may be used instead of crewels, and, if one were not anxious to follow the

FIGURE No. 7.—BLUE JAY IN SOUTH-KENSINGTON STITCH.

pattern set by Dame Nature, the bird might be of any gorgeous coloring desired.

Flower Spray, in Satin Stitch.

FIGURE No. 8.—A spray of flowers, that shows a pretty commingling of colors, is always a delight to the worker in crewels or silk. This is done in crewels, and the leaves and stem are of carefully selected dark green tones, the petals of the blossom are of deep yellow, while the hearts are of dark brown— a combination that must be a correct one, for it is copied directly from the flowers of the field. Any of the threads used for such work may form the pretty cluster, a consideration of the background and the use to which the

FIGURE No. 8.—FLOWER SPRAY, IN SATIN STITCH.

article is to be put deciding whether very simple or very elaborate materials be used.

Bunch of Oats, in Satin Stitch.

FIGURE No. 9.—A spray, especially pretty to have scattered over a tea-tray cover or pillow-sham, is here pictured. It is done in satin stitch with dark golden cotton in this instance, but could be of any color desired. On linen for pillow-covers it might be in clear white; on a tea-tray cover it could be in scarlet, olive or yellow; while on a table-cloth of felt, plush or any fine material, gold thread might be used with good effect. A straight

row of such sprays to form a border to a towel would be in good taste, and any colors

FIGURE No. 9.—BUNCH OF OATS, IN SATIN STITCH.

desired, that would stand laundering, could then be selected.

Flower Spray.

FIGURE No. 10.—This graceful spray is embroidered in the Kensington stitch, and,

FIGURE No. 10.—FLOWER SPRAY.

while the leaves should always be done in green shades, the blossoms may be white, pink, salmon or any hue preferred. The centers of the flowers are usually done in knot stitch. On table-scarfs, lambrequins, or any article preferred, this design may be embroidered as a corner decoration, or it may be repeated to form a graceful vine, with charming results.

may be introduced, with elegant effect. Beads may be used for the eyes. Both designs may be embroidered on a scarf, in the points of lambrequins, the centers of mats or the corners of handkerchiefs. The butterfly is usually surrounded by several wasps grouped in a fanciful manner. In the corners of hand-

FIGURE No. 11.

FIGURE No. 12.

FIGURES Nos. 11 AND 12.—BUTTERFLY AND WASP, IN KENSINGTON STITCH.

FIGURE No. 13.—DESIGN FOR OUTLINE EMBROIDERY.

Butterfly and Wasp, in South-Kensington Stitch.

FIGURES Nos. 11 AND 12.—The wasp and butterfly here illustrated are done in South-Kensington stitch, and the butterfly may be as brilliant in hue as desired. Several colors

kerchiefs the designs may be white or in natural tints, as preferred.

FIGURE No. 13.—Such a design as this, suitable for the edges of a towel, a tray-cover or, indeed, any article to which it adapts itself, may be done in one or many colors in the South-Kensington or outline-stitch. Its simplicity is as attractive as it is suitable, and will undoubtedly commend it to many.

table scarf, etc. It is done in the South-Kensington outline-stitch, with flosses, crewels, etc.

FIGURE No. 15.—Rose pink for the blooms

FIGURE NO. 14.—FLORAL DESIGN, IN SOUTH-KENSINGTON OUTLINE-STITCH.

FIGURE NO. 15.—BRIAR-ROSE DESIGN, IN SOUTH-KENSINGTON OUTLINE-STITCH.

FIGURE No. 14.—This pretty design may form a border to a table cover, piano cover,

and the tips of the buds, and olive for the out line of the buds and leaves, and also for the stems, are the natural combination of colors in a design of this kind.

Kensington outline-stitch. Golden yellow and dark olive are the proper colors. The work

FIGURE NO. 16.—BUTTERCUP DESIGN, IN SOUTH KENSINGTON OUTLINE-STITCH.

FIGURE NO. 17.—PANSY DESIGN, IN OUTLINE-STITCH.

FIGURE No. 16.—This engraving illustrates a pretty design of buttercups, done in South-

is simple, and the result, when neatly accomplished, very beautiful.

FIGURE No. 17.—On lambrequins, table-scarfs, chair-scarfs, table-covers, etc., this is The design of any of the five succeeding ones may be used as a border to lambrequins,

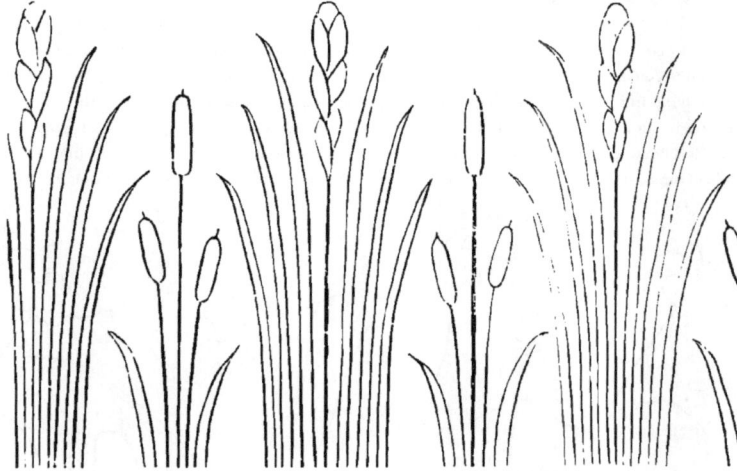

FIGURE No. 18.—SWAMP-GRASSES AND CAT-TAILS, IN SOUTH-KENSINGTON OUTLINE-STITCH.

FIGURE No. 19.—FLORAL DESIGN, IN OUTLINE-STITCH.

a pretty and graceful design. It is merely outlined with floss, embroidery silk or crewels. table-covers, piano-covers, etc., of plush, cloth, or velvet, and may be filled in with the much admired South-Kensington stitch when a rich, heavy result is desired.

FIGURE No. 18.—The grasses and cat-tails composing this design are simply outlined with colored floss or any embroidery fabric, in South-Kensington outline-stitch. The design may be filled in with the South Kensington stitch, and will look best so completed when a heavy effect is desired. On plush, cloth, flannel, damask, velvet, etc., the design

may be. Silk or linen floss, crewels, or very narrow ribbons are used for working such designs.

FIGURE No. 20.—This design is wrought in various shades of brown, but any combination of colors or any one color may be used for it. Its simplicity will commend it to those whose knowledge of embroidery is not great, while its correctness and beauty will find favor in the eye of the skilled work-woman. It may

FIGURE No. 20.—FLORAL PATTERN, IN OUTLINE-STITCH.

is very effective. When filling-in is followed, the colors should match the natural hues as nearly as possible.

FIGURE No. 19.—The daisy and cat-tail design here shown is in simple outline-stitch, it being a mere matter of taste as to whether it is done in that way or filled in. The foliage is dull green; the cat-tails, a golden brown; and the daisies, white with yellow hearts. Done in one color, this will be found a desirable pattern for towels or linen covers; and, when elaborated, it is a favorite on all artistic fabrics, no matter how elegant they

be suitably used on any article requiring a bordering.

Embroidery Design.

FIGURE No. 21.—A beautiful design for a border on table-covers, lambrequins, tidies, etc., of plush, felt-cloth, *momie* cloth, satin, velvet, etc., is here illustrated. The embroidery may be done with either satin or South-Kensington stitch in any preferred colors in floss, embroidery-silk, crewel or *filoselle*. The daisies, embroidered with yellow centers and white petals, and the leaves, in dark green, will produce a beautiful realistic effect on olive, red, brown or green. The daisy petals are effective, but not quite so complete in appearance, when formed of two long threads of floss; and in this event the rest of the caps or any decorative articles, with beautiful results. It is a tasteful selection for the embellishment of house coats or dressing gowns for gentlemen.

FIGURE NO. 21.—EMBROIDERY DESIGN.

pattern need only be outlined. This pattern is especially effective on a handsome table-cover.

Embroidery Design.

FIGURE NO. 22.—A handsome floral design,

Embroidery Design for Suspenders.

FIGURE NO. 23.—This design is done in satin stitch with silk floss of the realistic tones: the wheat being yellow, the forget-me-nots blue, and the thistle a dark purple. For

FIGURE NO. 22.—EMBROIDERY DESIGN.

done in South-Kensington stitch, is here illustrated. The design may be used for table-scarfs, table or piano covers, tidies, smoking-any article on which a vine pattern was desired, this would be especially suitable; and for ribbon strips to place as borderings on fancy aprons or drapery, it will be in good taste. Slightly enlarged, it would be pretty one for any garment or drapery requiring a running design, and to any one at all familiar

FIGURE NO. 23.—EMBROIDERY DESIGN FOR SUSPENDERS.

on a towel; and, in its present size, it is proper for a tea-tray cover. with the stitch will be found a very simple example of it. If desired, split zephyr may

FIGURE NO. 24.—FLORAL DESIGN, IN SOUTH-KENSINGTON STITCH.

Floral Design in South-Kensington Stitch.

FIGURE No 24.—This design of roses and be used, instead of crewels or floss, on flannels or any woolen materials.

FIGURE NO. 25.—DECORATED STRIP FOR BORDERS.

foliage may be done in fine white, or some taste may be displayed in the use of natural colors. The pattern will be found a pretty

Decorated Strip for Borders.

FIGURE No. 25.—This engraving illustrates a strip of velvet decorated with applied leaves of brilliant Autumn colorings. The leaves were selected from a line of manufactured floral *appliqués*, and may be obtained in every variety. They are arranged in a vine design, and the stems are done in outline-stitch. For a center strip for a chair, a border to a scarf, lambrequin or table-cover, etc., the strip is very handsome and graceful.

Design in South-Kensington Stitch.

FIGURE No. 26.—For the corners of hand-kerchiefs, or for decorating tidies, mats, lam-brequins, *mouchoir*-cases or any fancy article, this design is graceful and pretty. The bird may show the natural tintings of its plumage, and the bough, grasses, etc., may be olive

FIGURE No. 26.—DESIGN IN SOUTH-KENSINGTON STITCH.

green, dark green or any desirable shade in green or brown. Silver or gray is very pretty for the bough, with green and brown for the grasses and cat-tails. The stitch is the well known South-Kensington stitch, and is simple and effective. This design will often be developed in various colors, as corner decora-tions for handkerchiefs.

Cat's Head, in South-Kensington Stitch.

FIGURE No. 27.—This engraving shows a design that may be applied to the corners of handkerchiefs, or to the corners or centers of any articles for which such a design is required or considered appropriate. The tints selected must depend upon the taste, shaded gray, brown and wood colors being

FIGURE No. 27.—CAT'S HEAD, IN SOUTH-KENSING-TON STITCH.

generally used. The wood color is selected for the present example, with black for the eyes and tip of the nose, and red for the mouth.

Design in South-Kensington Stitch.

FIGURE No. 28.—The most brilliant shades of brown, together with dense shades of the same color, are selected in embroidering the

FIGURE No. 28.—DESIGN IN SOUTH-KENSINGTON STITCH.

butterfly and cat-tail here represented. The design may have gay colors for the butterfly, if desired. The plain Kensington stitch is here used, as by it the shading can be most properly done.

Design in South-Kensington Outline-Stitch.

FIGURE No. 29.—This design is done in straw color, and black, seal-brown and *écru* shades of silk floss. A trifle of green, needed for the wheat-leaves, is also seen. Any other

FIGURE No. 29.—DESIGN IN SOUTH-KENSINGTON OUTLINE-STITCH.

combination of colors may be used for the butterfly, and, as Nature has provided such a multitude of animated designs, we do not see the need of making original suggestions as to the colors to be used.

Embroidery Designs in Satin Stitch.

FIGURES Nos. 30 AND 31.—These two engravings illustrate rich and effective designs which are developed in satin stitch. They are adapted to the elaboration of any article for which a rich decoration is desired, and are especially suitable for the ornamentation of smoking-caps, being in the correct sizes for caps cut by pattern No. 1914 which is illustrated in the Metropolitan Catalogue and costs 15 cents. The designs being conventional ones may be duplicated in any color. Silks, crewels and chenilles are suitable for working them.

Kensington Painting.

ANY variety of decorative work having its name prefixed by the word "Kensington" is certain to receive attention, and when it possesses the artistic merits of Kensington painting it is equally certain of being permanently admired. A great many of the designs illustrated in this book as being suitable for Kensington embroidery are equally appropriate for Kensington painting. The shading in Kensington painting bears marked resemblance to the arrangement of stitches in Kensington embroidery, and any one who understands the latter kind of needle-work and has a general knowledge of the blending of shades and the merest rudiments of decorative painting may attempt Kensington painting with a certainty of success.

The designs that best repay the worker for her time and effort are those which permit of strong, bold touches. Amongst floral selections those with bright blossoms are preferable. Birds, cats, dogs' heads, etc., are effectively represented upon artists'-board, blotting-paper, felt, plush with a short, thick nap, and velvet. If one be skilled in drawing, the design may be roughly sketched in outline, but if not it may be stamped according to the directions for transferring and stamping given on another page.

Tube paints are used, being adapted to the work without being thinned or reduced. All the outlining and all the sharp strokes are done with a rather long steel pen, that is heavy enough to bear some pressure, without spreading so as to weaken the nib after the first stroke.

After deciding on the colors and mixing those that are necessary upon the palette, take the pen-holder in the hand, with the hollow side of the pen upward, and take up as much paint in it as it will hold without allowing any to run over the edges. Clean off the back of the pen thoroughly with an easel rag, and still holding it with the back downward in 'scoop fashion, draw the point ° back toward the material. After the outlining is done the pen is filled with paint, and the petals are filled or covered with paint, which is applied in pen strokes that are drawn

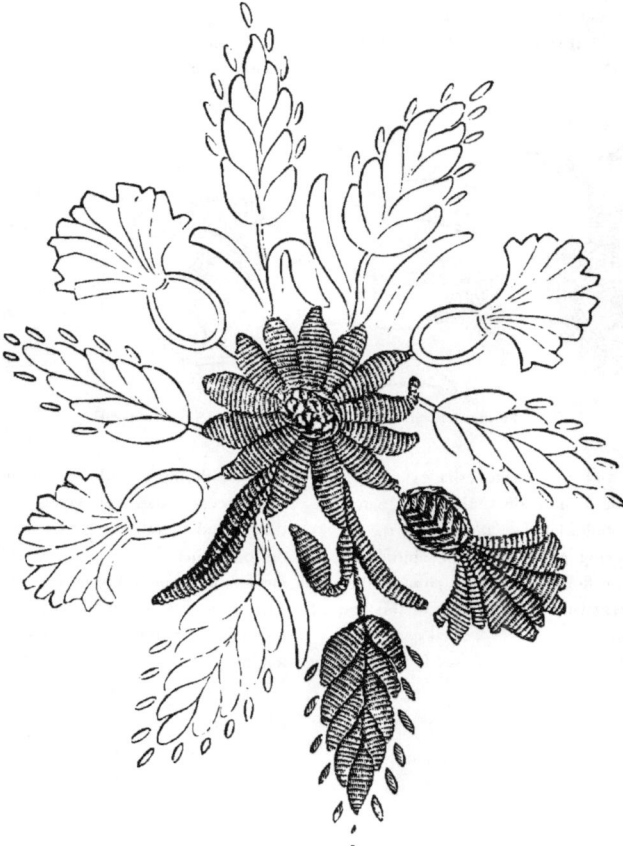

FIGURE NO. 30.—DESIGN IN SATIN STITCH.

over the outlines, turning the nib a trifle along the outside to produce distinct edges, and turning it to the right or left, according to the direction of these edges, but always keeping the toward the center in the same manner as the stitches are taken in embroidery, the embroidered effect being further heightened by scratching the blended paint with the point of the pen, or with a needle. The tendency of the paint to form itself into little rolls as it leaves the pen aids the worker in producing a realistic effect; and these rolls may be drawn toward the center in a way to greatly increase the light and shade effect, the thickest portion being left where it is desired to have the shade darkest. The principal colors are first of painting, although if the design be a large one the paint may be applied inside the outlines faster with a brush than with a pen; and for flowers with thick clustered blossoms, such as sumac and golden-rod the brush is essential, though the Kensington stitch effect is only attainable by the use of the pen. Good results cannot be assured unless plenty of

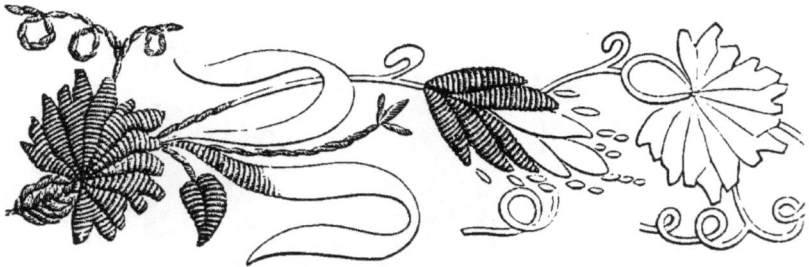

FIGURE NO. 31.—EMBROIDERY DESIGN IN SATIN STITCH.

applied and the darker shades next, after which the lighter tints are added and the shading and blending done, with the object that is being painted kept in mind. A good study or, if flowers are being painted, the natural blossoms, are useful aids in this part of the work.

Brushes are not much used for this variety time for drying be allowed, because part of the process consists in laying the paint on thickly and permitting it to remain in the little rolls which imitate stitches. The re-touching can be done a day or two after the first part of the work is completed, but the making up should be deferred if possible somewhat longer.

CHAPTER X.

Embroidery Designs, Especially Adapted to the Decoration of Articles of Dress.

THIS chapter includes descriptions and illustrations of several varieties of fancy-work and embroidery stitches which are often employed in the decoration or finishing of wearing apparel, and they are for this reason grouped by themselves instead of being distributed among those which are limited in their application to articles of household adornment.

Floral Embroidery Designs.

FIGURES NOS. 1 and 2. — These designs are here given in their proper sizes. The sprays are pretty and graceful, and may be done in solid embroidery, in outline stitch, or in a side stitch such as is shown in the flowers; or they may be cut from velvet, plush, satin or silk and applied with button-hole stitches. The leaves are usually veined after being otherwise finished. The centers of the flowers should be done in knot stitch to be effective. The "side" stitch combines long and short stitches in the manner illustrated; care must be taken to slant the stitches down the sides of the petals in the manner illustrated, or else the shape of the

petals will not be graceful. Sometimes flowers of this kind are embroidered in darning stitch, and the leaves are done in Kensington stitch or else in appliqué work. They are especially pretty upon tea-gowns and house jackets.

Spray of Roses for Decoration.

FIGURE NO. 3.—A rose with its buds and foliage is here shown developed in pink plush and shaded green arrasene for decorative purposes. Suitable for lambrequins, portières, cushions, or, indeed, any large background allowing such decoration, its uses are many. The rose and buds are cut from small pieces of plush, while arrasene is used in applying them and forming the leaves. Any shade of plush preferred may be chosen, clear white, deep cream and pale or deep yellow, all being colors that the queen of flowers takes unto herself.

Section of Rose-Bud.

FIGURE NO. 4.—The rose-bud petal in its full size, after the seams have been taken off, is here shown. Two or three are required for each bud, according to the size desired and the disposition of the sections.

FIGURES NOS. 1 AND 2.—FLORAL EMBROIDERY DESIGNS.

Section of Rose.

FIGURE NO. 5.—One section or petal of the rose itself is here shown in full size after the sewing; five such pieces are required, and, if artistically arranged, they may be of different shades, though a novice in doing appliqué work will be acting wisely in only having one tone.

FIGURE NO. 5.—SECTION OF ROSE.

FIGURE NO. 4.—SECTION OF ROSE-BUD.

FIGURE NO. 3.—SPRAY OF ROSES FOR DECORATION

Anchor and Star in Satin Stitch.

FIGURES NOS. 6 and 7.—These pretty ornaments in embroidery for the collars and cuffs of the sailor style of sea-side and mountain costumes are done in satin stitch with silk or linen floss in any preferred colors.

circles of the desired sizes are drawn on the article to be decorated, and the stitches, which are effective arrangements of the button-hole cord and long stitches, worked over them. Coins may be used to describe the circles, if a compass be not at hand.

FIGURE No. 6.—ANCHOR IN SATIN STITCH.

FIGURE No. 7.—STAR IN SATIN STITCH.

The designs will generally be used separately, and are of the proper size for girls'

FIGURE No. 8 illustrates the long stitches forming a star in the center of the design

FIGURE No. 8.   FIGURE No. 9.   FIGURE No. 10.   FIGURE No. 11   FIGURE No. 12.

 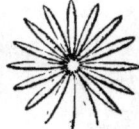 

FIGURE No. 13.   FIGURE No. 15.

FIGURE No. 14.
FIGURES NOS. 8 TO 15.—DESIGNS OF FANCY STITCHES.

and misses' costumes or for the costumes of ladies of small stature.

Designs of Fancy Stitches.

FIGURES NOS. 8 to 15.— These fancy designs in ornamental stitching, which may be used with gorgeous effect on tea and fancy-work aprons, as well as on table, chair and

and detached long stitches forming V's between the rays of the star.

FIGURE No. 9 shows a circle of chain stitches, which are made by sewing toward you and holding the thread under the needle to form a series of uniform loop stitches.

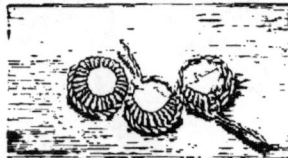

FIGURE No. 16.—STITCHES FOR EYELET-HOLES.

other scarfs, are illustrated in the above figures. In every instance circles or parts of

At Figure No. 10 is seen a circle of button-hole stitches, and Figures Nos. 13 and 15 illustrate parts of circles worked in button-hole stitch.

FIGURE No. 11 is a circle done in cord stitch, which is nothing more than slanting over-and-over stitches made close together.

FIGURE No. 12 is made of evenly spaced long stitches done between two circles of different sizes in pairs that form V's.

outline is first run by a single thread of floss, after which two or three other threads are run in at the lower half to make it appear wider and heavier. The cloth is then slightly cut, and the edges drawn in by the stitches. The thin part of the eyelet is worked in a plain over-and-over stitch, while the wide part is done in button-hole stitch.

FIGURE No. 17.—DESIGNED IN DAISY SPRAYS.

FIGURE No. 14 is a star formed of long stitches radiating from a center.

Stitches for Eyelet-Holes.

FIGURE No. 16. — This engraving shows a method of making the eyelet-holes seen in much of the French embroidery. The plain

This style of embroidery is considered pretty for making scollops and blossoms.

Design in Daisy Sprays.

FIGURE No. 17.—On any article of ornament this pretty design may be worked. A tea-gown having the center front similarly embroidered is especially artistic and does not require a large outlay. The daisy petals are formed of narrow gros-grain ribbon, known as 'daisy ribbon, and the centers are of golden floss in knot stitch. The petals and stems are worked in South-Kensington stitch with flosses, crewels, chenille or arrasene or embroidery silks in the required colors. The ribbon used for the petals is No. 1 in width, and a needle with an eye large enough to run the ribbon in is necessary in adding it. In using ribbon in this way, only short lengths should be cut, as, after having been drawn through several times, it is apt to curl up instead of being flat and smooth as the effect requires it to be.

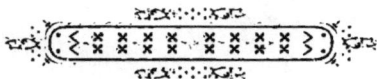

CHAPTER XI.

Designs Adapted to Kensington Embroidery or Painting.

Calendar.

FIGURE NO. 1. — This beautiful bit of artistic work is very simply made and will prove a handsome New Year's gift to either a lady or gentleman. A piece of cardboard of the size desired is covered on one side with velvet or plush embroidered with a graceful bird or other design, and the greeting, "Happy New Year." The other side is plainly covered with silk or satin, and a silk cord is sewed to the edges and coiled in a trio of loops at each corner. The pad may be purchased at almost any stationery store, and is neatly pasted in the upper right corner of the embroidered portion. Ribbons for hanging the calendar are fastened under bows to the top of the article and are regulated to be shorter at the side holding the pads, so that the calendar will hang straight. The ribbons are tied in a bow at the point of suspension. Such calendars may be of any color preferred, and hand-painting, instead of embroidery, may decorate them, with equally artistic results. An explanation and illustration of the bird decorating the calendar in this instance are given at Figure No. 2.

Embroidered Bird for Calendar.

FIGURE NO. 2.—South-Kensington and satin stitches are employed in embroidering this knowing-looking cockatoo, and as floss in all the brilliant tints peculiar to his lordship is artistically introduced, the effect is quite realistic. The bird is used in decorating the calendar pictured at Figure No. 1. It is a pretty and effective design on table-scarfs, lambrequins, sachet and handkerchief cases, etc.

Butterflies in South-Kensington Stitch.

FIGURES NOS. 3 AND 5.—Two sizes of the butterflies adapted to various articles are here illustrated, and both are reproduced in brown and gold coloring. Much taste may be used in the disposition of the colors, so that they may differ while yet of the same lineage and family. For the corners of handkerchiefs, especially the silk ones so much liked by gentlemen, either of these butterflies will form a pretty decoration. If one wished, a muffler might be made quite elaborate by having scattered all over it embroidered butterflies of the smaller size.

Humming-Bird in South-Kensington Stitch.

FIGURE NO. 4.—Brown and deep yellow tones are used for the delineation of this bird, which is wrought in South-Kensington stitch

FIGURE NO. 4.—HUMMING BIRD IN SOUTH-
KENSINGTON STITCH.

FIGURE NO. 1.—CALENDAR.

FIGURE NO. 5.—BUTTERFLY IN SOUTH-
KENSINGTON STITCH.

FIGURE NO. 2.—EMBROIDERED BIRD FOR CALENDAR.

FIGURE NO. 3.—BUTTERFLY IN SOUTH-KENSINGTON STITCH.

and which forms part of the design on the lambrequin illustrated. It would be quite pretty as a decoration on a sachet-bag or *mouchoir-case*, or, indeed, on any article needing a pretty but decided ornamentation.

Mats and Rugs.

Rugs are very artistic as well as very practical in their uses. They are too often disposed stiffly at the thresholds of living-rooms, where they are not needed for practical purposes, and where their artistic value is not recognized. A mat of white Japanese goat-skin is among the least expensive of handsome rugs. It is not a practical selection for a doorway mat, but it is a beautiful adjunct to the furnishings of a room in which ultra light colors do not predominate. Its disposal before the portière of an arch, in front of a couch or sofa, or across a corner in which stands a small table or a fancy chair, is certain to prove attractive. Of course, the handsomer the variety of mat the richer the effect, but an inexpensive selection has been mentioned to illustrate the point of properly placing such articles.

Sheepskin mats, dyed in various colors, are also among the medium-priced goods in these furnishings, and as they are not very wide they are especially suitable for threshold mats.

Any one who has become accustomed to seeing such articles always spread primly alongside the threshold of a door between a hall and parlor or living-room will be surprised at the improvement noticeable if they are spread over the threshold, with half their width inside and half outside. Such a rug may be made the harmonious link between carpets which are not at all connected in the scale of colors.

A couch in gondola shape, or one in low Turkish style, covered with a handsome rug and having upon it cushions that are not too decorative to be useful, adds an air of comfort and elegance to a library or study which seems more in keeping with the uses of such an apartment than lighter and more airy furnishings.

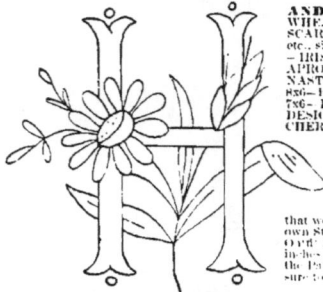

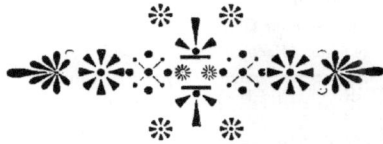

CHAPTER XII.

Illustrations and Descriptions of Various Designs for Canvas, Cardboard and other Embroideries.

THE designs presented in this chapter will be found very useful in making tidies, mats, bracket-lambrequins or anything requiring a border or center; and although they are represented as done on canvas, the stitch is suitable for any fabric, as it partakes of the South-Kensington method, except that the worsted covers the surface only and not both sides.

Design for a Corner or Center-Piece.

FIGURE No. 1.—This design may be used as illustrated for corners, or may be considered only as one quarter of a circle to be used for a center-piece. It is composed as follows, although any other combination of colors will prove as handsome if selected with taste : the zigzag outline at the outer edge is formed of three shades of red—the darkest at the inner edge and the lightest at the outer—a gradation not shown by the engraving. The outer points are crossed by yellow silk floss, while shaded blue silk floss is used over the inner points, each cluster of four

threads thus being of a separate shade, and six shades being therefore used in the example. A single stitch of yellow divides each cluster at the top. From each cluster to the corner two threads of two shades of blue zephyr, with one straight thread of gold-colored silk, are carried : while between these threads half-way down begin two threads of two shades of olive zephyr, crossed by a yellow silk thread; and these extend to a trifle below the cross-stitching, which consists of one row of the lightest red between two rows of yellow silk. From the cross-stitching to the corner the blue threads are over-stitched with yellow and magenta silk floss. Upon black, the effect is very Oriental. The design is charming for small lambrequins, mats, etc.

Design for a Tidy or Mat.

FIGURE No. 2.—The South-Kensington stitch in one of its many forms is here used. Three shades of red are used for the Grecian outline, and the shades are so distributed that sometimes the darkest is the outer thread, and sometimes the lightest, as will be seen by referring to the engraving. The stitches crossing the corners are in " new gold " silk floss, and the daisies are in pale olive and dull blue—the former being inside the Grecian outline and the latter outside. Each daisy

FIGURE No. 1.—DESIGN FOR A CORNER OR CENTER PIECE.

is also outlined with floss, and the leaf at the corner is made of the three shades of red and the floss. Any other combination of colors preferred may be used. The design

FIGURE No. 2.—DESIGN FOR A TIDY OR MAT.

is suitable for sofa-cushions, etc., as well as for the purposes mentioned in the title.

The other designs included in the chapter

will be found available in beautifying articles of use, such as tidies, covers, mats, cushions, etc., and also in making up portières or draperies where the canvas work will produce a neat finish, suggestive of embroidered tapestry. The following descriptions will make plain the colors used in the canvas work, and also simplify the details of the hem-stitching.

Design for a Tidy or Mat.

FIGURE No. 3.—There is nothing to be said in reference to the design here illustrated, as the engraving shows its appropri-

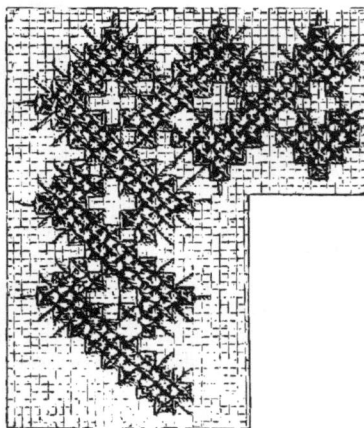

FIGURE No. 3.—DESIGN FOR A TIDY OR MAT.

ateness for the purposes mentioned in the title. The sample is done in olive zephyr, with an outline of old-gold silk floss. Any other combination of colors may be used, if preferred. The main portion of the design is done in ordinary cross-stitch, but the outlining runs straight along the sides of the stitches and also branches out between them in the manner illustrated in the engraving.

Spray of Forget-Me-Nots in Cross-Stitch.

FIGURE No. 4.—The flowers in this pretty little pattern are usually worked in pale blue, and the stem and leaf in olive-green. A cross-stitch of golden yellow in the center of the flower gives a charmingly realistic effect, and brightens the work beautifully. The design may be embroidered on canvas and perforated cardboard, and also on cloth and other textures. To render this kind of work neat and regular on cloth, flannel, etc., a section of canvas is basted on and the design then embroidered in; and when the design is completed, the threads of the canvas are carefully drawn out. In this way any pattern may be wrought without difficulty on any fabric.

Crown in Cross-Stitch.

FIGURE No. 5.—Five strongly contrasting colors in wool, floss, embroidery silk, filoselle or crewel may be handsomely commingled in a design of this kind. The squares marked alike are to be alike in color, and the colors may be whatever the taste desires. The design may be embroidered on canvas of any variety, or on cloth, felt, velvet, plush, etc.

Rose-Bud in Cross-Stitch.

FIGURE No. 6.—The colors blended in a rose-bud of this kind are usually those seen in a partially developed moss-rose bud. Pink or white, blended artistically with light and dark olive, produces a very realistic effect.

Design for a Canvas Tidy.

FIGURE No. 7.—This engraving illustrates a quaint design for the center of a tidy, toilette-mat, or a cover for a small table. The foundation is known as ordinary canvas, and single zephyr worsted in black, light and dark brown, red and salmon colors, is used for the embroidery. The stitch is the well-known cross-stitch, and the arrangement of the colors may be clearly understood by comparing the blocks under the engraving with those marked in the design. Two boys playing "see-saw" on a board that rests at the center upon a huge boulder, is the design represented. The colors may be whatever the fancy suggests, although those mentioned are especially appropriate.

Horse-Shoe Design.

FIGURE No. 8.—This pretty design may be embroidered on velvet, plush, satin, canvas, etc., and is done in the well-known cross-stitch. It presents a novel effect when embroidered on the front of a velvet slipper. The shoe may be embroidered in silver-colored floss, with gold-colored floss for the nails, or *vice versa*. It may also be done in any two hues for which a preference may be entertained.

Design for Canvas.

FIGURE No. 9.—A canvas-work design for two shades of wool is here represented. It needs no special explanation, the stitch being familiar to all, from those who indulge in fancy work at the present time back to those who worked samplers and pictures in our grandmothers' days. Tidies, mats, rugs, etc., may be prettily embellished by the design.

Sunflower in Cross-Stitch.

FIGURE No. 10.—The flower of the æsthete conventionalized is here given for the benefit of the industrious maidens who have reaped knowledge in decorative art from the æsthetic movement. While applicable especially to canvas working, this stitch is often made use of on towels and napery, and the sunflower as shown will form a pretty corner or center-piece done in crewels or working cotton. Here it is in proper colored silk flosses, the filling-in to be of a deep olive shade and the entire piece to be mounted as a footstool, several of the blossoms being scattered over the cover, while the mounting is gilded wood.

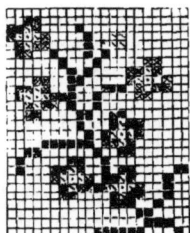

FIGURE NO. 4.—SPRAY OF FORGET-ME-NOTS IN CROSS-STITCH.

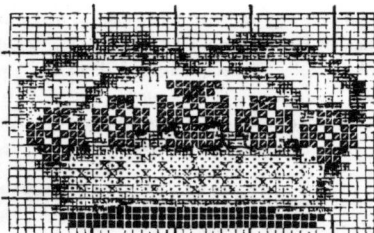

FIGURE NO. 5.—CROWN IN CROSS-STITCH.

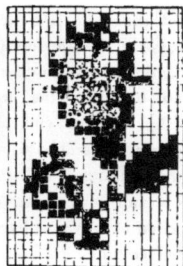

FIGURE NO. 6.—ROSE-BUD IN CROSS-STITCH.

Light Brown. Black. Red. Dark Brown. Salmon.

FIGURE NO. 7.—DESIGN FOR A CANVAS TIDY

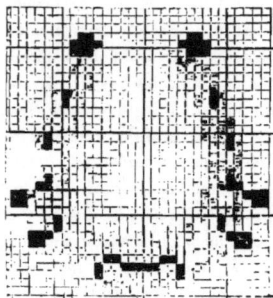

FIGURE NO. 8.—HORSE-SHOE DESIGN.

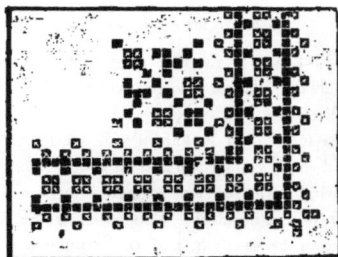

FIGURE NO. 9.—DESIGN FOR CANVAS.

Grade of Colors for Sunflower.

FIGURE No. 11.—The colors used in making the sunflower and the mark which in the design distinguishes them are here shown. The first in the scale is olive-green, then follow in regular order light orange, medium olive-green, light yellow, yellow, dark olive-green, light brown, and dark brown. A little care and there will be no trouble whatever in distinguishing just how the colors are used, and the growth of the sunflower will be quick and successful.

FIGURES Nos. 12, 13, 14 AND 15.—The borders illustrated at the corners of page 78 are neat headings to self-fringed tidies, mats and covers for cushions. Colors may be used in reproducing them, but on account of the fineness of the design, it is best to use split zephyr or Berlin wool. If done in black silk on white canvas, they look like strips of handsome lace insertion carried about the edges of whatever they decorate. Sometimes a wider border is placed between two of this description, with an excellent effect. Fancy card-receivers are made of white perforated cardboard, and these patterns are just delicate enough for such dainty affairs, and may be done in any colored floss or wool that may be preferred. In working Nos. 13 and 14 two tints may be associated in whatever materials are chosen, with specially good effect.

Border Design for Canvas.

FIGURE No. 16.—Of course all our readers are familiar enough with Java canvas to understand and follow the design as illustrated, so we will simply try to give the colors and their arrangement, as illustrated.

The button-hole stitches along the edge to hold the fringe are done with a pale wood-colored zephyr, probably as near the shade of the canvas as could be found. The bands are of black velvet, and the diamond outlines about the daisies, (which are yellow and white,) made with black zephyr. The long, branching design between the diamonds is done alternately in olive, red and blue, there being three shades of each color—dark, medium and light—in each design. The leaves at the points of the diamonds alternate in the same arrangement of color, the medium shades only being used. The yellow daisies have black centers, and each petal is overlaid with yellow silk, while the white daisies have yellow centers and are attached with white silk. The top band is cat-stitched on with yellow silk, and the clusters of stitches in the points are made alternately of the medium tints of red and blue silk. The lower band is also cat-stitched on with yellow silk, the latter also forming the clusters of stitches outside the edges of the band. In the upright points formed by the cat-stitches the medium and light shades of red alternate in the clusters of stitches, while on the inverted points between them the medium blue and olive tints are used. The star designs at the bottom are made of all the worsted colors in succession, but the clusters at the top and bottom of each are made of the medium shade of olive. The whole effect is showy and pleasing, and experience has proved that both the design and its development are very fascinating.

Design for a Border.

FIGURE No. 17.—As the engraving clearly delineates the manner of working this design as well as the center-piece, it will only be necessary for us to give an idea of the colors used in the sample. The rings and diamonds are formed of three threads of zephyr, the outer one seal brown, the next one pale brown, and the inner one white. The angles are all concealed by gold-colored silk, which, as will be seen by the engraving, is button holed

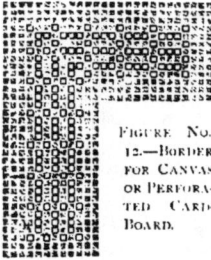

FIGURE NO. 12.—BORDER FOR CANVAS OR PERFORATED CARD-BOARD.

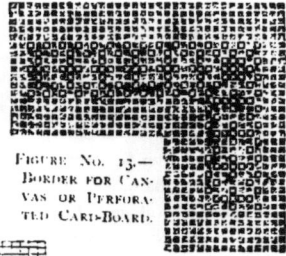

FIGURE NO. 13.—BORDER FOR CANVAS OR PERFORATED CARD-BOARD.

FIGURE NO. 10.—SUNFLOWER IN CROSS-STITCH.

| Dark Brown. | Light Brown. | Dark Olive-Green. | Yel-low. | Light Yellow. | Medium Ol-ive-Green. | Light Orange. | Olive Green. |

FIGURE NO. 11.—GRADE OF COLORS FOR SUNFLOWER.

FIGURE NO. 14.—BORDER FOR CANVAS OR PERFORATED CARD-BOARD.

FIGURE NO. 15.—BORDER FOR CANVAS OR PERFORATED CARD-BOARD.

FIGURE No. 16.—BORDER DESIGN FOR CANVAS.

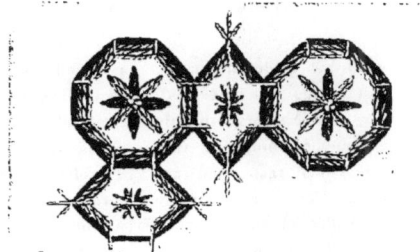

FIGURE No. 17.—DESIGN FOR A BORDER.

along inside of the white zephyr, and is also used to form the little prongs at the points of the diamonds. The stars within the rings are each formed of two shades of zephyr in three colors, arranged as follows:—one of scarlet, one of olive and one of blue, and so on, along the entire border. The center of each star is made with the silk. The little

Design for a Piano-Cover or Table-Cloth.

FIGURE No. 18.—This engraving represents a very handsome design for a table-spread, piano-cover or stand-cloth. The model from which this illustration was copied is made on garnet wool canvas with a rich, gold-colored floss, and is probably as effective a combination as can be suggested. However, personal

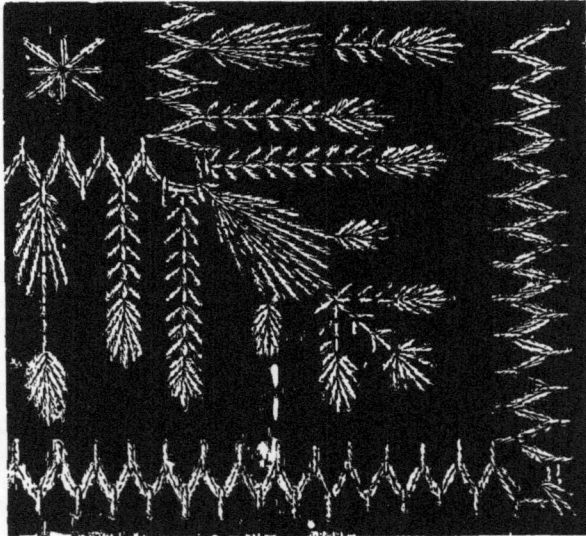

FIGURE No. 18.—DESIGN FOR A PIANO COVER OR TABLE CLOTH.

stars in the diamond are made alternately of the lightest shade of red and blue used, together with the silk. These colors form only one of many handsome combinations that may result from individual taste, and are therefore not the only ones that may be adopted. If three shades of one color be selected, the darkest should form the outline, the reason for such a gradation being readily understood.

taste, and the prevailing tint in a room where the article embroidered is to be used, must direct combinations. It is not necessary to use canvas, as cloth, felt or Canton flannel may be preferred; but the meshes of canvas will be found of great assistance in following the pattern with regularity of stitch. The work is all done in a long, back-stitch or a sort of Kensington stitch, and is extremely effective in appearance.

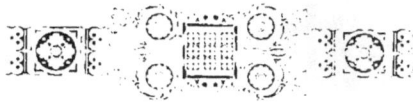

CHAPTER XIII.

SPECIMENS OF LACE AND METHOD OF MAKING.

HE engraving on this and those on the following pages illustrate a variety of fancy-work that seems to be both impractical and impossible for an amateur to undertake. It is, however, easily done, if one only knows what to get for it and how to begin. In the first place designs for lace work come stamped upon thick paper, for making

line of embroidery stuffs, you can purchase lace braid like the widest strips seen in the engravings, and feather-edge braid for the extreme border. The design is followed with the wide braid, which is flatly basted on ; and the outer border is produced by joining the loops of the feather braid to the edge of the lace braid.

FIGURES NOS. 1, 2, 3 and 4.—The specimens of lace pictured in these engravings indicate

FIGURE NO. 1.—CORNER IN LACE WORK.

barbes, collars, cuffs, etc., and one of these in whatever style of article you want must be selected. Then at any fancy-store keeping a

their special uses. The fine lines on these patterns are followed with single threads, the widest ones being two or three threads over-

FIGURE NO. 2.—DESIGN IN LACE BRAID.

FIGURE NO. 3.—DESIGN FOR LACE BORDER AND CORNER.

FIGURE NO. 4.—DESIGN FOR INSERTION OF LACE BRAID.

wrought closely in button-hole stitch. The dots seen are knots made at the crossings to keep the threads from slipping, and the dainty net-work about the inside of the border con-

pretty, and is much admired on dresses of gingham, print, cambric and other washable textures. The tape with a lace-edge finish may be purchased in any shop where lace-

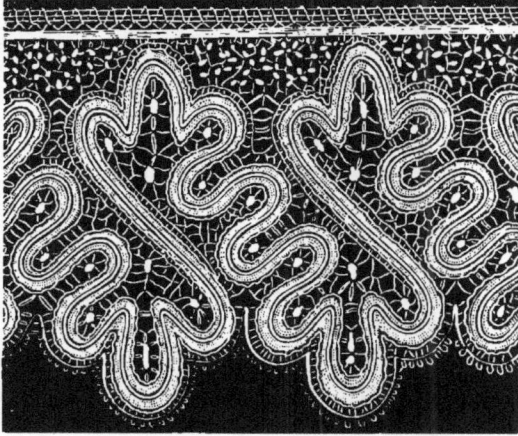

FIGURE NO. 5.—RUSSIAN LACE.

sists of a chain-stitch or lace-stitch done with a single thread.

Russian Lace.

FIGURE NO. 5.—This lace is durable and

makers' materials are kept, and the method is somewhat similar to that followed in making feather-edged trimming, a variety of fancy-work explained in another chapter of this book.

It cannot be denied that Fashion is very instrumental in shaping feminine fancies, but when the good dame exercises her influence in fostering such agreeable and harmless diversions as making some variety of fancy-work, which shall as long as it lasts be cherished as a souvenir of the worker's taste and skill by whoever is fortunate enough to become its possessor she is above censure. Just now,

in the name of sweet charity, many ladies are engaged in doing some variety of fancy-work in which they are especially proficient and disposing of it to the admirers of such work. Lace that has been made by some one who is known to the purchaser is especially liked, and the specimens illustrated in this chapter are among the patterns which the amateur lace maker most frequently selects.

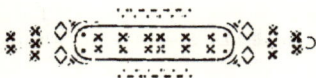

A Nest for a Cherub.

The cherub is only a little plaster figure, and his proper sphere seems to be illimitable space, but he has such a winsome face and is altogether so bewitching that although he is cast in plaster by the thousand he is sure to be admired, and whoever possesses him to look about for a place where he may swing without danger of colliding with less terrestrial beings. An arched doorway, a chandelier that is not hung too low, or an alcove where a tiny hook may be inserted is a fitting abode, and to make a bower suitable for such an inhabitant fasten cords about the arms or wherever they can be attached so as to hold the figure securely and suspend them from the hooks. Then cover the cords with smilax, or any climbing artificial vine and around the figure arrange a little nest or arch of ferns or any kind of greenery that will answer the purpose, being careful not to have the arrangement appear stiff or to obscure the figure; flying cupids, winged Dianas and various quaint little figures procurable in plaster, bisque and terra cotta at small expense may be artistically suspended in this way.

CHAPTER XIV.

EDGING AND INSERTION OF DARNED NET AND FANCY TIDY.

THE net used for this fancy-work is the kind known as "wash net" or "wash blond." Linen and silk floss are both used for the embroidery, but the linen is preferable, as it does not turn yellow like the silk. The lace edgings and insertions illustrated may be used on basques, skirts and dresses of thin lawn, muslin or nainsook, and are very dainty in appearance.

Darned Lace.

FIGURE No. 1.—This engraving shows the effect when the selvage forms the finish for the edging. The pattern needs no explanation.

FIGURE No. 2.—At this figure a more elaborate pattern for an edging is shown. The border is finished in button-hole stitch and the net below it may be cut away.

Tidy of Darned Net and Braid Rosettes.

FIGURE No. 3.—This engraving illustrates a dainty tidy of wash blond embroidered in a pretty and simple design to suggest rows of insertion, between which full, soft-looking rosettes of flat linen braid are fastened at equal intervals. A row of the rosettes is also arranged about all the edges of the tidy, and forms a rich-looking border. Pale blue surah silk is used for lining and forms an effective background, as it exhibits effectively the beauty of the design. Silesia, cambric, silk, satin or any similar fabric may be used instead of surah for lining, and may be of any delicate or bright tint most pleasing to the fancy or in accordance with the predominating colors in the room. The work must be neatly and carefully done to look well, and is so simple that only a little time and patience will be requisite to a pleasing result.

Design in Full Size for Tidy, Illustrated at Figure No. 3.

FIGURE No. 4.—This engraving shows the full size and pattern of the embroidery used in making the tidy represented at Figure No. 3. It is clearly illustrated, and its description in detail may be read at Figure No. 5.

Detail of Stitch and Design for Tidy, Illustrated at Figure No. 3.

FIGURE No. 5.—A thorough idea of the stitch and design used in making the tidy mentioned, is given by this engraving. The design combines the single and double stitches, the combination of the two being much more effective than if either were used alone. The single stitch is made by taking up two meshes of the net and leaving one be-

NEEDLE·CRAFT.

tween. In the double stitch all the meshes are taken up, the second stitch taking up the one left by the first stitch, and a solid and accurate all through. The necessity for doing this does not however add appreciably to the time consumed in doing such work, because a

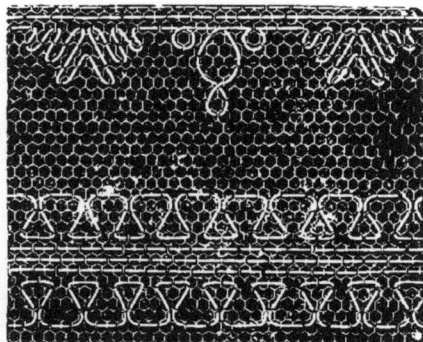

FIGURE NO. 1.—DARNED LACE.

FIGURE NO. 2.—DARNED LACE.

irregular result is obtained. The meshes should be counted in the same way as in embroidering canvas, so that the pattern will be little practice enables one to judge quickly of the space taken up by a certain number of stitches.

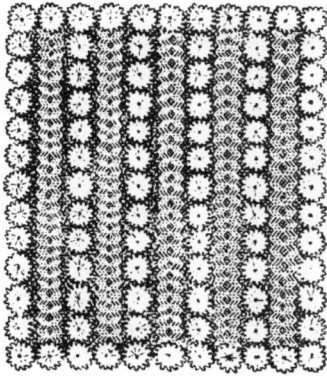

FIGURE No. 3.—TIDY OF DARNED NET AND BRAID ROSETTES.

FIGURE No. 4.—DESIGN IN FULL SIZE FOR TIDY ILLUSTRATED AT
FIGURE No. 3.

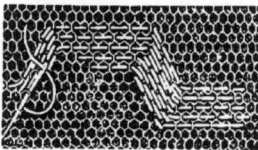

FIGURE No. 5.— DETAIL OF STITCH AND DESIGN FOR
TIDY ILLUSTRATED AT FIGURE No. 3.

FIGURE No. 6.—DESIGN FOR DARNED NET.

Design for Darned Net.

FIGURE NO. 6.—This design fully illustrates the double stitch in the border or margin. The stars have all the stitches radiating from one mesh, each stitch being "looped" through a mesh two or three holes from the center. This design may be employed for insertions—the engraving shows only half the figure—and applied to waists, childrens' dresses, skirts, etc., made of fine lawn or nainsook.

Rosette, in Full Size, used for Tidy shown at Figure No. 3.

FIGURE NO. 7.—This rosette is dainty and soft-looking in effect, and is made of flat linen braid, which is usually white, but which may

FIGURE NO. 7.—ROSETTE IN FULL SIZE.

be of any delicate or bright tint to match the lining of the tidy.

Detail of Rosette.

FIGURES NOS. 8 AND 9.—These engravings illustrate the method adopted in making the rosette. In Figure No. 8 the first step taken in making the rosette is shown. One side of the braid is gathered a little in from the edge with medium long stitches, and is drawn in as

FIGURE NO. 8.—DETAIL OF ROSETTE.

closely as possible to form the center, the ends being neatly joined so as not to be visible. Figure No. 9 illustrates the mode employed in shaping the outer margin of the rosette. The edge is caught down at equal intervals to the under side by stitches that are drawn only tight enough to retain them in place without wrinkling them. These ro-

FIGURE NO. 9.—DETAIL OF ROSETTE.

settes are much more easily made than those called "daisy" rosettes, and are fully as pretty in effect. The closeness of the rosettes and the actual width between every two rows are simple problems, quickly solved by a few trial comparisons on the worker's part.

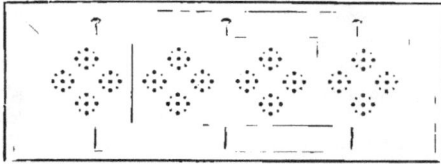

CHAPTER XV.

Crochetted Work. Explanation of Basis of all Crochetted Work. Illustrations and Descriptions of Star Stitch.

HOUGH knitted work is as ancient as art itself, it has, like art, progressed with age, and articles as fleecy as snow, airy and beautiful as floating S u m m e r clouds, and in usefulness, utility itself, have come into being by the aid of this simple and interesting domestic employment. The stitches, especially in crochet work, are manifold in variety and as beautiful as they are numerous, and, by combining two or three fancy stitches in one article, a very tasteful and artistic bewilderment of threads will result.

These engravings illustrate and the accompanying description explains a pretty and effective stitch called "star" stitch. The basis on which crochet work of all kinds is founded is also fully explained both by description and illustration, so that those who are in blissful ignorance of the work may become as blissfully wise.

An important item in the work is the crochet hook or needle. This should be fine or coarse to suit the worsted, thread, floss, cord or yarn selected ; and no matter how fine or how coarse it may be, the hook should be a perfect hook, or it will not "catch" well.

Saxony yarn, Shetland floss, split, double and single zephyr wools, thread, floss, macrame cord, etc., are all suitable for crochet work : Shetland floss and split zephyr wools resulting in the most exquisite of cloudy or fleecy effects.

Detail of Chain-Stitch.

FIGURES Nos. 1, 2 AND 3.—The fundamental principle of all crochet work, whether

FIGURE NO. 1.—DETAIL OF CHAIN-STITCH.

the pattern is simple or intricate, is the chain-stitch, the method of making which is fully illustrated by the engravings and accomplished in the following way : Take an end of the thread or wool to be used in the work in the left hand ; twist the thread so as to form a loop, and hold the loop between the left forefinger and thumb ; throw the thread *over* the first and second fingers, *under* the third finger and *over* the fourth finger. The fourth finger, by pressing against the third finger, serves as a sort of tension for the thread, so that the work may be done loose or tight, as desired. This is the method for holding the thread properly, and is illustrated at Figure No. 1.

Pass the hook through the loop, and under

Each time the hook is pulled through a loop counts as one stitch.

A single crochet is made by inserting the needle without throwing the thread over, and crochetting the two loops off at once. A double crochet is made by throwing the thread over the needle before inserting the latter and crochetting two loops off the needle at a time.

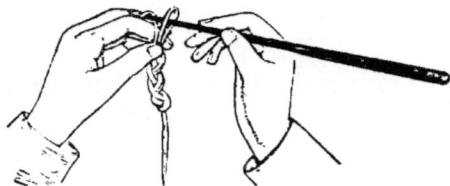

FIGURE NO. 2.—DETAIL OF CHAIN-STITCH.

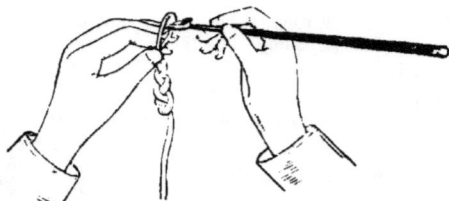

FIGURE No. 3.—DETAIL OF CHAIN-STITCH.

the loose thread over the first fingers, as shown by Figure No. 2.

Then pull the hook through the loop; keep the loop thus formed on the needle, and pass the needle under the thread and pull it through the loop, as shown by Figure No. 3.

Continue in this manner, till a chain of suitable length is obtained.

Method of Making Star-Stitch.

FIGURES Nos. 4, 5, 6, 7, 8, 9, 10 AND 11.— To make this stitch, first make a chain of stitches of whatever length the article to be made is to be. Then take up the first stitch in the chain nearest the hook, and pull the thread through the loop in the manner illustrated by Figure No. 4.

Then take up each of the next five stitches in the chain in the same way, retaining all

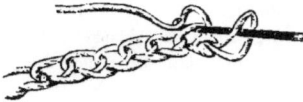

FIGURE NO. 4.

the loops on the crochet hook and carrying the thread on the hook as represented by

FIGURE NO. 5.

Figure No. 5 ; pull the hook through all the loops at one time, as illustrated by Figure No. 6.

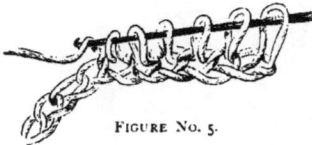

FIGURE NO. 6.

Then make one chain so as to close the star, as shown by Figure No. 7 ; take up each of the loops, lettered A, B, C, D and E, at

FIGURE NO. 7.

Figure No. 7, in the same way as the stitches just described, retaining all on the hook as shown by Figure No. 8 ; then draw the hook through, as described at Figure No. 6 ; and

make a chain-stitch to close the star, as described at Figure No. 7.

FIGURE NO. 8.

FIGURES NOS. 4, 5, 6, 7 AND 8.—METHOD OF MAK-ING THE STAR-STITCH.

Continue in this way till all the stitches in the chain have been used ; then fasten the thread by making a chain-stitch, breaking the thread and pulling the end tightly through the loop.

To make the second row of star-stitches : Draw the thread through the first loop of the

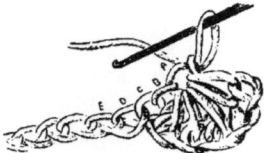

FIGURE NO. 9.

star-stitch first made, as shown by Figure No. 9 ; make three chain-stitches from this loop, as shown by Figure No. 10 ; and take up the

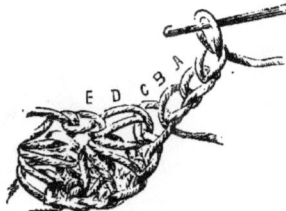

FIGURES NOS. 9 AND 10.—METHOD OF MAKING THE SECOND ROW OF STAR-STITCHES.

stitches lettered A, B, C, D and E at this figure keeping all the loops on the hook till the five stitches are taken up, then draw them off the needle and close them with one chain-stitch.

Take up the next five stitches from the star in the first row, and close this star like the other one.

The effect of the stitches, when several rows have been made, may be seen at Figure No. 11.

For nubias, shawls, fascinators, Afghans, baby-carriage robes and blankets, shopping bags, covers to hunting-bags, etc., this is a

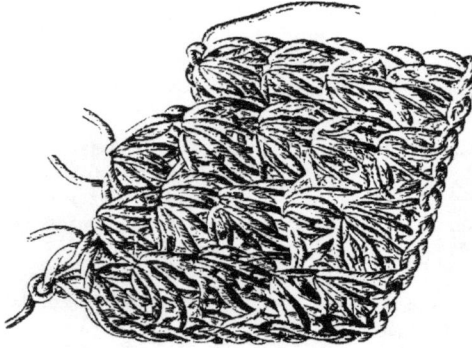

FIGURE NO. 11.—SHOWING THE EFFECT OF SEVERAL ROWS OF STAR-STITCHES.

Then proceed in the same manner all along the line, and, when finished, commence the third row in the same way as the second, and so on till the article is completed.

beautiful and effective stitch. Of course, cord is preferable for shopping and hunting bags, as it is very durable and can be easily renovated when soiled.

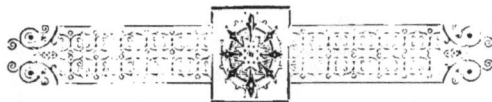

CHAPTER XVI.

Tam O'Shanter Hat and Method of Making It. Fancy Horse Reins and Method of Making Them.

F Robert Burns had an inspiration for every fancy and a music for every mood, he certainly also was blessed with the power to awaken artistic genius in one man who has been made famous by a most original piece of sculpture, which was the outcome of a true idea of the two jolly characters so vividly depicted in "Tam O'Shanter," and which gave, undoubtedly, the first fame to the picturesque cap crowning Tam O'Shanter's jolly head.

This cap has a style that is entirely its own, and it is a favorite with children of all ages and both sexes and is much affected by young ladies while skating, sleighing, etc. Crochetted in crimson, scarlet, brown, blue or any becoming shade of wool, it is most useful, and its only needful decoration is a large pompon.

In order to answer the numerous queries that have been asked in regard to directions for crochetting the cap, we have given its illustration and construction a prominent place in this book.

Tam O'Shanter Cap, and Method of Making It.

FIGURES Nos. 1, 2, 3, 4 AND 5.—The cap illustrated at Figure No. 1 is made of dark-blue Germantown yarn of heavy quality. Take a bone crochet-needle of proper size and make three chain stitches, as shown by Figure No. 2.

FIGURE No. 1.

Lift the first stitch on the needle, as shown by Figure No. 3, and draw it through the last stitch, as shown by Figure No. 4. Then in each of these stitches make two single cro-

FIGURE No. 2.

chets, and in each of these make two single crochets in the same way, working round and round, as shown at Figure No. 5, but not fastening at the ends of the rows. After the second row one single crochet only is made in each stitch, except when it is needful to widen so as not to make the work "cappy," two single crochets being made for this purpose whenever needed. All that is to be considered in the further progress of the crown is to have the work neither cap nor ruffle the least bit, and judgment will have to be exercised in introducing the two single crochets

FIGURE NO. 3.

in one stitch, as no rule can be followed in this matter. Crochet very tightly and evenly and do not widen regularly at certain places, for this will spoil the circular shape needful. Forty rows are necessary to complete the crown. The part for the side and brim is made separately from the crown. Start with a chain of as many stitches as there are in the last row in the crown and join the ends

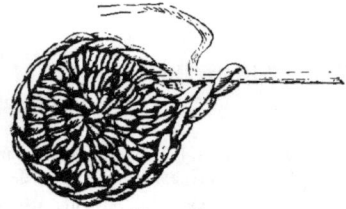

FIGURE NO. 4.

of the chain; then make a single crochet in each chain. In the second row make the same number of stitches as in the second row from the last in the crown, skipping a stitch when necessary to obtain the right number; each succeeding row should also contain only the same number of stitches as the corresponding row in the crown, until twenty rows are made. When correctly made this

portion will be perfectly smooth when laid upon the outer part of the crown. The twenty-first row is made without widening or narrowing, and seven other rows are needed to form the brim and complete the cap. In making these last seven rows widen a little on each row, only enough, however, to make a band that will fit the head of the person that is to wear the cap. When the last row

FIGURE NO. 5.

is made finish off securely and neatly. Then place this portion on the crown, with the right sides together, and sew the parts together with a piece of the worsted, or crochet them together by lifting together the corresponding stitches in the two parts and making half-

FIGURE NO. 6.

stitches. The cap is then completed and ready for the pompon, which should be sewed on with strong thread at the center of the crown.

Fancy Horse-Reins.

FIGURE NO. 6.—That the coming man will be fond of horses almost goes without saying, because from his youth up he displays a liking for their equipments, which is fostered by many a mamma and older sister. The reins shown have a pretty band of dark blue velvet, upon which is outlined a flying steed, whose record, it is fair to presume, has never been beaten. All around the edge are tiny bells that jingle with every movement of the prancing boy. The reins are crochetted of scarlet worsted, and are sufficiently easy for even a novice to attempt. The stitch used in making the reins is called the Afghan stitch, and is illustrated and described at Figures Nos. 7, 8 and 9 in this article.

Afghan Stitch for Horse-Reins.

FIGURES NOS. 7, 8 AND 9.—Illustrations are given of the stitch employed in making the play reins just described. First make a chain of five, six or more stitches, according to the width desired. Take up the stitch in the

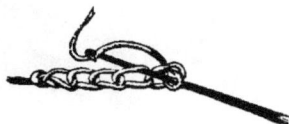

FIGURE NO. 7.

chain nearest the needle; throw the thread over the needle as shown by Figure No. 7, and draw the needle through the loop; take up

each stitch in the chain in the same manner till all the stitches are lifted on the needle, as shown by Figure No. 8. Then throw the thread over the needle and crochet two stitches off the needle, and proceed in this

FIGURE NO. 8.

manner till all the stitches are crochetted off. In the next row each of these stitches is lifted as shown by Figure No. 9, in the same manner as the stitches in the chain, and crochetted off as described. This is known as the

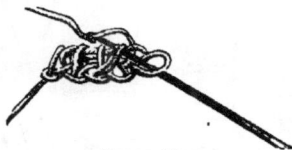

FIGURE NO. 9.

"Afghan" stitch, and is much used for carriage-blankets, lap-robes, etc. Zephyr wools are usually employed for this stitch. Care is required even in this, the simplest of crochetting, to do the work regularly and not have one line loose and another tight.

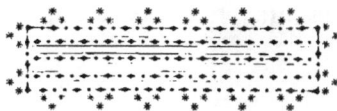

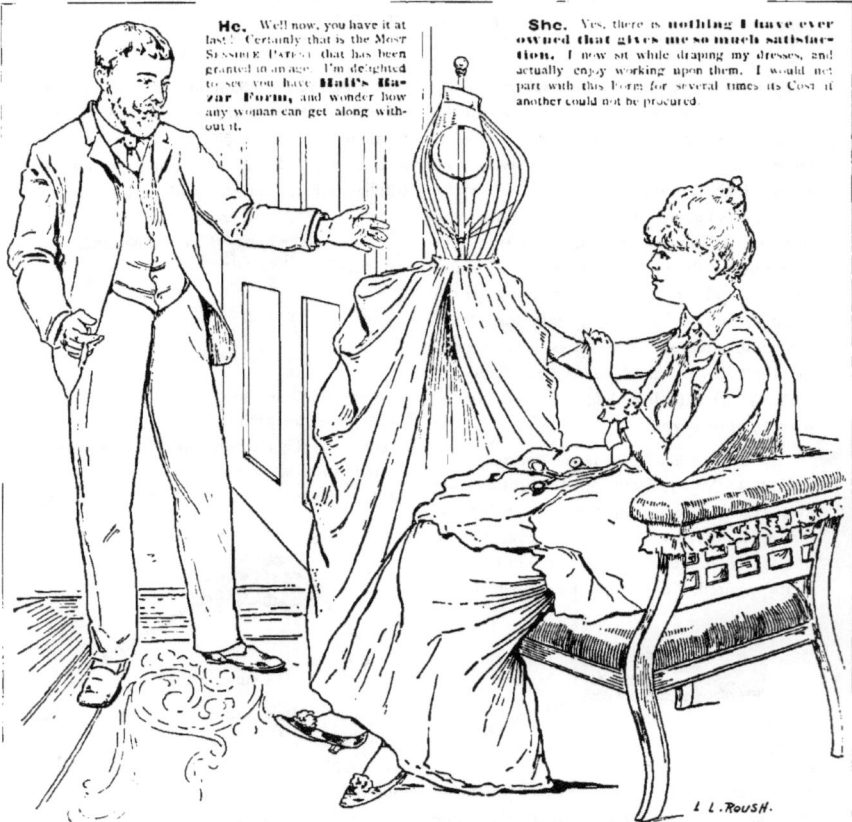

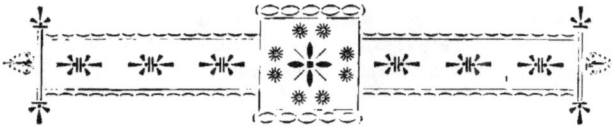

CHAPTER XVII.

CROCHETTED LAMBREQUIN, AND METHOD OF MAKING.

THE fundamental principles of crochet work which were fully described in a previous chapter, wherein also the method of making some fancy stitches was clearly shown, should be fully mastered before attempting this work, as some of these same stitches are used in making the lambrequin illustrated.

Crochetted Lambrequin.

FIGURE No. 1.—This handsome lambrequin is made of macramé cord and satin ribbon, and is very elegant in effect. The method of procedure is as follows:

Crochet a chain of forty stitches; then throw the cord over the needle and lift up the fourth stitch in the chain nearest the hook, as shown by Figure No. 2; throw the cord over the hook and pull the loose cord through the loops lettered A and B in Figure No. 2; throw the cord over the needle again, and pull it through the two loops remaining on the needle —this is called a "double stitch"; — make six more stitches in the same way in the same stitch in the chain to form a shell of seven double stitches, as shown by Figure No. 3.

Then throw the cord over the needle, and take up the third stitch in the chain, counting from the shell; throw the cord over the needle, and draw it through the nearest two loops on the needle, as shown by Figure No. 4; throw the cord over the needle again, and pull it through the remaining two loops, as shown by Figure No. 5. Then make two more stitches in the same way, taking up each consecutive stitch in the chain.

Now make a chain of seven stitches; throw the cord over the needle, and take up the seventh stitch in the chain, counting from the last stitch lifted, and proceed as shown at Figures Nos. 4 and 5, making three double stitches as shown by Figure No. 6.

Now throw the cord over the needle, take up the third stitch in the chain, and make six double stitches in this stitch to form a shell.

Then make three double stitches, taking up the third, fourth and fifth stitches in the chain consecutively, counting from the shell; and proceed in making the seven chain and three double stitches and then a shell of six stitches, as just described.

After this shell has been completed, make a chain of three stitches, as shown by Figure No. 7; throw the cord over the needle, put the needle between the third and fourth stitches in the shell just made, as shown by Figure No. 8, and make a shell of six double stitches.

Then throw the cord over the needle, and take up the first stitch in the group of three double stitches, as shown by Figure No. 9; and make a similar group of three double of seven stitches just beneath, as shown by Figure No. 10; then throw the cord over the needle, and pull it through all three loops on the needle *at once.*

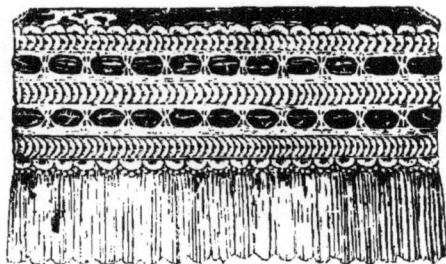

FIGURE NO. 1.—CROCHETTED LAMBREQUIN.

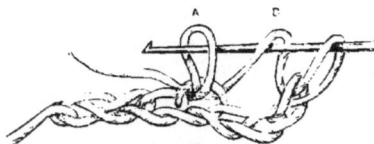

FIGURE NO. 2.

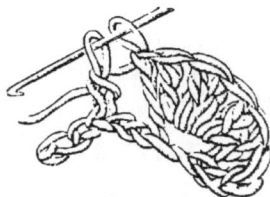

FIGURE NO. 4.

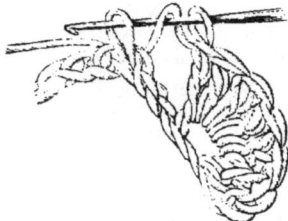

FIGURE NO. 3.

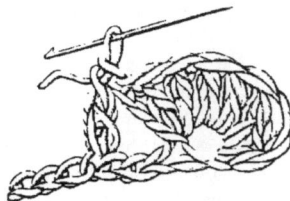

FIGURE NO. 5.

FIGURES NOS. 2, 3, 4 AND 5.—DETAILS OF CROCHETTED LAMBREQUIN.

stitches, taking up each of the lower stitches in the same way.

Then make a chain of three stitches, and take up the fourth stitch in each of the chains

Now make a chain of three stitches, throw the cord over the needle, and take up the stitches in the nearest group of three stitches, proceeding as shown by Figure No. 11.

Continue to the last shell in the first row in the same manner.

When the last stitch for the last shell in the second row is made, throw the cord over the

Then make a chain of three stitches, throw the cord over the needle, and make a shell of six stitches, as before, between the third and fourth stitches in the last shell made.

FIGURE No. 6.

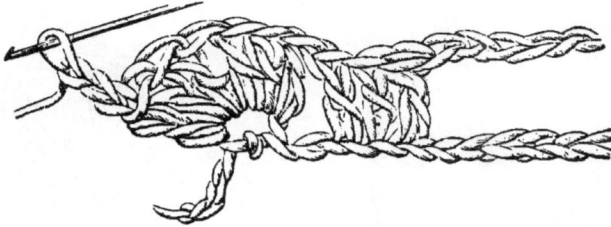

FIGURE No. 7.

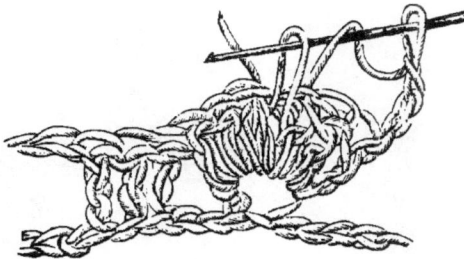

FIGURE No. 8.

FIGURES NOS. 6, 7 AND 8.—DETAILS OF CROCHETTED LAMBREQUIN.

needle, pass the needle between the first and second stitches made in the first shell in the first row, and crochet the loops off the needle as described for the double stitch.

Then complete this row in the manner described for the first row, making the chain of seven stitches between the groups of three stitches. When the last shell is made in this row, make another shell of six stitches in the hole made by the chain of three stitches at the turning of the first row to make the second row, commencing as shown by Figure No. 12.

crochet the loops off *at once*, as shown by Figure No. 13.

Then make another chain of three stitches, and pass the needle between the next two

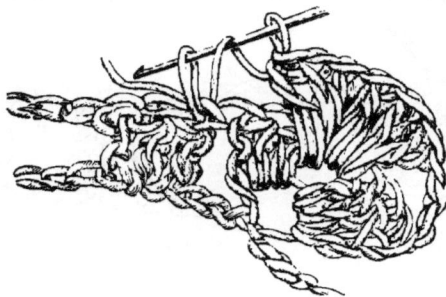

FIGURE No. 9.

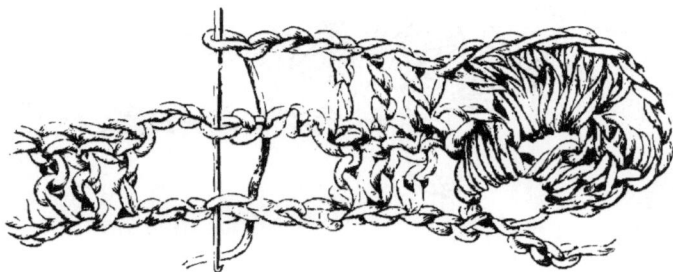

FIGURE No. 10.

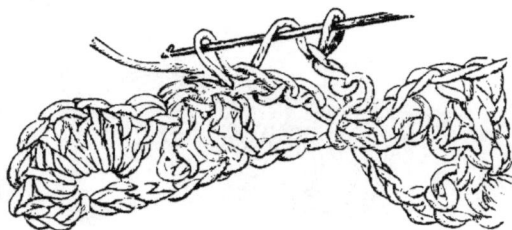

FIGURE No. 11.

FIGURES Nos, 9, 10 AND 11.—DETAILS OF CROCHETTED LAMBREQUIN

Then make a chain of three stitches, and pass the needle between the nearest two stitches in the shell just made, taking care *not* to throw the cord over the needle, and

stitches in the shell, and so on all along the shell, as shown by letters A, B, C and D in Figure No. 14. Then make a chain of three stitches, and pass the needle in the hole be-

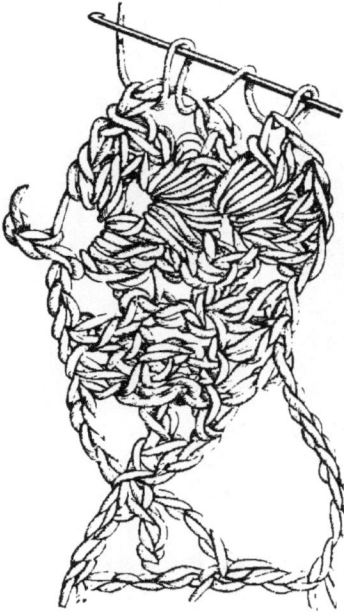

FIGURE NO. 12.

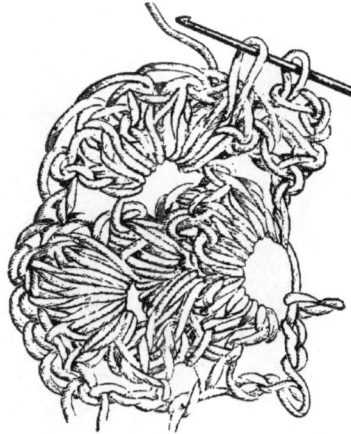

FIGURE NO. 13.

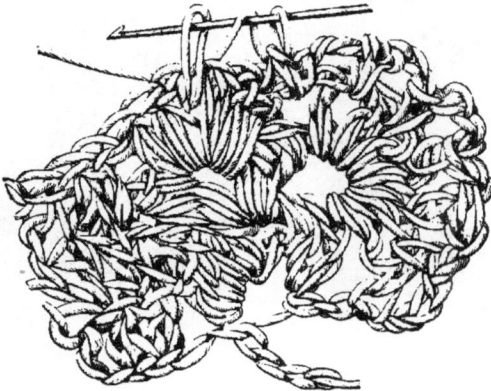

FIGURE NO. 14.

FIGURES NO. 12, 13 AND 14.—DETAILS OF CROCHETTED LAMBREQUIN.

tween this shell and the next in the same manner as shown by letter E in the same figure. These loops finish a scollop, and are

Now throw the cord over the needle, and make a shell of six stitches in the next shell, commencing as shown by Figure No. 14.

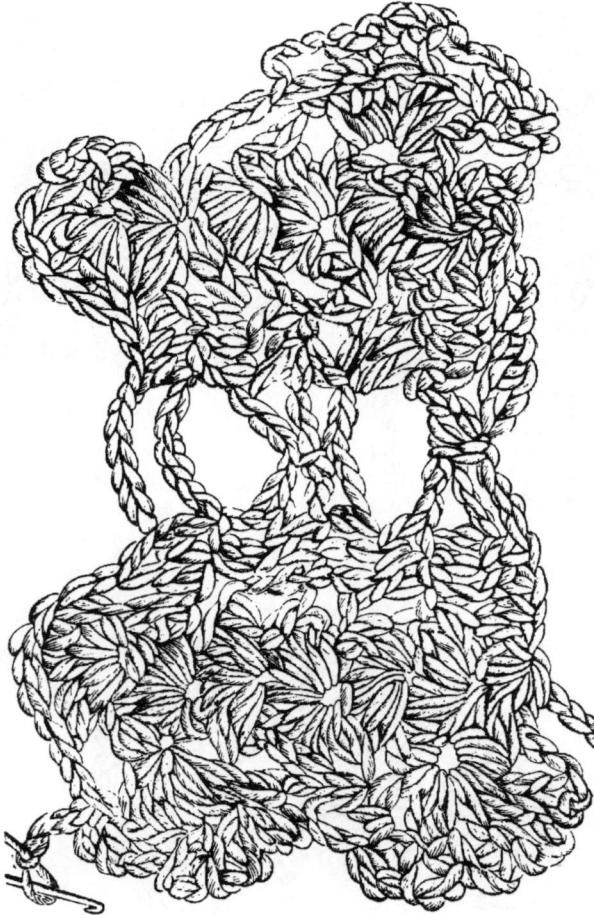

FIGURE No. 15.—EFFECT OF SEVERAL ROWS OF STITCHES.

used at one end of the lambrequin to attach the fringe and at the other end as a heading.

Continue to make this row in the same manner as the row just made : finish a scollop at the turning from this row to the next, as described at Figure No. 14; and then make this next row to correspond with the second row, by taking up the fourth stitches in the nearest two chains of seven stitches.

An idea of how the lambrequin looks as it increases in width is given by Figure No. 15. The method described provides for the use of two rows of ribbon. If only one row is desired, a chain of twenty-five stitches will start it. If a deeper lambrequin is desired, sixteen stitches, added to the forty used for the

double row, will provide for three rows of ribbon. The fringe is made by knotting several strands of the cord into the holes described as finishing the scollops, and may be of any desired depth. The ribbon may be of any color desired; pink, pale-blue, cardinal, orange, brown, peacock-blue, light-blue, olive, etc., being all pretty. The same pattern in crochet may be used in making tidies, with handsome effect.

A Pretty Easel.

THAT is, it became pretty after it had been decorated, but when it was first placed where the study of roses in a gilded frame, which it supported, would receive a good light, it was rather discouraging. The varnish was apparent, and yet the quality of the wood was apparent too, and neither were satisfactory. But it had to be adapted to the purpose, and this is how it was accomplished.

A glance convinced the furnisher that there were quite as many draperies in the room as its style and size permitted, so a scarf was not allowable, even if it would have answered the purpose of the decorator. Yet near a certain corner, but not *in* the corner, the easel must stand. Its lower part would be somewhat obscured by a chair drawn in front of it. The mass of bloom within the frame

would bear a subduing influence, and this was attainable in the shape of several long vines of artificial English ivy and a few fronds of maiden-hair. The ivy was twined about the upper portion as if it were a growing plant rooted in a concealed receptacle at the back, and the fronds of fern were deftly tacked to the back of the frame at one corner by pins, and bent to droop from the top and extend slightly along one side, their delicate foliage forming a slight screen over the roses but not obscuring them. The effect was not only improving, but positively beautifying. It betrays no hint that the means were resorted to for any purpose other than to develop a particularly effective background, and consequently it is worthy of being pronounced "artistic."

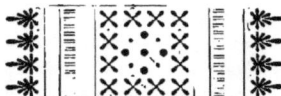

A Bit of Bloom.

THE modern fancy-worker may not be able to "paint the lily or gild refined gold," but the evidences of her liking for the golden finish are quite obvious.

A very pretty ornament for the corner of a room is made by gilding a fancy straw shade-hat and filling it with dried grasses, among which are set daisies that appear to be blooming naturally. One side of the brim may be turned down so as to allow the grasses to fall over it, and an Alpine staff may form the support, the hat being attached to it by a large bow of ribbon. Artificial wild-roses, thistles, milk-weed pods with their fluffy contents disclosed, or clover in masses of red and white, are all suitable blossoms for mingling with the grasses; the hat may be mounted upon a little easel, but it is more picturesque when the staff suggests its association with a summer's outing.

CHAPTER XVIII.

CROCHETTED WORK IN CRAZY STITCH.

A VERY pretty stitch known as the "crazy" stitch is introduced in this variety of crochetted work. Done in Shetland floss, split zephyrs, crewels, etc., it is beautiful and effective for shawls, Afghans and similar articles.

First, make a chain of stitches as long as desired for the article to be crochetted: then throw the thread once over the needle, as shown by Figure No. 1; take up the by Figure No. 3; throw the thread over again, and pull it through the nearest two loops on the needle, as shown by Figure No. 4; and crochet the remaining two loops off in the same way, as shown by Figure No. 5. This completes the double stitch, which is also fully described in another chapter on crochet work.

Make two more double stitches in the same loop, as shown by Figure No. 6.

Then take up the third loop in the chain, counting from the loop holding the three double stitches, and throw the thread over the needle, as shown by Figure No. 7; then

FIGURE No. 1.

FIGURE No. 2.

third nearest stitch to the needle; throw the thread over the needle, as shown by Figure No. 2, and pull it through the loop, as shown pull the thread through it and the loop on the needle, at *once*, to fasten down the shell thus made, as shown by Figure No. 8.

Then make a chain of three stitches; throw the thread over the needle; pass the needle through the loop holding the last stitch, and make three double stitches in this loop; proceed all along the chain in making the chain of the three stitches, a shell of three double stitches and the single fastening stitch, in order as described.

FIGURE No. 3.

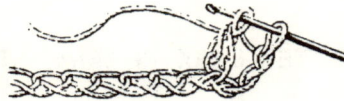

FIGURE No. 4.

FIGURE No. 5.

FIGURE No. 6.

FIGURES NOS. 1, 2, 3, 4, 5 AND 6.—DETAILS OF CRAZY STITCH.

FIGURE No. 7.

make the single or fastening stitch in the third stitch in the chain from this stitch, as shown by Figure No. 9.

Then make a chain of three stitches, and

When at the end of the chain make a chain of three stitches, as shown by Figure No. 10. Then turn the work and take up the third stitch in the shell of three double stitches last made, as shown by Figure No. 11; and pull the thread through, to make the fastening stitch described.

Then make a chain of three stitches, throw the thread over the needle, and pass the needle in the nearest hole formed by the

stitches in the next hole formed by a chain of stitches, and so on to the end of the row.

At the end of the row, take up the last stitch in the shell remaining, making a single stitch here.

Then make a chain of three stitches, turn

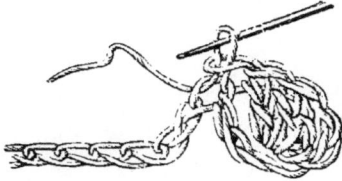

FIGURE NO. 8.

FIGURE NO. 9.

FIGURE NO. 10.

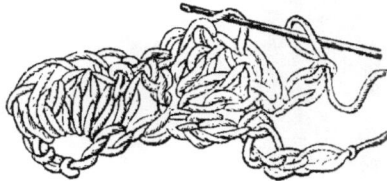

FIGURE No. 11.

FIGURES NOS. 7, 8, 9, 10 AND 11.—DETAILS OF CRAZY STITCH.

chain of three stitches in the first row, as shown by Figure No. 12; make three double stitches in this hole; then make a single stitch in the third stitch in the next shell, then a chain of three stitches, then three double

the work and proceed all through the line and all through the work, as described for the other rows.

This stitch is very simple indeed, and is also very effective, as may be seen by Figure

No. 13, where the appearance of several rows is shown.

In shawls, Afghans, nubias, fascinators and similar articles, a very rich and beautiful out the entire article, or in alternating stripes, as desired. Contrasting colors may be introduced in Afghans and carriage-robes with beautiful effect, making three or four rows

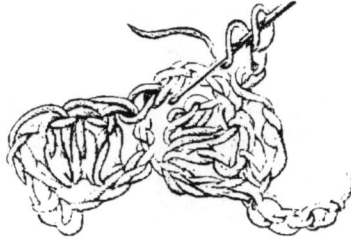

FIGURE No. 12.—DETAIL OF CRAZY STITCH.

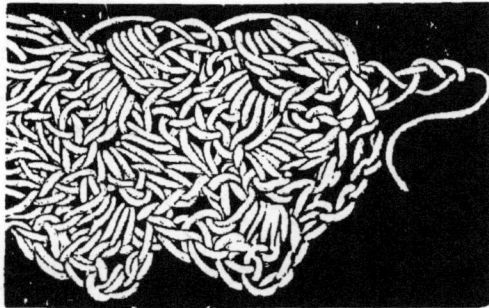

FIGURE No. 13.—EFFECT OF SEVERAL ROWS OF STITCHES.

effect may be obtained by using a thread of wool and thread of silk floss together in a stripe. This may be continued through- of one color for a stripe, and the same or a smaller number of rows of another color for another stripe, and so on.

CHAPTER XIX.

CROCHETTED LACE EDGINGS AND INSERTION.

THIS specimen of crochetted lace is done with Saxony yarn, and, while it may be suitably used on dresses, it is very appropriate as an edge to shawls having crochetted centers or centers of flannel, cashmere, merino, etc. It may also be appropriately used on underskirts or petticoats for the grown lady or the child, and may be made up in white or any preferred color. The pattern is simple, and the method of making it is here fully described, so that but little effort is necessary for a successful result. It would not be advisable to apply woollen lace upon any garment that is to be frequently laundered, as the design would soon become obscured by shrinking. There are, however, many articles to which such lace is particularly adapted that would not necessitate such a result. The scolloped portion is a light and airy garniture for infants' sacks, shawls and carriage robes, and also for ladies' house-shawls. The heading may be increased or decreased by beginning with twice or half the number of stitches.

Before entering upon the method of construction, it will probably be best to refer to the stitches employed, so that the amateur in crochetting will not meet with difficulties. A single crochet, as previously explained, is made by inserting the needle, *without* throwing the thread over, and crochetting the two loops off at *once*. A double crochet is made by throwing the thread over the needle before inserting the latter and crochetting two loops off the needle at a time.

Crochetted Lace Edging and Insertion.

FIGURES NOS. 1 and 2.—This pattern is simply executed and is very like torchon lace when made of linen thread. The engravings clearly illustrate the pattern and style of stitches, and any lady familiar with crochet-work can readily pick it out. Insertion to match the edging is represented at Figure No. 1. Made of coarse linen thread, the edging and insertion form a rich and handsome decoration for tidies, table and chair scarfs, and also for handsome scrim curtains.

Crochetted Lace.

FIGURE NO. 3.—Make a chain of stitches about two inches shorter than you desire the lace to be when finished; then turn and pick up the fourth stitch from the needle in the chain, making a single crochet stitch; make a chain of seven stitches, pick up the fourth stitch in the chain from the last stitch, mak-

ing only a single crochet stitch, and continue
in this manner all along the chain.

stitch in the nearest hole, making a single
crochet; then make a chain of seven stitches,

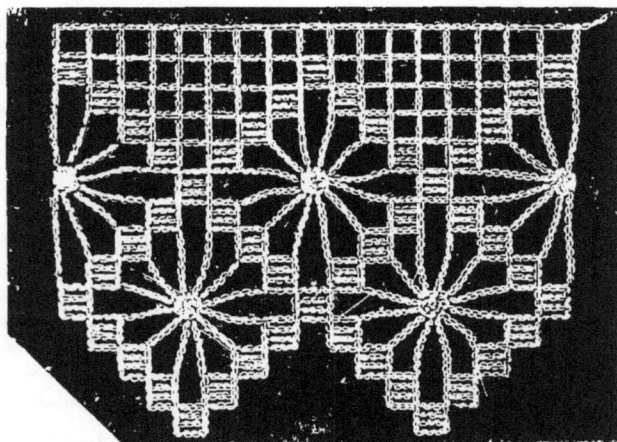

FIGURES NOS. 1 AND 2.—CROCHETED LACE EDGING AND INSERTION.

When at the end of the chain, make seven
rows and turn, and picking up the fourth

pick up the fourth stitch in the next hole, and
continue in the same manner all the way across.

Then make a chain of seven stitches, and turn and make another row of holes in the same manner.

When the three rows of holes are made, make a chain of five stitches; then turn and make four double crochet stitches in the nearest hole. Make one chain, and then make

for the second and third rows, and continue making the three rows of holes in alternation with the single rows of grouped stitches until a sufficient quantity of lace has been made.

To make the scollop: First row.—When the last row of the part just described is made, make a chain of five stitches, and then

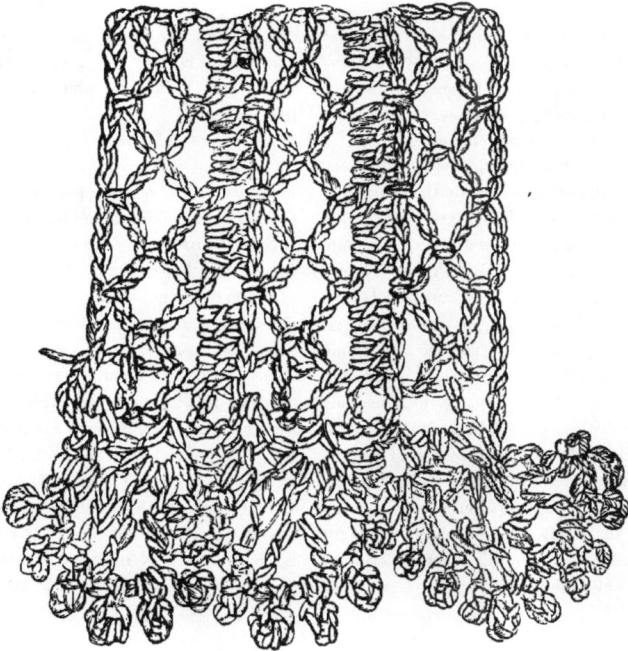

FIGURE No. 3.—CROCHETTED LACE.

four double stitches in the next hole, and so on to the end of the row.

Then make a chain of seven stitches, turn, and make a single crochet in the hole between the clusters of four stitches. Continue in this manner all the way across. Then make two more rows of holes in the manner described

make a double crochet in the nearest hole in the nearest long edge; then make a chain of two stitches, and make a double crochet in the right corner of the next hole; make a chain of two stitches; make a double crochet in the left corner of the same hole; make a chain of two stitches; make a double crochet in the next hole; make a chain of two stitches; make a double crochet in the next hole; make a chain of two, and a double crochet in the next hole; a chain of two, a double crochet in the right corner of the next hole; a chain of two, a double crochet in the left corner of the same hole; and proceed in this manner to the end.

A Home-Made Portfolio.

In the mind of the one who designed and executed it, "home-made" is not synonymous with poorly made, nor suggestive of any apology for the origin of whatever she undertakes; and her portfolio is an evidence of the creditable work that can be done by any one whose efforts are based on the same principles. Two narrow white wood frames, one considerably wider than the other, were procured and around the margin of each a conventional daisy design was hammered as it would be on brass. The surface of the rest of the frame was punctured slightly with a small nail, and then the woodwork was sized with white glue and thickly coated with metallic silver powder sifted through a piece of scrim. In the smaller frame a photograph of a woodland scene was placed within a mat of Gobelin blue plush, and in the larger one the owner's inter-linked initials worked upon satin the same shade, above a scroll which incloses the words "Ars Longa." The satin is mounted on a stretcher, as an artist mounts his canvas, backed with cardboard, and the nicety and precision with which the work is done gives no hint of the words which usually follow the quotation, for the worker apparently took plenty of time to do her best. There is no glass over the photograph, but upon the inside of its frame satin is tacked, and over the tacking a handsome silk cord is invisibly arranged. The two frames are hinged together at one of the longest sides of each, their positions being regulated to bring the larger frame at the back with the satin upon the inside while the photograph frame forms the front. Small silver screw-eyes are inserted in the ends of each frame, and through them are run small metal chains harmonizing in color, which hold the two frames at a proper angle. The stand is covered with Gobelin blue plush, and like the portfolio is almost entirely home-made. The entire affair is as attractive as it is useful, and may be duplicated with any variations in its details which personal taste suggests.

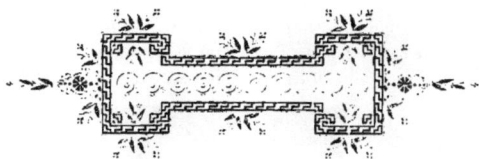

CHAPTER XX.

Crochetted Lace Edging and Insertion: Suitable for Linen, Silk or Cotton.

Crochetted Lace.

THIS lace is pretty for under-garments, aprons, pillow-cases, etc., and is made of fine linen or cotton thread, crochetted with a steel needle.

Make a chain of seven stitches, turn and make three crochets in the seventh stitch from the needle, throwing the thread over the needle each time ; then make six chain stitches, and turn as shown at figure No. 1; throw the thread over the needle, and make three crochets in the middle of the first three crochets; continue as shown at figure No. 2 until four loops are formed at each side as shown at figure No. 3.

Now make three chain stitches, and make nineteen crochets in the first loop to the left; beginning with the second of these crochets to make a chain of nine stitches into every alternating crochet, throwing the thread over the needle and crochetting the thread and loops all off at once for every crochet. Make a single crochet in the next loop.

Make a chain of three stitches and fasten in the middle stitch of the first loop of nine stitches as shown at the left of the scollop

pictured at figure No. 4. Continue in this way all around, until all the loops are taken up. Now to continue the heading make three chain stitches and then three crochets into the center of the three crochets forming the head-ing. Proceed by making six chain stitches and three crochets into the center stitch of the three crochets just made; make a chain of three stitches, fasten with a single crochet to the top of the first loop of the scollop. Throw the thread over the needle, put the latter through the first hole in the scollop, throw the thread over the needle again, draw it back through the hole and single crochet, and with it draw all the stitches off the needle. Repeat until four of these crochets are made in the hole. Chain one stitch and proceed as be-fore until all the holes of the scollop are filled as just described, and as pictured at the right of figure No. 4. Throw the thread over the needle, put it through the next loop in the heading, throw the thread over the needle, draw the thread through the loop, and with a single crochet take off the three stitches on the needle. Make a chain of seven stitches, turn, and take up the fourth stitch on the scollop. Continue in this way all around the scollop. Now to carry the heading along

make a chain of three stitches and three crochets, making the latter into the center of the
three crochets already made in the heading.
Make a chain of six stitches, and make three
more crochets into the last group described.

entire scollop. Now taking the first loop in
that portion of the heading originally formed;
turn, throw the thread over the needle, put it
through the first loop of the scollop, throw the
thread over the needle and draw it through

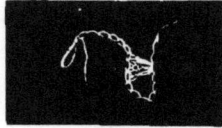

FIGURE NO. 1.

FIGURE NO. 2.

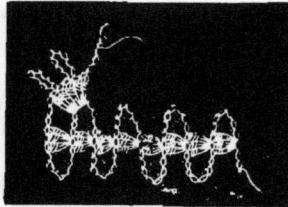

FIGURE NO. 3.

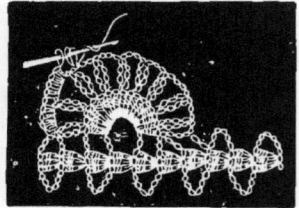

FIGURE NO. 4.

the needle and draw it through this loop with another double crochet; follow this with two single crochets to complete the filling-in of this loop. Then continue this process in every loop about the entire scollop, to complete the outer edging. Making a chain of three stitches and fasten to the crochet which

stage where the outer edging is begun. Then into the first hole of the second scollop make two single crochets, one double crochet and two chain stitches; take up the center stitch of the loop in the heading and the center stitch of the first loop in the edge of the completed scollop with a single crochet; make a

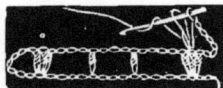

FIGURE NO. 6.

FIGURE NO. 7.

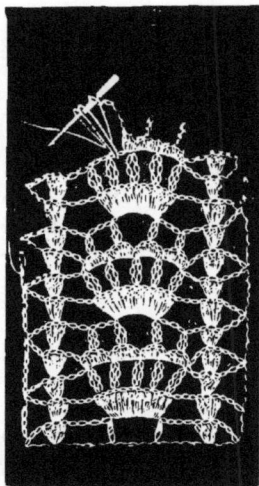

FIGURE NO. 8.

Figures Nos. 6, 7 and 8. Crochetted Insertion, and Method of Making It.

forms the end of the heading thus far made. To continue the heading make a chain of six stitches and three crochets in the center of the three crochets already made in the heading, and continue with the heading until four loops are formed on each side. Make the second scollop the same as the first, up to the

chain of two stitches, turn, make a double crochet and two single crochets in the hole into which the two single crochets and the double crochet have been previously made. To make the second joining of the scollops, make two single crochets, one double crochet and two chain stitches; take up the center stitch of the loop in the edging of the completed scollop with a single crochet. Make two chain stitches, turn and repeat the double and single crochets as explained for the first joining. Proceed by finishing the edging of the second scollop, and repeat the process until the requisite length has been accomplished. Then make a row of chain stitching along the top of the heading for sewing on the decoration.

Crochetted Insertion.

This insertion is to match the lace above described.

Make a chain of twenty-four stitches, then turn, and in the eighth stitch from the needle make three crochets, throwing the thread over the needle, as described for the heading of the lace.

Then make four chain stitches, and make a double crochet in the fifth stitch in the chain from the group of three crochets. Then make a chain of four stitches and another double crochet in the fourth stitch of the chain, counting from the last crochet; then a chain of four stitches and three crochets in the fifth stitch from this on the chain; this is shown at Figure No. 6, as is also the next step, which is as follows:

Make a chain of six stitches, turn, and make three crochets in the middle of the last three crochets made. Then make a chain of two stitches, and make eleven crochets in the second hole, making a loop of six stitches into the top of the second of these crochets and a similar loop into each alternating crochet, as represented at Figure No. 7.

Then make a chain of three stitches, and make three single crochets in the middle of the three crochets near the end. Make six chain stitches, turn, and make three crochets in the middle of the three crochets just made; then make a chain of two stitches, and fasten in the center stitch of the nearest loop; repeat the two chain stitches and fasten in each remaining loop.

Then make a chain of two stitches, and make three crochets in the middle of the crochets near the end. Make a chain of six stitches, and make three crochets in the middle of the three crochets just made. Make two chain stitches, and make six single crochets in the hole between the first two loops, making a chain of five stitches between the third and fourth crochets.

Repeat in each remaining hole as shown at the unfinished top row of Figure No. 8. Then make a chain of two stitches, and make three crochets in the middle of the three crochets near the end.

Make a chain of six stitches, turn, and make three crochets in the middle of the three crochets just made; make a chain of two stitches, and fasten in the first loop; make a chain of three stitches and fasten in the second loop; make a chain of four stitches, and fasten in the third loop.

Make a chain of three stitches, and fasten in the fourth loop; make a chain of two stitches, and make three crochets in the middle of the three crochets near the end.

This completes the pattern and the beginning row for the next pattern, which is done in the same way and is shown at Figure No. 8. A chain is crochetted along each side, for the sewing-on rows.

CHAPTER XXI.

Crochetted Laces, with Braid Headings, and Method of Making Them.

TO make this lace, a piece of fancy braid with a loop edge and some fine cotton or linen thread will be needed. Begin by fastening the thread into the first loop at one end of the braid, chain one stitch, throw the thread over the needle, fasten into the second loop, chain one again and continue in this way into the seventh loop on the braid.

double crochets, then another chain of three stitches and three double crochets, and still another chain of three stitches and four double crochets. Then take up the next loop with a single crochet. Make a chain of eight stitches, turn and fasten with a single crochet in the second loop formed in the first hole. Make a chain of three stitches, turn and fill in the hole with double crochets and loops as before. Make three

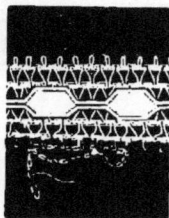

FIGURE NO. 1.

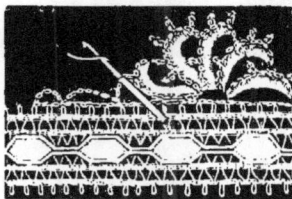

FIGURE NO. 2.

Figures Nos. 1 and 2 Represent Details of Crochetted Edging.

Now make a chain of five stitches, then turn back and with a single crochet take up the second hole on the braid, counting from the needle; make a chain of eight stitches and take up the last hole on the braid, counting from the needle, and make a chain of three stitches, as shown at figure No. 1. Turn and make three double crochets in the large hole just made; then into this hole also make a chain of three stitches and three

more shells in the same way, fastening in the same manner in this hole, to complete the group of five shells shown at Figure No. 2. Now make a chain of three stitches, and fasten the first loop of the fifth shell to the first loop on the braid with a single crochet. Now take up nine loops on the braid in the same manner as in beginning the work. Then make a chain of five stitches, turn and take up the second hole on the braid, count-

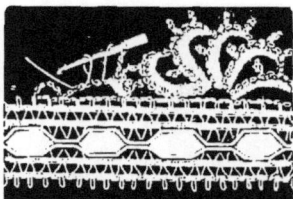

FIGURE NO. 3.—DETAIL OF
SECOND SCOLLOP.

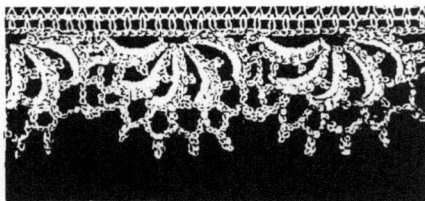

FIGURE NO. 4.—CROCHETTED EDGING, WITH ONE
ROW OF SCOLLOPS AND HEADING.

FIGURE NO. 5.—CROCHETTED EDGING, SHOWING DETAIL OF
SECOND ROW OF SCOLLOPS.

Figure No. 2. Then a chain of two stitches, and into the hole formed by the loop of eight stitches make three double crochets; chain two stitches, turn and with a single crochet take up the remaining loop in the fifth shell of the first scollop. Then make pleted, and make each succeeding scollop in the same way. This width when provided with a heading, such as is illustrated at Figure No. 7, and finished with an edging in the manner shown at Figure No. 4, is pretty for underwear, aprons, etc., and is edged with a row of holes and loops as pictured at Figure No. 4. This edging is made as follows: when the last shell in the row is made, make a chain of eight stitches and turn; then take up the fifth stitch in the chain, counting from the needle, with a single crochet, and make a chain of three and then a single crochet in the nearest loop in the shell. Repeat in each of the loops along the edge of the scollop.

If a deeper pattern be desired, make a row of loops along the tops of the shells

FIGURE NO. 6.—CROCHETTED EDGING, SHOWING TWO ROWS OF SCOLLOPS AND HEADING.

by making nine chain stitches for the chain connecting the scollops; eight chain stitches for the next loop, which takes up the first loop in the third shell; eight chain stitches for the next hole, which takes up the first loop in the fourth shell; eight chain stitches for the next loop, which will form the center of the scollop in the added row and is caught to the second loop of the fourth (same) shell in the scollop above; then repeat these four loops all along the lace, as shown at the right end of Figure No. 5,

before beginning to make the shells of the second row.

The shells are connected in the same way as in the first line, and the finish is as described at Figure No. 4. The rows may be repeated until the lace is as deep as desired, and the method of making the rows for the second depth of the pattern is clearly shown at Figure No. 5. The lace completed with the heading is shown at Figure No. 6.

To make the heading: make a row of loops on the braid, using six chain stitches for each loop, and taking every third loop on the braid up with a single crochet;

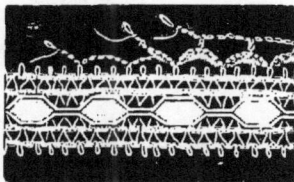

FIGURE NO. 7.—SHOWING DETAIL OF HEADING.

then in each crochetted loop make four double crochets, a chain of three stitches and four double crochets. To complete the heading, make a sewing-on row of chain stitching, as shown at Figure No. 7 in this chapter.

Crochetted Lace, with Braid Heading, and Method of Making It.

FIGURES NOS. 8, 9, 10 and 11.—This lace is crochetted back and forth on fancy braid that should be the length required for the lace. Begin by fastening the thread in the first loop of the braid; then make a chain of ten stitches and fasten in the second loop of the braid with a single crochet; make a chain of twelve stitches and fasten in the fourth loop (omitting one) with a single crochet;

then make a chain of ten stitches and fasten in the next loop.

Chain two stitches, fasten in the next loop of the braid; chain two more and fasten in the succeeding loop, and continue in this the first loop, crochetting all the stitches off the needle at once for the first and twelfth crochet. Into the next loop of twelve stitches make twelve double crochets, chaining one stitch between the sixth and seventh

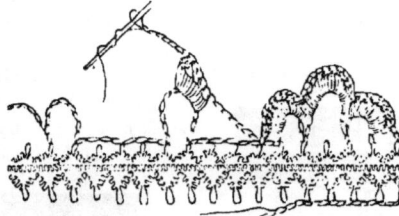

FIGURE NO. 8.

FIGURE NO. 9.

way until you have taken up five loops. Chain twelve stitches and fasten in the next loop; then take up five more loops, chaining two stitches between every two loops. Chain ten stitches, fasten in the next loop, chain twelve and fasten in the next loop (omittting one), chain ten and fasten in the next, and so on for whatever length is required. When this has been done, chain two stitches and fasten in the last loop on the braid. Turn, and make twelve double crochets in

FIGURE NO. 10.

crochets, taking all the stitches off the needle at once for the first and twelfth crochets. Into the next loop of ten make twelve crochets in the same manner as in the first loop of ten, and fasten with a single crochet into the adjacent short loop previously formed by the chain of two. Next chain seven stitches and fasten with a double crochet into the next large loop. Now into this same loop make three double crochets in the same manner and then two double crochets, putting the thread over the needle twice for each of the latter two and crochetting these two off, two stitches at a time. Chain six stitches, make two more double crochets, throwing the thread over the needle twice for each crochet and crochetting off two stitches at once as before; then make four double crochets into this

Turn, and chain eight stitches and fasten with a single crochet between the sixth and seventh stitches of the last scollop made; chain eight more and fasten with a single crochet between the sixth and seventh stitches of the center scollop; chain twelve stitches and fasten with a single crochet in the

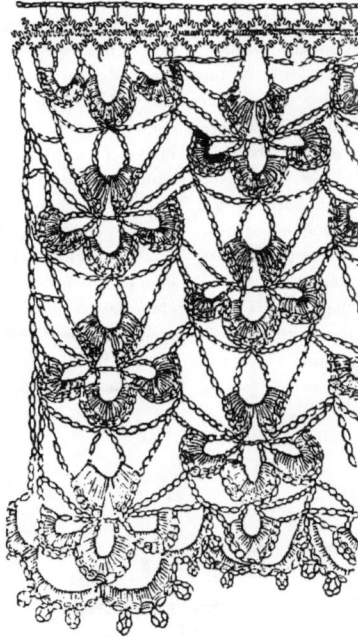

FIGURE NO. 11.

Figures Nos. 8, 9, 10 and 11.—Crochetted Lace, and Detail of its Construction.

loop in the ordinary manner. Chain seven stitches and fasten with a single crochet into the fourth of the adjacent small loops. Proceed by duplicating the processes employed in the first two parts of the design until the end of the braid is reached. Make a chain of two stitches and fasten.

same hole as the last; chain eight stitches and fasten with a single crochet between the sixth and seventh stitches of the next scollop; chain eight more stitches and fasten with a single crochet in the large loop at the center of the adjacent design. Chain ten and fasten with a single crochet into the same hole as the last; chain twelve and fasten with a single crochet also into the same hole, and lastly, chain ten and likewise fasten into this hole, with a single crochet. Chain eight and fasten between the sixth and seventh stitch of the next succeeding scollop and repeat the looping as for the first scollop, continuing as before to the end of the braid, and fastening.

Turn and chain seven, fasten with a double crochet into the loop at the center of the last scollop; proceed by making three other double crochets into this loop. Now into the same loop make two double crochets, throwing the thread twice over the needle each time and crochetting the stitches off, two at a time. Chain six and repeat the two double crochets with the thread thrown over the needle, etc., and follow by making four double crochets in the ordinary way. Then chain seven and fasten with a single crochet in the next loop; chain three and fasten with a double crochet in the first of the group of three loops following. Repeat to whatever depth is desired; and, having completed the last row, make a chain of ten stitches, turn, and fasten into the nearest loop with a single crochet; chain ten and fasten with a single crochet into the center of the chain connecting the two parts of the design. Chain eight, fasten between the sixth and seventh crochets in the first scollop, chain eight, fasten into the center of the next scollop, chain eight, fasten into the center of the next scollop, chain eight and with a single crochet fasten to the chain connecting the two designs. Continue in this way to the end of the braid. Turn, and into the loop last formed make three double crochets, chain five, make three double crochets, chain five, make three double crochets, chain five and three more double crochets; then with a single crochet fasten into the center of the first scollop. Now fill the next loop in the same manner as the one just described and so continue along the entire margin.

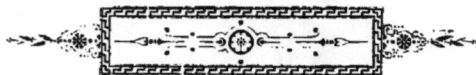

CHAPTER XXII.

Collars, Edgings and Insertion of Feather-Edged Braid.

Child's Collar.

FIGURE No. 1.—This figure represents a pretty, round collar for a little boy or girl. It is made of feather-edged braid crochetted with fine thread, and is shaped to the neck by a cord with tassels, that passes through tiny openings a little below the upper edge. These collars bear a close resemblance to Russian point lace, and can be obtained at very reasonable prices at any of the fancy dry-goods stores : but will cost but a trifling amount, if the lady constructs them herself.

Child's Sailor Collar.

FIGURE No. 2.—This engraving shows a pretty collar for a youngster. It is made in the sailor shape, and is crochetted with white cotton and feather-edged braid.

Full Size of Scollops for Sailor Collar.

FIGURE No. 3.—This engraving shows the details of the construction, which may be thus easily wrought out by any one accustomed to this class of work. The braid appears to be cut after forming the loops and points, but the row is really placed directly under the one seen in the engraving and is fastened there by the crochetted stitches, which are taken up through the loops of both rows. Colored cottons are sometimes used in making these collars, and for edgings designed for trimming gingham and seersucker dresses. When white thread is used, however, care should be exercised that the same shade is used throughout, as some is blue-white and some cream-white, and the result of their admixture is not pleasing. This difference is, of course, obliterated when the article is laundered ; but as considerable wear may be obtained before washing becomes necessary, it is well to remember the caution to which we have just given expression.

Child's Fancy Collar.

FIGURE No. 4.—This illustrates another pretty collar, for which the feather-edged trimming has been used as decoration. It is of the charming sailor shape and is made of linen ; but may be of Valenciennes or Torchon lace, or of piqué ornamented about the edges with lace or embroidery.

Trimming of Feather-Edged Braid.

FIGURE No. 5.—" Feather-edged braid " is the basis of this pretty trimming, and crochet-work forms it into the graceful outlines illustrated. The design is easily followed, as the engraving is very plain. By adding to   every lady knows how prettily this braid

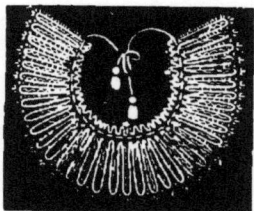

FIGURE No. 1.—CHILD'S COLLAR.

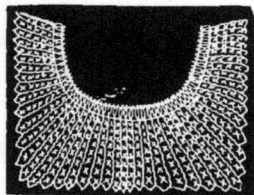

FIGURE No. 2.—CHILD'S SAILOR COLLAR.

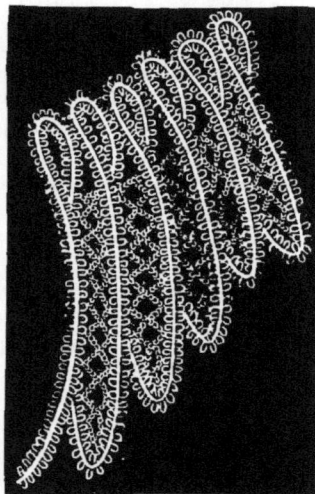

FIGURE No. 3.—FULL SIZE OF SCOLLOPS
FOR SAILOR COLLAR.

Edging and Insertion.

FIGURES NOS. 6 AND 7.— An edging and an insertion formed of crochet work and feather-edged braid are here illustrated. The engraving explains the details better than words. The insertion is made just like the edging, except that a chain is added to both sides instead of one. For children's dresses cardinal, pale-blue or pink cotton may be used for the crochet part, but white is selected for all other purposes, because of its harmony with all tints.

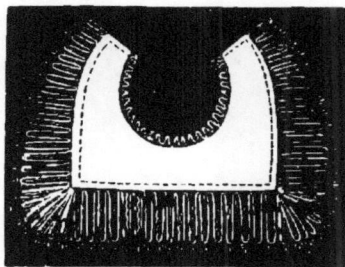

FIGURE NO. 4.—CHILD'S FANCY COLLAR.

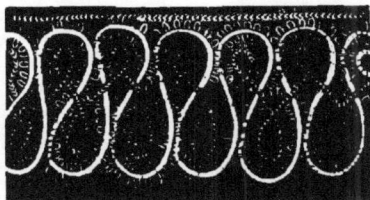

FIGURE NO. 5.—TRIMMING OF FEATHER-EDGED BRAID.

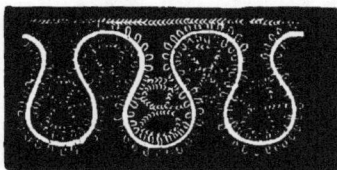

FIGURE NO. 6.—DESIGN FOR EDGING.

FIGURE NO. 7.—DESIGN FOR INSERTION.

Fancy Wall-Pockets.

A PRETTY wall-pocket, large and strong enough to hold trifles that one desires to keep, is made as follows : Take a shallow paper box that is square or nearly so and from the cover separate the edge which slips over the box proper. Finish the margin with a fancy cord or with a binding of velvet or plush, and then run narrow ribbons through corresponding holes made in both the box and cover, tying them so as to bring the two portions together at the bottom and leave them far enough apart at the top to permit of inserting whatever the pocket is intended to hold. Suspend it by cord or ribbons to a fancy-headed tack. A box that has a pretty picture on the top or is covered with fancy paper may be utilized for this purpose with pleasing results. If the edge of the cover is very shallow it need not be removed.

Two flat pieces of Bristol board may be joined by gore-shaped pieces of plush, velvet or strong fancy paper, and upon that which is to form the front may be neatly gummed a portrait of some celebrity, such as is often published in the best illustrated periodicals of the day, or a small landscape engraving, which may be obtained from the same source. A band of ribbon velvet or of velvet paper, in some rich tint, forms a pretty framing, and a fancy cord provides a neat bordering for all the edges and also the means of suspension. If the board be strong enough and the decoration artistic, a very durable and pretty pocket may be thus made at a trifling expense. Scraps of velvet and tinsel paper, and the numerous varieties of wall paper in art tints which may be left over from making borders, friezes, dadoes, etc., may be utilized for such articles with good results.

CHAPTER XXIII.

MACRAMÉ LACE WORK

AS far back as history takes us, lace seems to have held sway over the human affection for things beautiful. The Egyptians, Romans, Israelites, all indulged in the luxury of lace embellishments; and many of the beautiful laces which appear quite modern to us are revivals of those of ancient days.

Among the most easily made laces, and one that, owing to its simplicity of formation, is within the reach of rich and poor alike, is that called Macramé. This lace is formed by knotting threads together, and many and beautiful are its patterns. It may be used in beautifying the toilette of my lady, and also in making lovely her *boudoir*, her parlor or her sitting-room. Lambrequins, table-covers, whisk-broom holders, shopping-bags, game-bags for the sportsman, shawl-cases and bags for the traveller, hammocks, etc., may all be made of this handsome lace.

By studying these engravings and following closely the accompanying descriptions, success will surely attend those who seek to unravel its mysteries.

The requisites for making the lace are a desk, pins and cord. The desk, with the pins, may be purchased; but a lady of ingenu-ity can easily make one for herself in the following manner: A smoothly planed board, about twenty or twenty-five inches long and twelve or fourteen inches deep, with nicely rounded edges, is the first requirement. Cover the upper side of the board with several layers of flannel or cloth, drawing all sufficiently taut to avoid wrinkles, and securing them perfectly so that not a wrinkle will ruffle the surface in the working. If the regular pins cannot be procured, small nails, carpet tacks or stout common pins may be used. Arrange the pins at equal intervals across the upper edge of the desk, and also at the ends wherever cross-threads are to be fastened.

Tying cord and softly twisted fishing cord are sometimes used, and so also are the coarser threads in white or delicate tints either singly or combined. The finer the thread, however, the closer the pins should be placed. The cord or thread usually employed is known as the "Macramé," and may be obtained in fine and coarse, as well as in medium grades.

Attachment of the Threads.

FIGURE No. 1.—This engraving illustrates how the threads are attached and the work begun. After arranging the pins according to previous instructions, fasten two threads of equal lengths about the pins as shown by Figure No. 1—A. Then tie them in a single knot, as shown by Figure No. 1—B, and in a second knot as shown by Figure No. 1—C, to produce an ordinary double knot. Now arrange a cord across the desk, tying its ends securely to pins fastened in the ends at a depth sufficiently low to permit the cord to cross over the threads and just below the double knots. Then proceed as in Figure No. 1—D,

It is not unlikely that even as early as this stage of the work the hands will feel the effects of drawing the cord, especially if it is of the firm, hard, twisted variety, and to the novice the advice not to attempt too much without permitting them time to recover, may be given. There is a knack in handling the cords so as not to cut or chafe the hands, and until it is acquired many ladies protect the palms and fingers by wearing old gloves, from which the tips of the fingers have been cut.

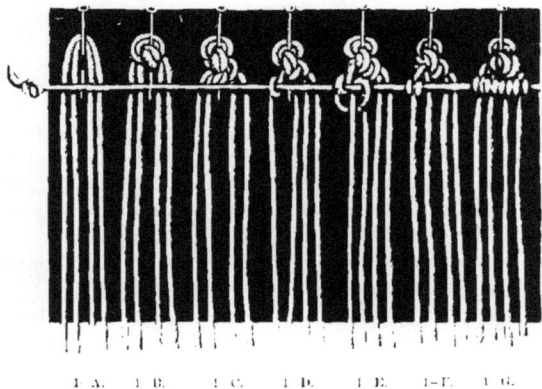

1 A.   1 B.   1 C.   1 D.   1 E.   1—F.   1 G.

FIGURE NO. 1.—ATTACHMENT OF THE THREADS.

commencing with the first left-hand thread, bringing it over the cross-thread and under toward the left, as illustrated; using the same thread to tie the knot as illustrated at Figure No. 1—E, drawing this thread very tightly, and producing the double coil as shown in Figure No. 1—F. Then take up each of the succeeding threads in a similar manner, producing the result seen in Figure No. 1—G. This completes the first unbroken cross-line cord from which the next stitch is worked, as shown by Figure No. 2.

The work is not retarded by such a course, indeed it is advanced, because the hands thus protected can withstand the influence of constant friction from the material. It may not be amiss to add that if before beginning lace-making each time, the hands are bathed in warm water, and while still moist, rubbed with cold cream, or whatever emollient experience has proven best adapted to them, the cuticle will be less liable to break beneath the tension of a cord drawn too quickly or too tightly.

Diagonal Pattern.

FIGURE No. 2.—This illustrates the diagonal pattern, which in this instance is produced by the use of twelve threads. Selecting the first thread at the left as the leader or the thread over which the others are to be knotted, take up the next thread at the right, and tie it over the leader as seen at figure No. 2—A, and draw it closely as directed for the cross-lines. Then take up each of the four succeeding threads separately, and continue with each in a similar manner, produc-

No. 1—F, the result of which is also shown at Figure No. 2—D.

Although this may be properly termed only a preliminary to more elaborate patterns, it is in itself a very pretty and effective design and it is especially adapted to the embellishment of such articles as are constructed with a view to showing some delicate and bright color through its meshes. As it does not however permit of running ribbons into the heading it is less in favor than some others for decorating articles for which an elaborate finish is

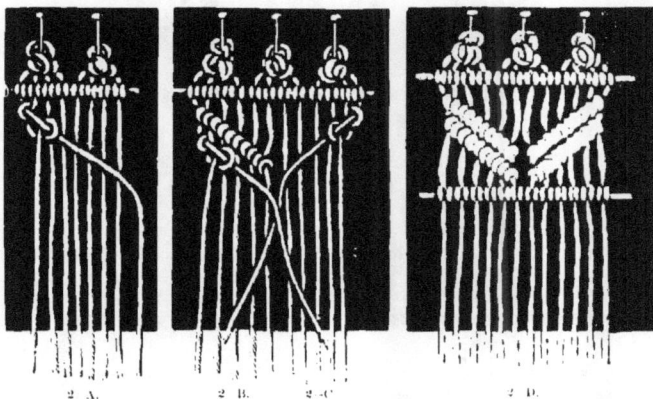

2 A. 2 B. 2 C. 2 D.

FIGURE No. 2.—DIAGONAL PATTERN.

ing the first diagonal pattern as shown by Figure No. 2—B. Then again, take the left-hand thread as the leader, and proceed with the succeeding five threads as already described. Then take the right-hand thread of this cluster of twelve threads already selected, bring it over the five at the left nearest it; then take up the first of these five threads nearest the leader, and knot it over the leader with a reversed knot, as illustrated in Figure No. 2—C. Then proceed as directed in Figure No. 2—B, producing the result as illustrated at Figure No. 2—D. Below this arrange another cross-thread, over which tie each thread, as directed for the first at Figure

required or desired. It is however commendable for the ease with which it may be freshened by the most simple laundry process.

All macramé lace may be renovated by washing it in water in which a little soap and borax have been dissolved. The dust should be shaken from it before it is wetted and it should be moved up and down vigorously after being allowed to soak for some time. Several rinsings and a thorough squeezing are in order, and before it is hung to dry it should be well shaken. When dry the pattern may be drawn into shape with the fingers and the fringe clipped to give it a fresh and attractive appearance.

Tape or Braid Pattern.

FIGURE No. 3.—This illustrates the tape or braid pattern, which in this instance is formed by selecting clusters of four threads

and proceed with the same stitch to produce the effect as shown by Figure No. 3—C, below which attach a third cross-cord.

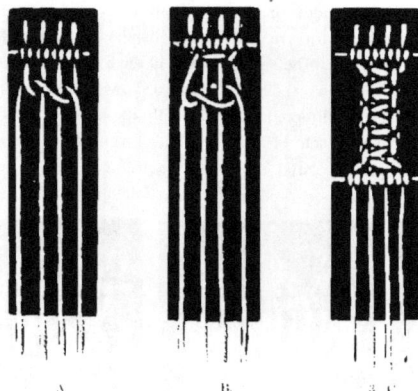

FIGURE No. 3.—TAPE OR BRAID PATTERN.

each. Of these clusters take the middle two threads, over which knot the outside threads, disposing of the first as in Figure No. 3—A,

Lace Pattern.

FIGURE No. 4.—This illustrates the lace pattern. Separate the threads into clusters

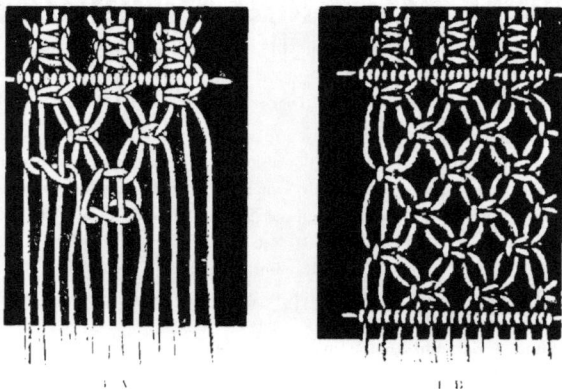

FIGURE No. 4.—LACE PATTERN.

drawing it closely to the cross-thread and again tying the same two threads, as seen in Figure No. 3—B, also drawing this tightly;

of four, and tie a double knot over each of the middle two of the clusters, as illustrated at Figure No. 3—B, to form the heading or commencement of the pattern. Then leave the two threads at the left, and take up the next four, over the middle two of which tie the two outer threads, as illustrated at Figure No. 4—A. continuing this method as a second line of knots across the length of the desk. Then, taking up the two threads at the left, which were dropped at this row, take the two next to the right, to form a cluster of four; then proceed to tie the first knot in the third row, combining the same to produce the nec-

the tape pattern as illustrated in Figure No. 3—C, to the amount of nine knots or stitches. Then take the two leaders, bring them up over the tape, insert them through the space between the lower diagonal cords, and draw the ends of the tape closely to the first stitch of the same, as seen at Figure No. 5—B. Then, take the two working threads or cords, bringing them outside the commencement of the tape pattern, and tie them around the two leaders in the double knot to make the

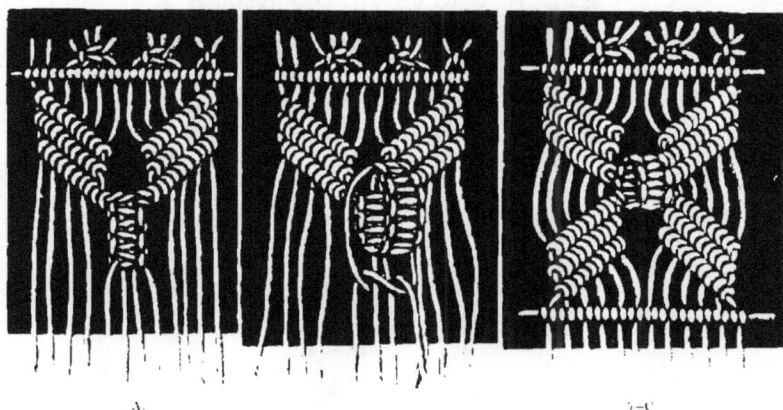

A.   5—C

FIGURE No. 5.—TAPE OR BRAID KNOT.

essary depth of this pattern, the completed result of which is shown at Figure No. 4—B, which also discloses the fourth cross cord.

Tape or Braid Knot.

FIGURE No. 5.—This illustrates the fifth pattern in the series, the first arrangement of which is produced as in Figure No. 2, but discloses three diagonal cords, instead of two, with the tape or braid knot introduced, the production of which is attained as follows: Select the middle four threads of this double cluster of the diagonal pattern, and compose

fastening, and complete the tape knot, as shown at Figure No. 5—C, which also discloses a second line of diagonal cords, made as follows: Take the twelve threads, and work each of the six outward from the knot to complete this section of the pattern, which is divided by the fifth cross-cord from the tassel fringe that completes the series.

It is always best to use the same make of cord throughout for each piece of lace as different makes are apt to vary in closeness of twist or some equally important particular.

Tassel Fringe, for Finishing Macremé Work.

Figure No. 6.—This illustrates the construction of the tassel fringe. Select twenty-four of the threads at the left hand and divide

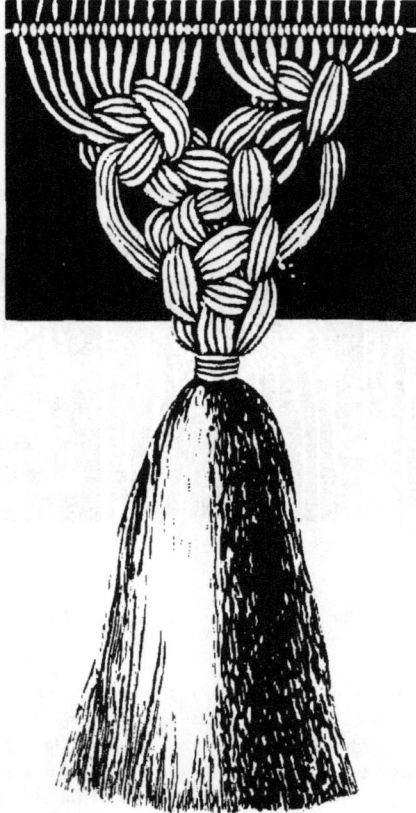

FIGURE No. 6.—TASSEL FRINGE, FOR FINISHING MACREMÉ WORK.

them into two groups of twelve threads each. Then subdivide each of these groups into three clusters of four threads each, and proceed to knot them as illustrated. This forms the heading. Then untwist and comb the threads below the last knot, to form a light, fluffy tassel.

The knots or stitches described are among the simplest varieties, and by the exercise of a little ingenuity on the part of the lace-maker, many beautiful results and quite an assortment of very pretty patterns will be obtained. It would be well for the worker to remember, however, that every thread should be knotted twice, and that the knots or stitches should be tightly drawn, to keep them from slipping during the progress of the work or afterward.

CHAPTER XXIV.

FRINGES AND THEIR CONSTRUCTION.

Ball for Tassel Fringes, etc., and Method of Making It.

FIGURES Nos. 1, 2, 3, AND 4.—In making the ball illustrated at figure No. 1, worsted of any variety may be used in single colors or in two or three shades as preferred. First cut from card-board a circular piece about one inch in diameter, and cut a large hole in the center; run the worsted in and out through

FIGURE No. 1.

the hole, about the solid portion of the section, as shown by Figure No. 2, until the section is very thickly and uniformly covered. Then run a thread of the worsted under the

worsted on the section, as shown by Figure No. 3, being careful to put the needle back in the place where it comes through till the thread comes out at the starting point; then cut the worsted all around the edge of the section, and tie the thread run round the hole as tightly as possible. The manner of putting in the tying thread and cutting the

FIGURE No. 2.

worsted is shown at Figure No. 3, and the manner of tying the thread when the worsted is cut is shown at Figure No. 4. After cutting the worsted, pull it through the hole at one side; clip the threads evenly and closely with a sharp scissors, rolling the ball between the palms of the hands to shape it; then shake it well. The balls may be made any size desired by increasing or decreasing the size of the card-board section upon which the worsted is wound. Many persons make the balls by winding the worsted in and out between the prongs of a fork and tying the

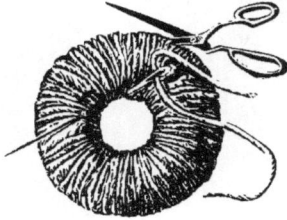

FIGURE No. 3.

entire mass through the center. The cutting, clipping, rolling, etc., is the same as that

shown by Figure No. 5 may be used entirely as lambrequins or as edges for them, or they

FIGURE No. 4.

may edge table-scarfs, chair-scarfs, work-baskets, etc. The method of constructing the

FIGURE No. 5.

directed for the balls just described. The effect of the balls made in fringes is shown at Figures Nos. 5 and 6.

balls for these fringes is illustrated at Figures Nos. 2, 3 and 4. Worsteds of all varieties may be used in making such fringes, and the

FIGURE No. 6.

FIGURES NOS. 5 AND 6.—STYLES FOR BALL FRINGES.

Styles for Ball Fringes.

FIGURES NOS. 5 AND 6.—Fringes made as

balls may be of one color or may show two or three colors, as preferred.

Knotted Fringes.

FIGURES NOS. 7, 8 AND 9.—Three different ways of knotting fringes are here shown. The fringe is formed by ravelling the ends of the article to be so completed, quite deeply, separating the fringed part into clusters of equal numbers of threads and then knotting them in any of the ways illustrated. If it be

Bag for Soiled Clothes.

FIGURE No. 10.—A very useful article is pictured in this engraving. It may be made of towelling, duck, crash, linen, canvas or any similar fabric. The section, which should be more than twice as long as it is wide, is folded up quite deeply, and the edges are seamed together. The top is then folded over

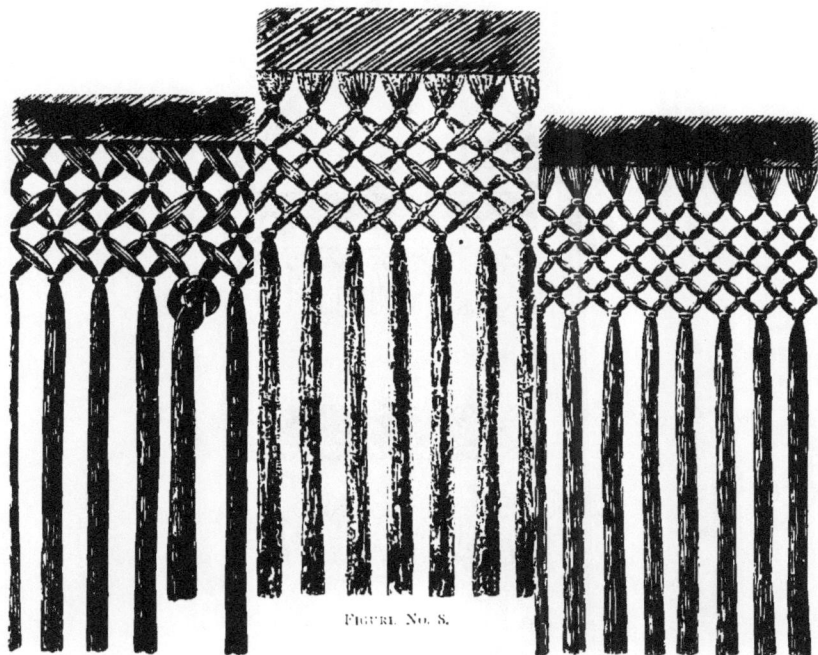

FIGURE No. 8.

FIGURE No. 7.

FIGURE No. 9.

FIGURES NOS 7, 8 AND 9.—KNOTTED FRINGES.

not desirable to ravel the edge of the article, threads of silk, floss, etc., may be run through the edge until a heavy fringe is formed, and similarly knotted. Fringe, knotted in the manner represented at Figure No. 9, is used in decorating the bag pictured at Figure No. 10 in this chapter.

a rod in cover fashion, and to the ends of the rod are attached the suspending ribbons. The edge of the cover and the lower end of the case are trimmed with fringe, and a little above the fringe are applied, with herring-bone or other fancy stitches, strips of ribbon that are embroidered along the center with daisies or

other flowers. If a fancy ribbon be used the
application stitches only are necessary. The
fringe is made of a strip of the material, fringed

ornamented with simple designs done in outline stitch; or such a bag may be made of
towels having colored borders.

FIGURE NO. 10.—BAG FOR SOILED CLOTHES.

out and knotted to a depth sufficiently effective for a heading. Various styles of knotted
fringes are illustrated elsewhere in this
chapter. As a bag devoted to the purpose
for which this is constructed is itself apt to
need laundering occasionally, the ribbon decoration may be omitted in favor of linen bands

Tassel for Fringes, etc., and Method of Making It.

FIGURES NOS. 11, 12, AND 13.—In making
the tassel shown at Figure No. 11, many
strands of wool, floss or embroidery silk are
laid evenly and thickly together. Then a
piece of pretty silk cord or of the tassel

material is tied around the middle of the bunch, as shown by Figure No. 12. Then the bunch is doubled and tied around in the manner illustrated by Figure No. 13, the worker tying it as tight as possible. Such tassels may be sewed along the edges of lambrequins,

passed under and over the meshes of the canvas in the manner depicted in the engraving, the point at which each strand passes under and over the canvas being calculated by counting the bars in the fabric. A regular gradation, which is one of the chief charms of the

FIGURE NO. 12.

FIGURES NOS. 11, 12 AND 13.—TASSEL FOR FRINGES, ETC., AND METHOD OF MAKING IT.

FIGURE NO. 11.

FIGURE NO. 13.

table-covers or scarfs, to make a heavy, handsome fringe ; or they may be fastened to cords to be used as festoons or other decorations. The material used for the tassels may be left in the natural state, or it may be carefully combed out. When used as decoration for the ends of cords, the cord should be used for the tying illustrated at Figure No. 12. Such tassels are often utilized in making fringe.

Fancy Fringe.

FIGURE NO. 14.—This fringe is easily made and is effective as a finish to portières, shelf-draperies or any hanging requiring such a completion. The foundation is canvas, and the fringe itself is formed of worsted in two shades cut in graduated lengths, as indicated by the engraving. Each strand of worsted is

decoration, is thus obtained. The threads of canvas which are thus brought over the

FIGURE NO. 14.—FANCY FRINGE.

worsted are concealed and the beauty of the fringe enhanced by making a stitch of silk directly over each thread of canvas visible upon the surface. The engraving explains the process so clearly that elaborate instructions regarding its details are unnecessary. It may be suggested, however, that the worsted is most easily slipped under the canvas by threading a canvas or embroidery needle with it, and that the fringe is rendered more firm looking by making each silk stitch through a half square of the canvas instead of merely around the mesh that crosses the worsted strand. Several shades of color or several contrasting colors may be united in a fringe of this style. The canvas may be trimmed off far enough from the ends of the strands to permit of their falling free, and the spaces between the irregular lengths may be filled in

the width of the section depending somewhat on the thickness of the worsted used. A bit of pasteboard or, what is better still, a smooth match-shaped bit of wood is then laid in the center of each section and a needle threaded with worsted is passed through the meshes nearest it on one side, brought to the surface through the corresponding ones on the other side, carried over the wood to the opposite side and passed under and over in this way for the length of the enclosed section. The process is repeated through the next succeeding row of meshes or openings on each side and so on until one half the space on each side has been worked over. The process is

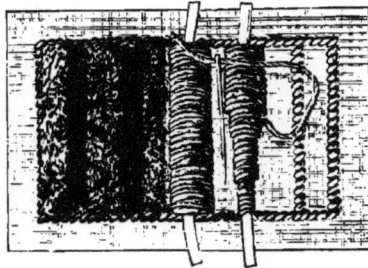

FIGURE NO. 15.—FANCY HEADING FOR FRINGE.

with any variety of embroidery stitch adapted to the texture.

Fancy Heading for Fringe.

FIGURE NO. 15.—Although the title denominates this as only a fancy heading for fringe it will quite as often be developed as a border for shelf draperies and other hangings or as a finish for fancy rugs. The foundation is canvas, the fineness or coarseness of the mesh being decided by the variety of worsted chosen. The thick, fuzzy pile is produced in the following manner: The canvas is marked off into narrow bars or sections by rows of stitching as indicated at the right side of the engraving,

clearly delineated by the partially completed bar shown in the engraving, the needle being passed under a thread of canvas in the act of bringing the worsted from one side to the other. When all the canvas has been worked over a pair of sharp-pointed scissors is needed to cut the stitches as they lie upon the bit of wood, and care should be taken to insert the lower blade so as to cut them evenly. When thus cut they will form the short thick pile represented by the left end of the engraving. Two or three colors, or several shades of the same color may be combined in this variety of work with tasteful results. Such a border forms a handsome finish for a portière of billiard cloth or for one of tapestry embroidery. Made of very thick worsted or carpet ravellings it would be very effective about a rug. Of course such a finish would not be desirable for rugs that were to be subjected to constant use, but for the long narrow ones which look so well under mantels it would be quite suitable. If a fringe finish were in order one like that pictured at Figure No. 14 might be developed with especially harmonious results.

Drapery Fringe.

FIGURE NO. 16.—This fringe is one of the

graduating their distance apart by estimating how large a diamond shape they will form when brought together for the first row of lattice work. After they have all been attached begin to form the lattice work by bringing the corresponding cords together as if they were to be netted, but instead of knotting them fasten them securely with a few stitches done with a needle and thread : care is necessary in this part of the work that they be not lapped nor stretched but simply brought together and fastened. In this way make as many rows of the lattice or diamond work as

FIGURE NO. 16.—DRAPERY FRINGE.

easiest for the home decorator to make and one of the most effective which she can employ in the ornamentation of any furnishings which require or suggest such an addition. It is made of silk cord and in attempting its construction it is best to start with a correct idea of how long a piece of fringe is needed. When this is decided upon procure a piece of tape or gimp of the same length and as much silk cord as the quantity required suggests. Cut the cord in lengths corresponding with the depth the fringe is to be when finished and attach the sections to the tape at intervals,

are desired and finish the lower row by bringing the ends of contiguous cords together and fastening them so as to permit of tying tassels over them. Wherever stitches have been taken twist bits of chenille or finer cord, and when the fringe is applied tack a row of mossheading or fancy gimp to conceal the foundation. Fringe of this style is used to drape very expensive furniture, to form mantel lambrequins, and for a variety of purposes suggested by its beauty. The engraving does not give a good idea of its rich effect, but any lady who has observed the beauty of such a decoration can readily obtain from it the requisite insight into its construction. The ends of the cord may be allowed to hang free so as to tip each one with a tassel, or they may be graduated in length, and finished with tassels of different colors.

Fancy Fringe.

FIGURE NO. 17.—A dainty fringe, suitable of crochetted loops, which are done in chain stitch and attached along its lower points. The second row of crochetted loops are much deeper, and each one forms a tiny circle at its lower extremity. The arrangement of the ribbon, which is of the narrow purl-edged variety, is clearly explained by the engraving. The upper row is tacked securely to the edge

FIGURE NO. 17.—FANCY FRINGE.

for finishing a chair or bureau scarf or any article requiring an especially pretty and delicate completion is here illustrated. The engraving suggests the manner of its attachment, the plain upper portion representing the article to be finished. Upon it is worked with rope silk a pretty design which is clearly portrayed, and apparently supports the first row of the fabric at every third crochetted loop, and the lower rows are knotted through the little circles, a brass ring being slipped on the ribbon before it is knotted each time. The irregular lengths of the lower ribbons are obtained by skipping every alternate ring when the first row is inserted, and taking the omitted ones up when the second row is arranged.

CHAPTER XXV.

ORNAMENTAL PORTIÈRES.

MONG the most beautifying adjuncts to the furnishings of a house or apartment are draperies and hangings harmonizing with the general tone of the upholstery. Very often it is such hangings which give to an otherwise cold appearing interior its most cheerful and satisfying effect.

When it is practicable to remove doors that do not slide in panels it is always well to do so, but as it is not always permissible to do this a few suggestions regarding the next best course may be of value.

When a uniformly good effect from both sides is desired, hang the curtain from a pole set in sockets screwed into the casing, midway between its inner and outer edges, instead of upon brackets at either side. If it is an arched opening let the pole go as high as it will, and have the curtain only long enough to extend from it to the floor, unless it be arranged to drape in some artistic fashion above the pole, which may be accomplished in a variety of pretty ways, one that is very easily developed being arranged by means of a gilded rope and rings which screw into the top of the casing. The rope is passed through the rings and enough slack allowed to permit of throwing the top of the hanging over it; a few stout pins will maintain this portion in position, but a curtain thus arranged does not permit of being drawn out of the position in which it is hung. It is not therefore an advisable disposal for doorways which must sometimes be entirely screened. A pretty device for filling in the space above a pole thus placed consists of Japanese fret-work, which may be purchased by the foot and fitted to any outlines. It may be gilded or finished in any other way desired, and is in itself very attractive.

After any hanging is adjusted care should be taken not to draw it out of its plaits or cause it to sag by careless handling. A dexterous movement will suffice to draw a heavy drapery which refuses to yield to misapplied efforts, and as rings and all the other fixtures required for perfect manipulation may be procured at a moderate outlay there is no reason for an unsatisfactory disposal or an unsightly appearance.

Among the materials which are utilized by people of artistic tastes who are not deterred from asserting their fancies by dread of being unconventional, are plain ingrain carpetings.

These goods are woven in a variety of colors and drape handsomely.

Embroidered Portière.

FIGURE No. 1.—The elegant portière here shown is made of Gobelin-blue plush, rich'y

or they may be worked through on canvas, which may be withdrawn, thread by thread, when the embroidered figure is completed. The natural colors of the flowers should be copied to achieve the desired result. Felt,

FIGURE No. 1.—EMBROIDERED PORTIÈRE.

embroidered with detached sprays of different kinds of flowers, with their special foliage. The designs may be *en appliqué* if preferred,

cloth, satin or any preferred plain material may be used instead of plush, with handsome effect.

Handsome Portière.

FIGURE No. 2.—This engraving illustrates a sumptuous door-drapery of crimson plush. The curtains are embellished near the top with a large floral design *en appliqué*, and small detached flowers and leaves *en appliqué* are strewn all over in an apparently careless but carefully studied manner. The rod is ebony,

in raw silk, satin, *crétonne* or any suitable curtain fabric, the material being usually selected to accord with the furniture of the rooms.

Instead of the decoration illustrated an effective design in fruits or flowers or in geometrical or other conventional outlines, might be applied by a lady who is clever

FIGURE No. 2.—HANDSOME PORTIÈRE.

and above the curtain is a smaller rod, from which a width of plush droops in a handsome festoon at the center, the ends being thrown artistically over the curtain rod. Cord and heavy tassels drape the curtains back, and a lining of crimson satin is added both to the curtains and to the lambrequin drapery. The same effect in drapery may be achieved

with the brush. Lustra-painting is a most beautiful means of ornamenting such a drapery.

Decorated Portière

FIGURE No. 3.—This handsome portière is made of China silk, and is rendered very rich and elaborate by four bands of velvet which cross the bottom, the lowest band being about a quarter of a yard wide and the other three about one-third as wide. The wide band is enriched along its lower edge with plush ball-

is achieved with fancy stitches done with vari-colored flosses. The curtains are attached to brass rings run over a brass rod, and may be tied back with wide ribbon or allowed to

FIGURE NO. 5.—DECORATED PORTIÈRE.

ornaments and a handsome appliqué design, the appliqué decoration being selected from among a variety of silk-embroidered appliqués. Between the narrow bands a rich effect

fall loose, as preferred. Sateen, damask, *cretonne* or any fabric may be similarly embellished. Japanese silk, which is now procurable in a great variety of artistic tints makes a pretty portière for an upper room. So does scrim and prettily figured madras.

Portière for Book-Case.

FIGURE No. 4.—The handsome portière

lambrequin effect is achieved by a facing of velvet cut in fancy tabs at the bottom, each tab being decorated with an embroidered medallion. A deep band of velvet faces the

FIGURE No. 4.—PORTIÈRE FOR BOOK-CASE.

here illustrated is made of Turcoman silk and suspended with rings on a brass rod. A

bottom of the portière, and from its top depends a row of Turkish fringe. Above the band is a row of velvet discs that are curved out at one side and arranged to appear as if they overlapped, a row of fine cord edging them. A row of cord also borders the edges of the lambrequin-like facing. Plush, silk, reps, etc., may be used for such portières, with

pretty. The rod is suspended below the arch. The material used is pongee silk on which acorns and oak leaves are applied in a most effective manner. The shapes of the acorns and leaves are shown in the correct sizes at diagrams A and B. The leaves are

FIGURE NO. 5.—PORTIÈRE FOR AN ALCOVE.

some pretty contrasting material for the bands, discs and facings.

Portière for an Alcove.

FIGURE NO. 5.—The pictured method of arranging portières for an alcove is new and

cut from plush or velvet of an olive shade, and the upper parts of the acorns are olive and their lower parts of golden brown plush. Two shades of brown may be used for the acorns, and bronze green and olive for the leaves. The acorns are applied all over the

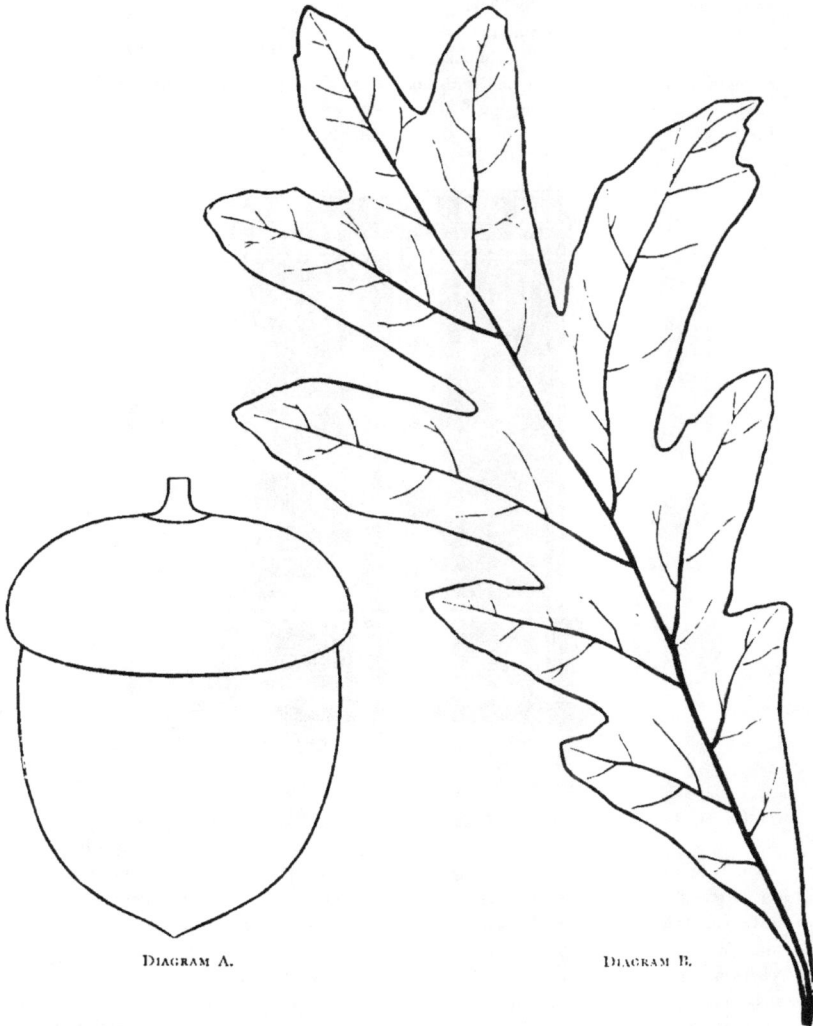

DIAGRAM A.

DIAGRAM B.

DIAGRAMS A AND B.—OUTLINE OF ACORN AND LEAF FOR DECORATED PORTIÈRE—FULL SIZE.

curtains at intervals with invisible stitches, and the leaves are arranged to form a graceful border across the top. The effect is very rich, and the tones of the plush and the pongee form a wonderfully beautiful combination of color. The leaves are veined with embroidery silk or floss in Kensington outline-stitch.

acorns may be used as effectively as on the portière, and they may be cut from cloth, flannel, velvet, plush, silk, satin, etc.

Embroidered Portière.

FIGURE No. 6.—This portière, suitable for doorway or embrasure, is illustrated as being on a cabinet, for which it is particularly well

FIGURE NO. 6.—EMBROIDERED PORTIÈRE.

Outline of Acorn and Leaf for Decorating Portière.

DIAGRAMS A AND B.—These diagrams show the correct shapes and sizes of the acorns and leaves used in decorating the portière pictured at Figure No. 5. The veining of the leaves is done in outline-stitch with flosses or silks to harmonize with the shade of the material from which they are cut. For table-scarfs, chair-scarfs, lambrequins, etc., the leaves and

adapted. It is of bronze felt, embroidered in many colored flosses in set patterns and finished at the lower edge with a broad band of crimson plush. Brass rods and rings are used for the mounting, though, if preferred, ebony or wood matching the cabinet might be substituted. Cloth, flannel or any fabric in use for portières may take the place of the felt, and the border may be of silk, satin, velvet or any material decidedly contrasting in color and quality.

CHAPTER XXVI.

MANTEL LAMBREQUINS AND DRAPERIES.

THE rich and handsome lambrequin, shown on the following page may be used for the mantel, the window, etc. In the making of the fringe, odds and ends of zephyr worsteds, embroidery silks, flosses, crewels, etc., may be utilized ; but the one variety of material must be used throughout, although it may be in many colors or shades of one color. Very elegant fringes may be made by commencing with the lightest shade of the selected color and grading the rows to the very darkest. For instance, taking the gold shades, begin with white and shade down to the deepest orange ; for the red shades, begin with the lightest pink and shade down to the deepest crimson ; in blue, purple, green and gray the same method of shading may be pursued. Shading from light to dark is more effective than from dark to light, but either method may be followed. If the fringe fabric has to be purchased, it will probably be well to know that in shading from light to dark, the second shade will need to be double the amount of the first, the third three times that of the first, the fourth four times that of the first amount, and so on. Brass rings of any preferred size may be used, but they should all be alike. Small rings may be covered with embroidery silks or flosses, but for large rings this would be a very expensive covering, so crewels, zephyrs, worsteds, Saxony yarns, chenilles or any of the thick embroidery goods may be used. For brackets or small lambrequins the small rings are prettiest. Rings may be made of ordinary thick wire, if the rings cannot be readily purchased ; but care should be taken to have them perfect in shape, otherwise they will not look well. The tassels may be made at home, but, as they are not expensive, they are generally purchased. Full directions for covering the rings are given and the method illustrated at Figures Nos. 2, 3, 4, 5, 6 and 7.

Mantel Lambrequin.

FIGURE NO. 1.—This lambrequin is made of heavy reps, and decorated above the lower edge with an embroidery design of pansies and leaves. The embroidery decoration may be selected from manufactured appliqués or the lambrequin may be painted or embroidered by one's self, the outline of a portion of the design being given at Figure No. 8. The method of making the fringe is illustrated and described at Figures Nos. 2, 3, 4, 5, 6 and 7. the worsted about the ring, as represented by

FIGURE NO. 1.—MANTEL LAMBREQUIN.

The tassels are heavy and large, and are suspended from and high up between the fringe points. The lambrequin may be of any color and of any preferred material, and the embroidery may be of any pattern desired.

Figure No. 2. With a crochet hook catch the worsted, as shown by Figure No. 3; draw the

FIGURE NO. 2.

worsted under the ring, and throw the worsted over the needle as shown by Figure No. 4; and crochet the loop off the needle as

FIGURE NO. 3.

FIGURE NO. 4.

Method of Making Fringe Illustrated at Figure No. 1.

FIGURES NOS. 2, 3, 4, 5, 6 and 7.—Fasten

shown by Figure No. 5. Make single crochet stitches in the same manner all round the ring, until the latter is well covered. An illustration of the ring partly covered may be seen at Figure No. 6. The ring entirely covered is shown at Figure No. 7. When the required number of rings are covered, they are sewed together to form the pointed fringe decorating the lambrequin shown at Figure No. 1. Care should be taken to make the crochetted stitches even and close together. The hands should be smooth and in good condition before attempting silk embroidery. The slightest roughness is sure to cause the twist to loosen and the filaments to separate.

satin they are joined together so as to bring the two sizes in alternation both cross-wise and lengthwise and to form them into a square the size of the cushion, to the sides of which the outer rings are tacked. Ordinary embroidery silk, rope silk, Bargarran cotton, crewels and worsteds may be used for cover-ing the rings. Heavy silk works up more effectively for the purpose than any other working material.

A fringe formed by knotting strands of embroidery silk into a row of small covered

FIGURE No. 5.   FIGURE No. 6.   FIGURE No. 7.

FIGURES NOS. 2, 3, 4, 5, 6 AND 7.—METHOD OF MAKING FRINGE ILLUSTRATED AT FIGURE NO. 1.

There are many uses to which the cro-chetted ring-work may be applied with very effective results, one being the elabora-tion of handsome sofa cushions. A rich looking cushion, thus elaborated, is covered with satin of one of the lightest shades seen in growing ivy, but not the very lightest. The upper side has an outer covering com-posed of rings in two sizes, one being about as large as the top of a number seven thimble, while the other is a little smaller than a silver quarter of a dollar. After an equal number of each size has been prepared by crochetting over them with silk a shade darker than the

rings is an exquisite finish for a delicate silk scarf or drapery, and for cushions that are to be set upon dainty toilette tables or dressing cases.

Pansy Design for Embroidery.

FIGURE No. 8.—This design is very grace-ful and may be either outlined or solidly embroidered. The natural hues of the pansy blossom and leaves should, of course, be used, but, as there are numerous varieties of the blossom, many different effects may be achieved. The design is in the correct size for use.

FIGURE NO. 8.—PANSY DESIGN FOR EMBROIDERY.

Mantel Lambrequin.

FIGURE No. 9.—This lambrequin is made of velvet and is cut in square and tongue-shaped tabs in alternation. The square tabs are gathered up closely at one side edge—that toward the center of the mantel—so as to drape them in wrinkled points. A row of cord borders all the edges of the tabs, and is coiled in trefoil design above the separation of the tabs. The points are all tipped with heavy tassels, and the floral decorations are selections from floral appliqués, and are not

as elaborate may be developed without excessive outlay. Silk embroidered appliqués or silk or chenille hand-embroidery is, when indulged in to a lavish extent, rather costly, but there are exquisite appliqué decorations of chenille which can be purchased ready for application for a very moderate sum. They are mostly in floral patterns, and are excellent reproductions of daisies, buttercups, roses and various other blossoms and their foliage. They are mounted on wire and can easily be manipulated to appear naturally poised in any

FIGURE No. 9.—MANTEL LAMBREQUIN.

large in size. The mantel-board is also covered with velvet, and the lambrequin is neatly fastened on. Plush, pongee, velveteen, felt or any preferred material may be used for the lambrequin, and any other style of floral decoration may be followed. Pendants of any kind may be used instead of tassels.

At first inspection the cost of a lambrequin made up in this fashion may seem rather heavy, but a little reflection will convince anybody familiar with fancy-work that one quite

position where their decorative effect is desired.

A finish for the pointed sections, quite as effective as the tassels and less expensive in their requirement of silk, may be obtained by using brass rings that are much wider along one edge than along the other, and knotting into each one of them about one-fourth of a skein of embroidery silk. The silk is knotted into the narrower side and is cut to fall a little shorter than the tassels pictured in the present instance.

Mantel-Drapery.

FIGURE No. 10.—This drapery is very effective and may screen a fire-place when not in use, or it may be simply ornamental if there is no fire-place beneath the mantel. The mantel is covered with felt, at the edge of which is fastened, either invisibly or with mantel-band trims each curtain or drapery above the hem finishing the edge, and a little above this band is another band, which is applied by fancy stitches along the edges. These bands may be of wide velvet ribbon or of some fancy ribbon, if preferred; and the drapery may be of felt, cloth, pongee, plush,

FIGURE No. 10.—MANTEL-DRAPERY.

brass-headed nails, a deep band of velvet elaborated with fancy stitches carefully made with colored flosses. The drapery is plaited at the top so as to fall in graceful, careless folds, and descends to the floor. It is in two sections, and is attached to the mantel underneath the velvet band. A wide band of velvet corresponding in decoration with the silk, crétonne, canton flannel, etc., as is most in accordance with the furnishing of the room.

Mantel-Drapery.

FIGURE No. 11.—This handsome and graceful mantel-drapery is made of plush. Where the lambrequin is draped is placed a bunch of cord loops, and at the opposite side, where the slash is made, the edges are laced

together with cord run through eyelets
and tied at the bottom, the ends being tipped
with large plush balls. A beautiful spray of
flowers *en appliqué*, in two parts, decorates the
fits the mantel perfectly is covered smoothly
with the plush, and to it the lambrequin is
secured. A few pretty ornaments on the
mantel is all that is desirable, and when the

FIGURE No. 11.—MANTEL-DRAPERY.

lambrequin. The spray is a selection from
manufactured satin floral appliqués of which
there is a very large variety. A board that
fire is not lighted in the grate a Japanese par-
asol will make a charming screen. China or
India silk, Surah, cloth, crétonne, velvet,

plush, pongee or any preferred material may be used for the lambrequin. On thin goods painting or outline-embroidery is very effect be used instead of the cord, with good effect. The lambrequin was cut by Pattern No. 1451, price 7d. or 15 cents.

FIGURE No. 12.—MANTEL DECORATION.

ive, and a fringe of small ornaments may be added to the edges if desired. Ribbon may

Mantel Decoration.

FIGURE No. 12.—This rich mantel decoration consists of a scarf of deep-green plush allowed to hang gracefully at one end—where it is decorated with a ball fringe of the same color—and raised at the other end, being caught by a large bow of rose-colored satin ribbon. Where the scarf is uplifted there is shown a satin lambrequin elaborately deco-·rated with crimson roses and their foliage. These flowers are selected from manufactured floral appliqués. The peacock which so finely fills the fire-place is of brass, the out-spread tail being of natural feathers.

The novice at embroidery is so much helped to-day by the appliqué flowers and the threads that with very few stitches make stems and outlining. that even so-called elaborate pieces of work are not impossible to her. and. if she be ordinarily careful and has the determinati on to succeed. it is very certain that all difficulties will fly before her.

Implements have much to do with success in w rking, and to keep one's scissors sharp and one's temper _vice versa_. one's needles pointed and one's tongue still, one's silk out of tangle and one's mind to match. will aid in reaching that which is hoped for. When there is pasteboard to be cut a very sharp knife is the best to use.

A new departure in decorative needlework is worthy of note because of its truly artistic nature. It consists of the arrangement of special designs on panels of plush, velvet or other material so that each is a picture in itself. These decorated panels are applied with fancy or invisible stitches to the article they are to embellish. A beautiful specimen is among the contributions to this chapter, and the work will be found easier to do in these small sections than in a single large design. Although very elaborate in effect, such work may be accomplished with a small outlay. The panels may be all of the same color or they may represent a finely graded

contrast, in developing which odd pieces of plush or velvet or even of felt or billiard cloth may be utilized. Any lady who does fancy work understands how rapidly remnants accumulate. Each design in such a piece of work as that on the succeeding page suggests how such accumulations may be used to good advantage. Short pieces of wide satin ribbons may be employed for the panels, and being usually of firm weave are exceptionally desirable for painting upon, when the lambrequin is to be thus enriched.

Similar pieces of ribbon or short lengths of narrower ribbon are also of special value to any lady who estimates aright their value as a foundation for outline or side-stitch embroidery, or for one or both varieties of stitches in conjunction with purlette work or any of the fancy darning and overlaying stitches included in the chapter devoted to embroidery stitches in this work. The pattern traced by the weaver is an excellent guide for such decorations, and but a little needle-work is needed to develop an especially elegant effect. In a lady's sitting-room where the prevailing tint is pink the mantel lambrequin is made of pink ribbon and white Florentine lace insertion over pink sateen. The pattern of the ribbon is brought into striking prominence by an outlining of purlette work and an overlaying of fancy darning stitches. and while the effect is elaborate the actual cost of such a mantel decoration is not excessive, because its greatest value lies in the daintiness and precision with which the work is done. White or colored silk or cotton cord varying in circumference from the size of fine darning cotton to that of a thick round lamp-wick may be used for purlette work.

Rapid progress may be made in doing purlette work, and it is a variety of needle-work that repays the worker for every minute devoted to it.

Mantel Lambrequin.

FIGURE NO. 13.—The engraving illustrates a handsome lambrequin of peacock-blue felt cloth. The lower part is cut out in large oval scollops with uniform spaces between them, and above each of the spaces is a narrow strip of velvet applied with fancy stitches, thus continuing the effect of the scollop to the top.

There are many little items of economy which may be kept in mind by ladies who take a justifiable pride in keeping the productions of their needle within a moderate sum, and one of them relates to the making of ornaments for finishing points, tipping cords, etc. Metal foundations in various pretty shapes may be purchased for a small sum and

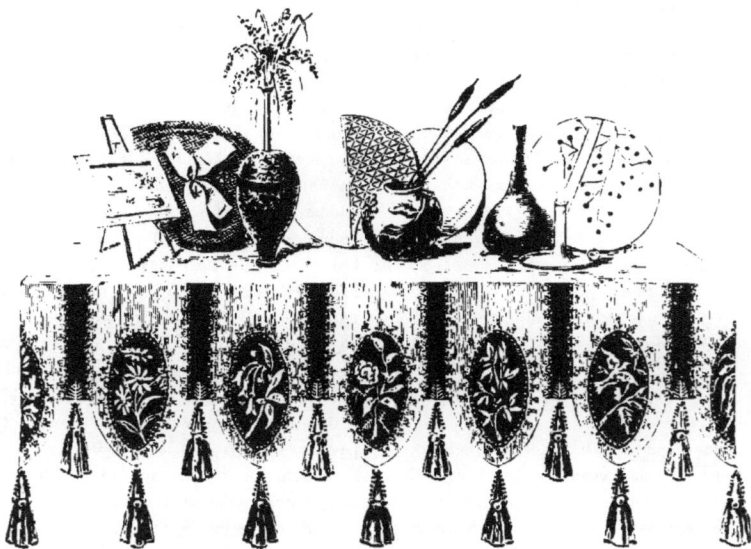

FIGURE NO. 13.—MANTEL LAMBREQUIN.

Upon each scollop is an oval panel of velvet applied with fancy stitching, which forms an effective background for embroidered or painted floral sprays. A handsome tassel-ornament depends from each of the strips of velvet, and also from the tip of each scollop. The designs for the panels are given in full size at Figures Nos. 4, 5, 6, 7 and 8. The cloth may be of any preferred shade.

the tassel portions attached at home with but little additional cost. The floss, worsted or silk that is to be used should be made into little skeins only long enough to permit of knotting them into the metal and leaving the length required for the tassel. The falling end is then cut to perfect the appearance. Regarding the cutting of silk—never attempt it with scissors that are at all dull.

Designs for Embroidery on Lambrequin.

FIGURES NOS. 14, 15, 16, 17 and 18.—These suitable for ornamenting other articles of a similar nature. The spray of handsomely

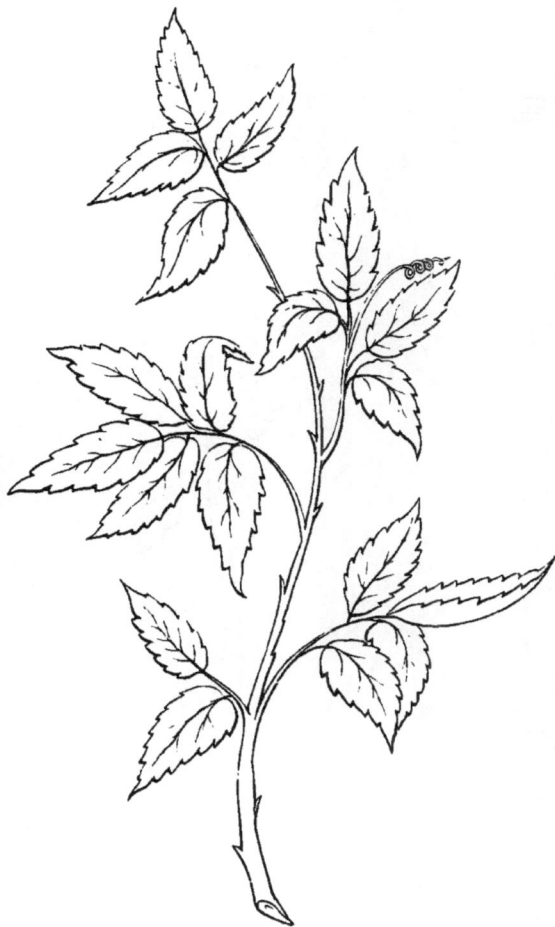

FIGURE NO. 14.—DESIGN FOR EMBROIDERY ON LAMBREQUIN.

designs are graceful in effect and are shown in the proper sizes for decorating the lambrequin illustrated at Figure No. 13, though they are also crenelated leaves illustrated by Figure No. 14 suggests rose foliage, but wide latitude is allowable in embroidering foliage.

FIGURE No. 16.—DESIGN FOR EMBROIDERY ON LAMBREQUIN.

FIGURE NO. 17.—DESIGN FOR EMBROIDERY ON LAMBREQUIN.

FIGURE NO. 18.—DESIGN FOR EMBROIDERY ON LAMBREQUIN

"BUBBLES"
FROM THE CELEBRATED PICTURE BY
SIR JOHN MILLAIS BART. R.A.
AND GOLD MEDALLIST &c
[IN THE POSSESSION OF THE PROPRIETORS OF
PEARS SOAP
PURCHASED BY THEM FOR $11.000]

CHAPTER XXVII.

WINDOW DRAPERIES.

LTHOUGH heavy curtains and cumbersome draperies made up so elaborately as to form receptacles for dust are no longer in vogue, Fashion and good sense unite in paying considerable attention to the curtaining and draping of windows. Charming effects are produced without large outlay. India silk, plush, scrim, and Madras are among the materials which are oftenest selected for draping and curtaining, and it is safe to say that the simpler textures are susceptible of quite as artistic treatment as the richer fabrics. Here are a few things which purchasers should bear in mind in selecting window draperies :

That very cheap lace curtains are less desirable than those of scrim or muslin.

That any lady who is clever with her needle can make handsome window curtains.

That she must take every stitch and measure every part with precision if she hopes to win approval for her work.

That fluted ruffles are very pretty upon cottage curtains, but that they should be full enough to flute evenly.

That the narrow margin projecting beyond the work upon lace curtains should be hemmed under or moistened with gum arabic water and pressed underneath, but not cut off.

That dark heavy curtains may make a large room look cosy, but they decrease the apparent size of a small room.

That lace curtains—unless they be of the finest quality—always hang a little stiff when first put up.

That they will fall into more graceful folds after a short time.

That they should either be draped back, or allowed to fall straight permanently. Frequent changing stretches them.

That the extra length should be folded in-and-in at the top—not allowed to drag upon the floor—never cut off, as it will be needed when the curtains are laundered.

That écru and all shades of cream and gold are obtainable in lace curtains, but that it is always safe to select a pure white tint in fine curtains.

That the effect of a narrow window may be broadened and a low one heightened by having the poles extend beyond it, or placing them a little above it.

That a curtain or shade which is worked on rollers should not be jerked or drawn sideways, if its easy and satisfactory management is to be perpetuated.

Window-Drapery.

FIGURE No. 1.—A full drapery of Madras is often placed before the lower part of the window when the room is on the ground floor and a certain amount of privacy is desired. The curtain drapery is then hung from the silk are selections from manufactured silk floral appliqués. One need not necessarily be an adept at needle-work in order to be able to make such a drapery. The lining is of brown sateen. Of course, individual taste will dictate other combinations, but the colors

FIGURE No. 1.—WINDOW-DRAPERY.

top of the window and falls over the Madras. It is mounted on its rod, and, being in two parts, may, therefore, be pushed aside to permit the light to stream in. The material is felt of a dull mode color, and the velvet band is of a golden-brown shade; while the background of the appliquéd figure is velvet of the same color and the pansies of yellow mentioned are most in vogue and are of a variety of which the eye will not soon weary.

Appliqué for Window-Drapery.

FIGURE No. 2.—The flat appliqué here pictured shows the correct size of those decorating the window drapery pictured at Figure No. 1. It is of yellow silk, and the flower is well brought out by the golden-brown velvet background. These flowers may be utilized and, indeed, any of the numerous "bits" that seem to call for embroidered ornamentation.

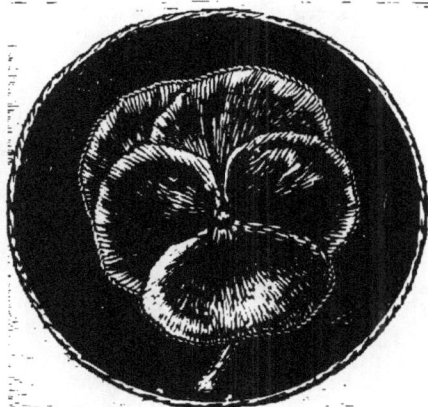

FIGURE NO. 2.—APPLIQUÉ FOR WINDOW-DRAPERY.

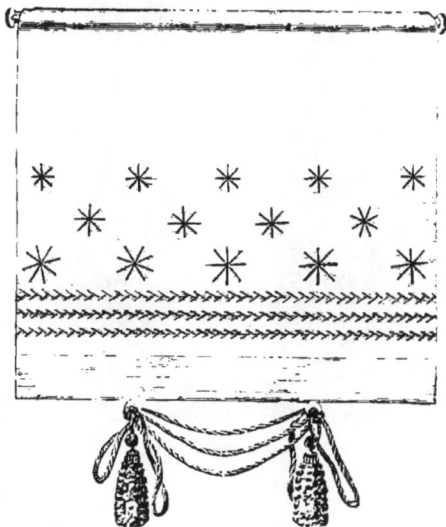

FIGURE NO. 3.—DECORATED CURTAIN.

for all decorative purposes and will be found desirable on rugs for lounges, on crazy quilts,

Decorated Curtain.

FIGURE NO. 3.—This curtain is made of

dru linen, its deep hem having above it three
rows of feather-stitching done in very heavy
scarlet crewels. The daisies, graded as illustrated, are of scarlet and white in the long
outline-stitch usually chosen for them. The

Window-Drapery.

FIGURE No. 4.—The engraving illustrates a
rich and handsome drapery for a window.
The curtains are of Madras in Persian colors,
and are edged all round with tiny, fluffy

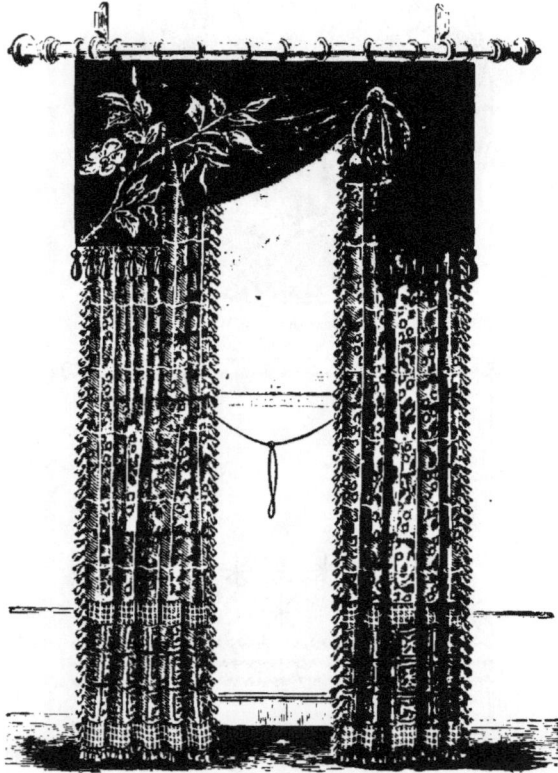

FIGURE No. 4.—WINDOW-DRAPERY.

cord and tassels are of scarlet and white,
looped through the brass crescents in an
artistic manner. Dark brown and yellow,
blue and yellow, or all crimson crewels may be
used if preferred to the colors illustrated.

tassels of floss showing all the colors of the
material. The lambrequin is of plush lined
with silesia. It is mounted on a pole with
rings and is elaborated by a decoration of
very natural looking satin floral appliqué

embroidery at one side, a bunch of cord tipped with large pompons where it is plaited up, and a row of pretty pendants along the lower edges of the tab-like sides. The pattern of this lambrequin is No. 1452, price 7d.

or 15 cents, and will develop handsomely in all materials used for lambrequins. Any style of pendants may be used, and ribbon may take the place of the cord introduced in its garnitures.

Choice Napery.

LUNCHEON sets show many pretty novelties, but none that entirely eclipse pure white damask, with hemmed edges or drawn-work borders. A handsome set of napery suitable for luncheon or tea is of plain linen that is soft and smooth and of rather heavy weave. The border consists of a row of fringe headed by three rows of drawn-work in an open pattern. All the threads pulled out in making the drawn-work were saved and some of them used in fashioning the threads left in the ravelled portion into a delicate lace-like design. The remainder, after being cut in lengths corresponding with the depth of the fringe, were knotted with the latter into handsome, heavy tassels. The tassels were made according to a method illustrated and described on another page, and their effect much improved by the addition of the extra threads, which increase the size to advantage. A cover could be easily decorated in this way at home by any lady who could give the requisite time to the work. Napkins or doilies to match are made with a narrower fringe and one row of drawn-work. The initials or cypher in medium sized letters, which are worked in solid embroidery, are added to the

ends of the cover and the corners of the napkins. Damask cloths with well defined borders may be elaborated by following the design of the border in outline-stitch with cotton or linen embroidery thread, or with washable embroidery silks. Sometimes the design is still further emphasized by associating a side stitch with the outline-stitch.

Pure white napery is always good form for dinner service. It may have no decoration, or it may be enriched by a border of heavy lace or Mexican work, the latter being drawn work, much elaborated. If spotlessly white, and ironed so as to bring out the beauty of the satin-like weave, unornamented damask is always beautiful. Various styles of letters for marking are given in another part of this book, and from them may be selected several varieties adapted to this department of table furnishing.

Silk-and-linen covers and napkins are woven in exquisite styles and colorings, and their lustre rivals the richest satin. They cost more than all-linen sets, which are much more durable, and they cannot be laundered, though they may be freshened by a dry process to look very well.

Brushes for Fabric Painting.

THE brushes most frequently used in fabric painting, are sizes Nos. 2, 4, 6 and 8. They should be thoroughly cleansed every time they are used, before they are put away. As an amateur advances in proficiency, the other sizes that will be required for various kinds of work will suggest themselves.

Sizing for Silk or Satin.

To prepare silk or satin for receiving paint to good advantage, it is often desirable to apply a sizing, which renders the surface receptive.

A good sizing may be made by dissolving in very hot water, equal quantities of powdered alum and isinglass. As the alum hardens the water the moment it touches it, the isinglass should be put in first. If the design is to be stamped, the stamping should be done before the sizing is applied. A brush is used for applying the liquid and is moved in quick regular strokes *with* the nap of the goods.

CHAPTER XXVIII.

TABLES AND TABLE SCARFS.

HE prevailing fashion of decorating fancy tables with scarfs is conducive to charming effects, which do not demand a large outlay of money, provided time and taste can be expended freely.

Table Scarf.

FIGURE No. 1.—Reps of the shade of yellow fashionably called pumpkin yellow was chosen for this pretty scarf, and the ends are decorated with a row of deep antique lace, above which is a handsome decoration of appliqué pansies with embroidered leaves arranged in single file. The pansies used were selected from manufactured floral appliqués. Any other preferred appliqué flowers or other designs may be used, or the entire decoration may be hand-embroidered or hand-painted, as preferred. Fringe, ornaments, etc., may be used instead of lace, and instead of the reps, felt, plush, silk, satin or any preferred material may be used.

Scarf for Square Table.

FIGURE No. 2.—This scarf is designed especially to meet the requirements of the small, square table that is so prominent a feature in many houses. The square in the center defines exactly the part that will cover the table. The scarf is of dark green plush, and the ribbons applied upon each corner are of shrimp satin, silk floss in the same shade and in one of the fancy appliqué stitches being used to hold them. After they are finished, the center square is laid over and fastened down with the same stitch. All this may be done over a lining of thin muslin, and the real lining of satin-finished silesia need not display stitches. For the distances indicated, the edges are ornamented with crescents of green plush, caught securely and yet so loosely that they hang easily. Any favored combination of colors, or one that will suit the furnishing of the room, may be substituted for this, though the shrimp of the sea and the green of the ivy form a combination that is approved by high art.

Decorated Scarf.

FIGURE No. 3.—A handsome white towel having floral sprays woven in it in white is used for this scarf. The pattern is outlined with scarlet and green, the green being used for the leaves, which are also veined. A pretty dash of color is also given the ground by running it with scarlet, but to look nice the work must be done carefully. Other patterns may be obtained, and the colors chosen are usually in accordance with the pattern. However, scarlet is much used, for it is very effective and bright-looking.

are the proper kind for this beautiful work. The pattern is outlined with red, blue, pink, green, brown or any other preferred color or

FIGURE NO. 1.—TABLE SCARF.

Some beautiful towels may be purchased with floral patterns the shade of the cream or white groundwork woven in them, and these colors, and then the ground is rendered bright with dashes of the color run in broken lines through it.

Pongee Scarf.

FIGURE NO. 4.—On this pretty écru pongee scarf, with its hem-stitched outlining, are applied morning-glories in purple and pink, forms the necessary finish. Such scarfs are so easy to make and so decorative that their desirability is conceded by all who admire pretty surroundings. Sometimes the flowers

FIGURE NO. 2.—SCARF FOR SQUARE TABLE.

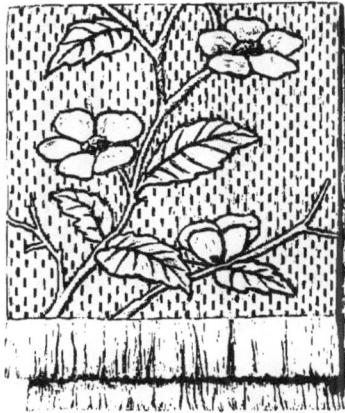

FIGURE NO. 3.—DECORATED SCARF.

clambering over a trellis of gilt. The flowers are machine-made floral appliqués, and the pretty trellis is outlined with gilt thread. The fringe is gilt and pale purple chenille, and are outlined with silk and their natural colors reproduced with paint. The effect of such a combination is beautiful, and is easily developed on all smooth materials.

Bureau Scarf.

FIGURE No. 5.—For the bureau or dressing table this is a very dainty-looking scarf. A long, narrow Turkish towel is widened on either side with three rows of ribbon of as many different shades, joined together by line over-and-over stitches. The ends of the ribbons extend below the fringe and are finished in long points that are each tipped with a obtainable in fine grades and in various colors as well as in white. A white towel elaborated with bright yellow ribbon and stitching develops handsomely.

Table Scarf.

FIGURE No. 6.—This handsome scarf is of heavy satin and has a dado decoration at the end done with colored embroidery silks. The

FIGURE No. 4.—PONGEE SCARF.

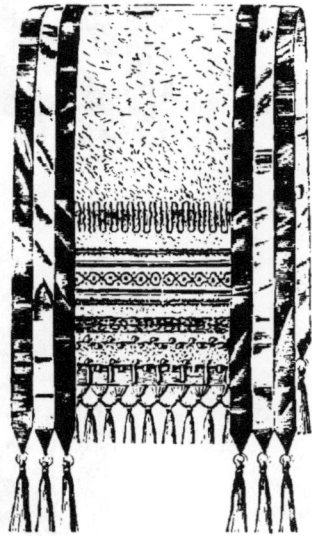

FIGURE No. 5.—BUREAU SCARF.

brass ring through which silk floss is pulled and tied to form a heavy tassel. The ends of the towel are embroidered over the border stripes with simple fancy stitches, and a band of ribbon applied with fancy stitches heads the fringe, with very handsome effect. The ribbons may combine any three harmonious shades, and all sorts of colors may be blended in the embroidery stitches. Such towels are irregular pattern is done in chain-stitch with gold silk; the circles are done with crimson silk in the same stitch, and filled in with a rainbow combination of colors in knot-stitch. A row of deeply netted fringe is added to each end, and may be made of silk in one color or a combination of colors. Any variety of fringe may be used, and velvet, plush, silk, cloth or any preferred material may be selected for the scarf. Metallic or tinsel cord adapted to portions of this work may be obtained for a small sum. It is in various shades and does not soon lose its brilliancy.

Ornamented Scarf.

FIGURE No. 7.—To throw over a towel-rack,

tassel. A tassel made of floss is also fastened where the discs touch and also at a similar point to the outer discs. The other end, which falls much deeper, is bordered with two bands of velvet edged at each side with tinsel cord arranged in a single scroll. The lowest band is directly at the edge, and pendants

FIGURE No. 6.—TABLE SCARF.

FIGURE No. 7.—ORNAMENTED SCARF.

a table or the back of a large chair, this scarf is useful and decorative. The fabric is China silk, and the end which hangs over is decorated with a row of applied velvet discs edged with tinsel cord. A crochetted ring is fastened to the bottom of each disc, and through it is fastened a bunch of silk floss to form a large

formed of crochetted rings and floss tassels are tacked to form a fringe all across the edge. The other band is a short distance above, and a row of crochetted rings depends from it. The method of crochetting the rings is illustrated and described in another chapter of this book.

Plush Table Scarf.

Figure No. 8.—Purple plush is used for
this scarf, the lining being of pale yellow
sateen. Satin is laid under the plush, and the
lines drawn in the fancy outlines represented
as sewn upon the satin, and an entwining
gold thread is then used to produce an
effect like that of the fine black lines in the
engraving. The fringe is of plush, showing
the two colors, the long pendants swinging
from the ends of the little brass crescents by

pattern may easily be obtained by folding a
piece of paper and cutting out the combined
designs with the edge having the crosses on
on the fold. The cross marks show the
center of the pattern, while the figures at the
end should fit to those corresponding on the
other portion of the design. The figures
should fit exactly to each other, and, if care
be taken, the result will be as pretty and
dainty as possible. The yellow satin is laid
under the plush before the lining is put on.

FIGURE NO. 8.—PLUSH TABLE SCARF.

which they are fastened to the edge of the
scarf. Any colors suited to one's drawing-
room may be developed in silk and velvet,
satin and plush.

Sections of Design for Cutting the Ends of a Table Scarf.

Figures Nos. 9 and 10.—Half of the pattern for cutting out the ends of the table-scarf
shown at Figure No. 8 may be obtained by
combining these two designs, and the entire

and the plush *cut out* in the fancy design and
outlined with gold braid, showing in what
sculptors call very low relief. The necessity
for sharp, pointed scissors to do the cutting is
imperative, as the edges should be absolutely
true, and the nap of the plush not broken or
matted, a result which is sure to follow the
use of dull implements, the blades of which
do not work easily. Plush having a short
nap is the most desirable to use for this kind
of work.

FIGURE NO. 9.—SECTION OF DESIGN FOR CUTTING THE ENDS OF A TABLE SCARF.

FIGURE No. 10.—SECTION OF DESIGN FOR CUTTING THE ENDS OF A TABLE SCARF.

FIGURE NO. 11.—TABLE SCARF AND LAMP SHADE.

Table Scarf and Lamp Shade.

FIGURE No. 11.—Very rich and handsome are these accessories to a table and a lamp. The scarf is of crimson plush, and is bordered at each side with a wide band of gold satin ribbon, handsomely embroidered with moss-roses and daisies *en appliqué*, and their foliage done in Kensington stitch. At the ends of the decorated bands the scarf is cut in handsome points, and between the bands it is somewhat shorter; the points and shorter portions being bordered with rich fringe. The

FIGURE No. 12.
FIGURE No. 12.—FLORAL
APPLIQUÉ.

FIGURE No. 13.
FIGURE No. 13.—FLORAL
APPLIQUÉ.

FIGURE No. 14.

FIGURE No. 15.

FIGURES NOS. 14 AND 15.—LEAVES IN OUTLINE, AND METHOD OF EMBROIDERING THEM.

embroidered and appliqué decorations are fully illustrated and described at Figures Nos. 12, 13, 14 and 15. Plush, velvet, felt, cloth, canvas, raw silk, pongee or any preferred material may be used for such scarfs, and on silk the border bands will usually be velvet or plush. These bands may, of course, be embellished

fringe may be whatever are most pleasing to the taste.

The lamp shade is made of two deep,

FIGURE No. 17.—EMBROIDERY DESIGN.

FIGURE No. 16.—FANCY TABLE SCARF.

with embroidery. Ornaments of any preferred variety may be added as a fringe, and the colors introduced in scarf, bands and

flounces of lace mounted on a section of bobbinet that is almost as deep and just as wide as the upper flounce. Heading the upper flounce is a row of lace beading that is edged with a row of narrow lace, and through the beading is run a narrow ribbon that ruffles the lace prettily and is tied at one side in a cluster of pretty loops and ends. A row of tiny pom-pons is fastened along the scollops of the lace flounces, with pretty effect. Any kind of lace may be used for such lamp shades, which are as dainty as they are beautiful, and the ribbon may be of any preferred color.

Floral Appliques.

FIGURES Nos. 12 and 13.—These pretty floral appliqués are selected from the usual machine-made varieties, and are used to decorate the table scarf illustrated at Figure No. 11. They may be used as decorations on scarfs, lambrequins, etc., and are very rich in effect. The foliage to accompany them is usually stamped and embroidered in South-Kensington stitch, as shown at Figure No. 14.

Leaves in Outline, and Method of Embroidering Them.

FIGURES Nos. 14 and 15.—These leaves represent the foliage of the moss-roses and daisies decorating the scarf illustrated at Figure No. 11. They are of the correct sizes, and are filled in with the South-Kensington stitch as shown by Figure No. 14. The natural shades are selected for them in filoselle, crewel, embroidery silk or floss, etc. This is the mode usually adopted in providing foliage for applied flowers, but sometimes the leaves are cut from velvet, etc., and also applied. The result is, however, much handsomer when the foliage is embroidered.

Fancy Table Scarf.

FIGURE No. 16.—This handsome scarf is made of reps and is bordered at each end with a broad band of plush or velvet. The upper part of the band is decorated with a handsome design in embroidery, and the ends

are bordered with a row of thick caterpillar fringe. The ends are slanted so that the scarf is much shorter at one side than at the other, and the effect is unique and pretty. A painted plaque on an easel, a handsome lamp or any preferred ornament may be placed upon the table. The embroidery design used in decorating the scarf is illustrated at Figure No. 17.

Embroidery Design.

FIGURE No. 17.—This engraving illustrates the design used in embellishing the scarf represented at Figure No. 16. It is in the correct size, and may be very easily repro-duced. The stitch is the well-known Ken-sington stitch. Such a design may be worked on lambrequins, chair or table scarfs, etc., and may be used as a center decoration or as a border, as preferred.

Decorative Scarf of India Silk.

FIGURE No. 18.—This scarf is particularly beautiful for the use illustrated. It consists of a width of silk decorated at either end with a row of lace headed by a light metal gimp, and fringed with tiny, fluffy tassels. On one end is pictured a vase containing leaves sim-ilar to those in the vase holding the scarf. Any shade of silk may be used, and the lace and painted decoration may be varied to please the fancy.

Table Scarf.

FIGURE No. 19.—Crétonne in two contrast-ing patterns and colors is combined with black velvet ribbon, cord fringe and heavy tassels in making this beautiful table-scarf. The crétonne is cut in strips—two of each pattern—of equal widths, and the strips are neatly joined together, the two kinds being arranged to alternate. Over the seams are herring-boned with gold-colored floss strips of velvet ribbon, which impart a rich and elegant

FIGURE NO. 18.—DECORATIVE SCARF OF INDIA SILK.

FIGURE NO. 19.—TABLE SCARF.

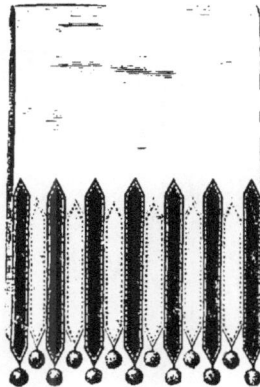

FIGURE NO. 20.—TABLE SCARF.

effect. A row of fringe borders the ends of the scarf, and over the fringe at each corner of the scarf and at the end of each strip of velvet ribbon is fastened a heavy tassel. The scarf may be lined with silesia or cambric, if desired; and, when a lining is used, the *cré-tonne* may be cut away beneath the velvet ribbon. Such scarfs may be as brilliant in hue as desired, and the fringe may be of any preferred variety. Plush and felt cloth, plush in two contrasting shades, velvet or plush and satin, make very rich and elegant scarfs; and the ends may be decorated with fringe or plainly finished.

Table Scarf.

FIGURE NO. 20.—This scarf is made of a width of India silk of the needed length for the table which it is to adorn. The ends are decorated with alternate strips of velvet and silk of equal width, but of different lengths, the silk strips extending not quite as far below the edge nor so far up on the scarf as the velvet strips. All the strips are finished in points at both ends, and all the edges are stitched with coarse silk of a contrasting color. The lower ends of the strips are tipped with chenille pompons. The velvet and silk may be of contrasting shades, and the pompons may be the color of each or of both. On each end the strips and pompons may be of different colors. This is a most decorative method of utilizing scraps of silk or velvet, or odds and ends of ribbon of any variety one may have on hand.

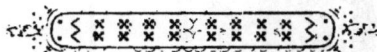

CHAPTER XXIX.

Fancy Scarf, with Crazy Embroidery. Group of Fancy Stitches.

HE furor prevailing in woman's kingdom for "crazy" effects—otherwise known as mosaic and oriental effects—in portières, quilts, sofa-cushion covers, etc., has brought into use every kind of stitch hitherto employed in embroidery, and has developed many pretty new stitches. The well-known darning stitch has become quite a favorite and effective embroidery stitch, and is used for decoration in all its stages, from the first simply crossed threads to the heavier and completed stage ordinarily called the "basket" stitch. Feather, herringbone, button-hole, cross, satin, Kensington and cat stitches are all used, and a little ingenuity and artistic taste will, out of these and the excellent variety of stitches which are illustrated in this chapter, create the most fascinating mosaic effects that could be imagined. All sorts of shapes in scraps of velvet, silk, satin, Surah, fancy and plain ribbons, pretty brocades in silk and wool mixtures, etc., are used in mosaic patch-work. They are basted to blocks of muslin, crinoline or sheet wadding; the edges slightly turned under and then applied in any and all the fancy stitches mentioned, with flosses in a veritable rainbow of colors; and the result is brilliant in a bewildering assortment of hues, shapes and embroidery. Birds, animals, Japanese figures, flags, stars, ships, monograms, Greenaway figures, flowers, single and in sprays, fruits, vegetables, etc., are introduced in this peculiar patch-work, and the more varied the effect, the more perfect the Oriental result will be. The blocks are usually square and may be of any size preferred; and, in uniting them, care should be taken that no suggestions of their joining be apparent. A broad band of brocaded, plain or fancy velvet, silk, plush or satin is a handsome bordering for the work, and should be monochromatic in its coloring, as the solid tone affords an artistic framing for the brilliant work and heightens the Oriental look. Black, dark garnet, deep crimson, navy-blue, ruby, violet, olive, purple, dark green, cardinal and brown are especially effective colors for borderings, the depth of their hues softening the brilliancy of the work, yet bringing out its beauty in the same way as a suitable frame shows off a handsome painting. Neatness in application and general work is an absolute necessity.

Fancy Scarf.

FIGURE NO. 1.—A handsome scarf, as appropriate for a mantel, piano, etc., as it is for a table, is here illustrated. It is made of felt cloth, edged at the ends with a fringe formed of heavy silk tassels, alternating with large plush pendants. A little above the fringe is applied a broad band of "crazy" patch-work embroidery, formed of three blocks of patch-work separated by bands of velvet ribbon ap-

any color desired, and the velvet ribbon may be like it or a contrast in color. Any kind of fringe preferred may be substituted for that illustrated.

Block in Crazy Patch-work.

FIGURE No. 2.—This engraving shows how

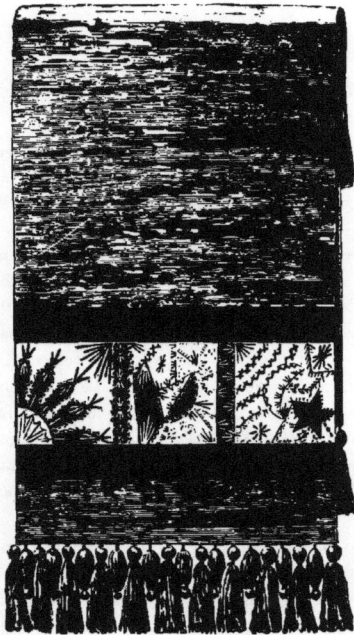

FIGURE NO. 1.—FANCY SCARF.

Embroidery in Darning Stitches.

FIGURE NO. 3.—This design forms an effective decorative feature in the block shown at Figure No. 2, at which it is worked on a plain piece of silk or satin. It is first outlined, and then the spaces are embroidered with the stitches described at Figures Nos. 4 and 5.

Darning Stitch.

FIGURE NO. 4.—This is the ordinary basket

through at the point where the next stitch is to be made, as illustrated.

Embroidery Stitch.

FIGURES NOS. 6 AND 7.—These engravings illustrate a pretty stitch formed of three long stitches and a loop, the method of making the loop being clearly pictured at Figure No. 6.

Embroidery Stitch.

FIGURE NO. 8.—In making this stitch, the short stitch is made first, and the needle car-

FIGURE NO. 2.—BLOCK IN CRAZY PATCH-WORK.

darning-stitch used in darning hosiery, etc. It is a well-known stitch, and a little study of the engraving will soon make it clear to any one who is not familiar with it.

Embroidery Stitch.

FIGURE NO. 5.—The long threads in this design are run in like darning stitches, only farther apart, so as to form diamond shapes, and are caught down at the crossing with a simple back-stitch : the needle being drawn

ried through at the point locating the end of the loop to be made; the needle is then carried back under the short stitch and down to the end of the loop.

Embroidery Stitches.

FIGURES NOS. 9 AND 10.—These illustrations show how a variety of stitches may be developed from that shown at Figure No. 8. The long stitches may be made in any direction.

Embroidery Stitch.

FIGURES NOS. 11 AND 12.—Figure No. 11

carried through at a point showing the length of the stem or middle stitch; the needle is

FIGURE NO. 3.

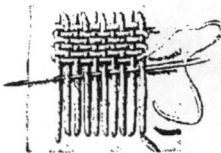

FIGURE NO. 4.

FIGURE NO. 5

FIGURE NO. 6.

FIGURE NO. 7.

FIGURE NO. 8.

FIGURE NO. 9.

FIGURE NO. 10.

FIGURE NO. 11.

FIGURE NO. 12.

FIGURES NOS. 3, 4, 5, 6, 7, 8, 9, 10, 11 AND 12.—EMBROIDERY STITCHES.

shows the method of making the stitch at Figure No. 12. In making the last stitch in a figure, it will be observed that the needle is then carried back to the end of the last stem or middle stitch in order to complete this stitch properly.

Figures in Embroidery.

FIGURES NOS. 13 AND 14.—These figures are effective on applied ribbons, bands, etc., more shorter stitches, as preferred. Figure No. 15 illustrates the method of putting in the long stitches.

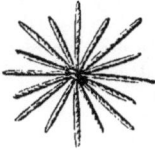

FIGURE NO. 13.

FIGURE NO. 14.

FIGURE NO. 15.

FIGURE NO. 16.

FIGURE NO. 17.

FIGURE NO. 18.

FIGURE NO. 19.

FIGURE NO. 20.

FIGURE NO. 21.

FIGURE NO. 22.

FIGURE NO. 23.

FIGURES NOS. 13, 14, 15, 16, 17, 18, 19, 20, 21, 22 AND 23.—EMBROIDERY STITCHES.

and also as center pieces to sections in mosaic patch-work. The stitches are all run out from a common center, which is crossed by one or

Embroidery Stitch.

FIGURE NO. 15.—These stitches all radiate from a common point, and may be of equal lengths, or the center one may be the longest. Three, five or more stitches may be grouped in a pattern, and, while they may vary in length, the corresponding stitches at the sides should be alike.

Embroidery Stitch.

FIGURE No. 16.—In making this pretty stitch, the needle is carried down *over* the thread, as illustrated. The stitch is pretty and simple, the only care being to take up the stitches in a line and to make them even in length.

Combination of Embroidery Stitches.

FIGURE No. 17.—This engraving illustrates an effective combination of the stitches explained at Figures Nos. 15 and 16. The combination is very effective and may include one or two colors.

Combination of Stitches.

FIGURE No. 18.—The stitch explained at Figure No. 15 is here combined with a knot-stitch to form a very effective variety in stitches.

Embroidery Stitch.

FIGURE No. 19.— Another very effective arrangement of the stitch described at Figure No. 15 is here portrayed. The stitches are made at regular intervals at each side of the edges to be appliquéd, the lower stitches being made so as to come midway between those of the upper row.

Embroidery Stitches.

FIGURE No. 20.—This stitch is commonly known as the "herring-bone" stitch, and is simple and one much used in decorating flannel under-garments, as well as for appliqué work.

Combination Stitches.

FIGURE No. 21—This engraving illustrates a combination of the stitches explained at Figures Nos. 15 and 20. The stitches may be of contrasting colors, and are particularly effective combined in this way.

Embroidery Stitch.

FIGURE No. 22.—The engraving clearly illustrates the method of making this pretty stitch. Care should be taken to make all the stitches even.

Combination Stitches.

FIGURE No. 23.—The diamond outlines are each made with four long stitches, carrying the thread under the needle at the corners. A simple cross-stitch, made in the center of each, completes this simple but pretty combination.

Group of Fancy Stitches.

Group of Fancy Stitches.

FIGURES NOS. 1 TO 13.—Those who are making "crazy" quilts or covers for chairs, pillows. etc.. will appreciate the novel combinations of stitches illustrated in this group. They are very effective when done in gold thread or, indeed, in silk, so that all the short bits left in the work-basket may be used up by the aid of such stitches and a decidedly oriental effect achieved.

For the application of ribbons, etc., they are equally effective. They are all formed partly or entirely of the well-known herring-bone, knot-stitch, feather-stitch, and long stitches grouped artistically. A careful study of the engravings will aid the searcher after

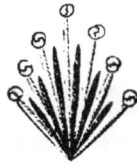

FIGURE No. 1.

FIGURE No. 2.

FIGURE No. 3.

FIGURE No. 4.

FIGURE No. 5.

FIGURE No. 6.

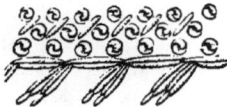

FIGURE No. 7.

FIGURE No. 8.

FIGURE No. 9.

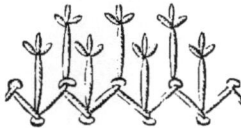

FIGURE No. 10.

FIGURE No. 11.

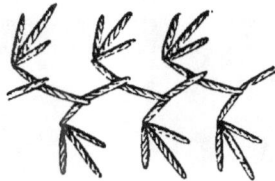

FIGURE No. 12.

FIGURE No. 13.

GROUP OF FANCY STITCHES.

pretty stitches in obtaining a variety of effects, and in either grouping one, two or several colors may be attractively introduced. It would seem as though the management of the needle had reached such a point of excellence that fine work done with it is no longer mentioned without its prefix of "artistic." Such work is the successor of "plain sewing," for the study of which, by-the-bye, classes are frequently formed, because without a proper knowledge of "plain sewing" one can have no certainty that, if she only knows how to do fancy work, she will always do it well. The dainty finish and the ease with which linings, especially, are made to retain their proper position are, in nearly all instances, due to knowledge obtained when the worker has been properly taught to hold the needle. At that time one learns to have the thread short, not to moisten the end of her silk so it will fray, and above all things to give thought to that which she is doing, else it will be a failure.

A Mosaic in Crochet Work.

A SOFA cushion suggestive of mosaic, or as it is more commonly termed crazy work, is covered with crochetted squares measuring a little more than three inches on each side. The squares are crochetted in the well-known shell-stitch and each one displays variety of colors arranged so as to present a striking difference to the others. Here are a few examples of the arrangement of colors. One square is black for half its dimensions, measuring diagonally from one corner to another; the other half shows a diversity of tints, one shell being orange, another white, another cardinal, and still another purple. Another square is composed of alternating shells of salmon and moss-green around a smaller solid square of darker green. Odds and ends of worsted, embroidery silk, chenille and all sorts of crochet and embroidery materials left over from various pieces of fancywork may be utilized to good advantage in mosaic work. Of course some dark color may be selected and used as a setting for the brighter and lighter tints, and a worsted cord of this color, or of all the tints combined may finish the edges.

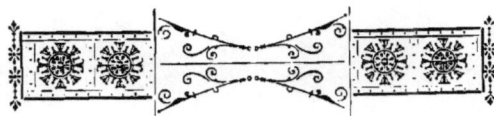

CHAPTER XXX.

ALPHABET FOR MARKING.

T is essentially a womanly weakness to like one's initials upon one's belongings, but she—that mysterious and universal she—has also cultivated this pretty taste in her brothers and father and husband by making them gifts of silk or linen handkerchiefs, with the letter or letters deftly embroidered in one corner. There seems something especially womanly in this work, and the constant demand of the fair workers is for new designs in letters and new combinations in coloring.

While the letters are more mediæval when done in wonderful browns, and sages, and blues, and scarlets, still it is well to remember that white washes the best, and that no other color can be cited as infallible. Next in order to the white comes scarlet and then sage, but the best blues and browns will be apt to grow dingy and disagreeable-looking.

Those who have had much experience in using various embroidery materials make it a rule not to use two different makes or brands in the same piece of work, even though they may seem identical in color, twist and texture, because the process of working or the effect of laundering is sure to emphasize any differences which may exist. They affirm that this rule is especially applicable to embroideries which are liable to form acquaintance with soap and water, though quite worthy of consideration in the use of silks, chenilles and arasenes, some being quite close and somewhat stiff, while others are loose and flexible. The eye of the needle should be large enough to permit of the thread moving freely in it and the point sharp enough to penetrate the fabric easily.

Alphabet No. 1.

The letters here shown are sufficiently artistic to appear as if they had been copied from some old missal where they had been gorgeously illuminated. The outlines of the letters are done in plain over-and-over and stem stitch, while the inner portions are in seed stitch. Individual taste must govern largely when combinations of coloring are used, but it would seem proper to make all the outlines and the large dots of one shade and the small dots of another, or each of a different one. All white is, however, considered in best taste. These letters are suitable for use on towels and table-cloths.

ALPHABET NO. 1.

Alphabet No. 2.

The letters here illustrated are intended for marking handkerchiefs, napery, under-garments, etc., and may be done either in white or colored embroidery, cotton or floss as pre-ferred. The method is simple, the embroidery, being done by an over-hand stitch, which increases in length to form the heavier parts of the letters or what in ink would be the shading. It is well to fill in this portion with

ALPHABET NO. 2.

running before making the embroidery, so that the latter will have a round raised surface. The finer portions are done with stitches taken through only two or three threads of the fabric, so that the lines will be delicate, while the leaves are fashioned in the same manner as the thick parts of the letters. In transferring the designs the outside lines must be followed in every instance in order to produce the requisite sizes.

  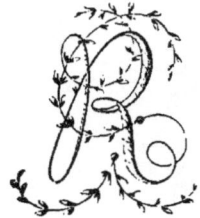

Alphabet No. 3.

The tiny forget-me-nots which give such a graceful, floriated effect to this alphabet may always be made in their natural colors when the letters are done in silk or crewels, but if it be desirable to use all white in working with cotton, no fear need be felt that the effect will not be good. Such letters are especially pretty for souvenir marking, but they are equally well adapted to napery, etc. White and colored floss and marking cotton are used in their development. The work is done in an over-and-over stitch and it always comes out most effectively, when the design is run with floss or filling cotton before the actual embroidery is begun.

ALPHABET NO. 3.

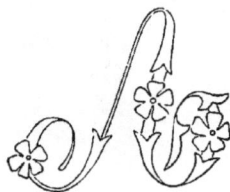

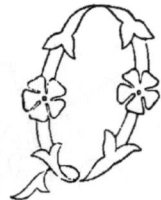

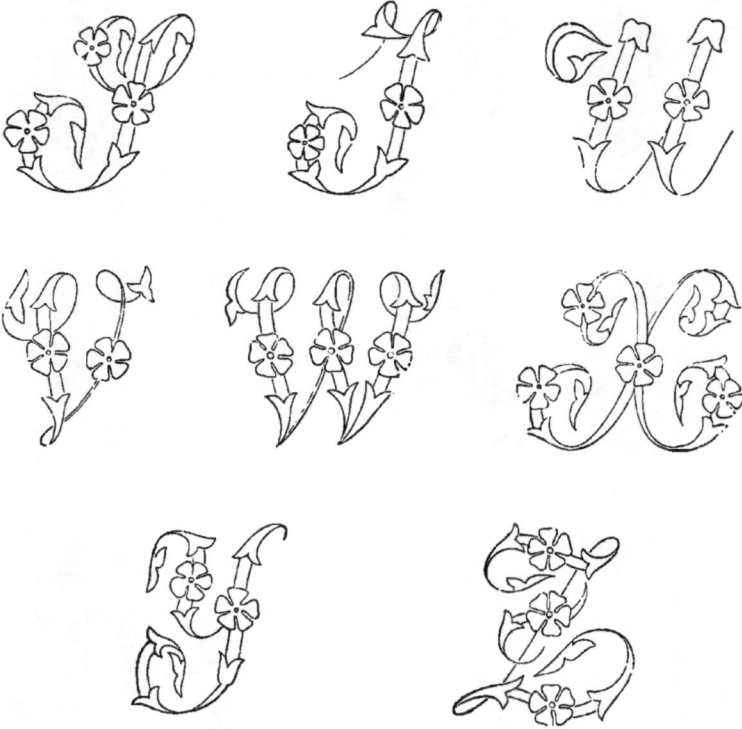

It is to the proper filling-in of the raised portion of the work that finely executed embroidery owes much of its good effect. Too often this portion is slighted, because it is to be overlaid by the final stitches; a smooth firm finish is not obtainable unless the filling-in be well done. Such work may be done rapidly after the necessary skill has been acquired, but the beginner should not permit herself to be controlled by a desire to do more than she can do well. Fine blue chenille makes very natural looking forget-me-nots, though, of course, it is not recommended for any article that is to be laundered. Two or three shades of blue may be introduced in making several of these dainty blossoms, as nature does not limit herself to a monochrome.

ALPHABET NO. 4.

Alphabet No. 4.

This alphabet is very artistically designed for working in outline stitch. Any article, whether for ornament or use, becomes emphatically one's own when the monogram or initials are upon it; and these letters are of a desirable size for all kinds of marking, and may be used as initials or combined in monograms. The making of monograms has always been thought much trouble, but these artistic letters are especially adapted to the purpose, and may be associated in any way admired. Of course the space between the outlines may be filled in and worked solid if preferred, or French knots may be scattered through these open spaces with good effect.

NEEDLE-CRAFT.

ALPHABET NO. 5.

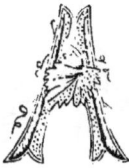   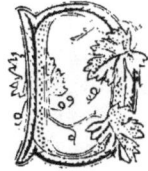

Alphabet No. 5.

These letters are embroidered in satin stitch and French knots, and while not difficult to do are elaborate enough to serve for marking souvenir or gift articles which one may wish to render particularly attractive. They are also adapted to handsome napery and may be worked all in white or in a uniform color or a combination of tints, according to the fancy of the worker.

CHAPTER XXXI.

RECEPTACLES FOR SHOES, UMBRELLAS AND CANES.

T HE articles illustrated in this chapter, will without doubt be much prized for their usefulness and the tasteful manner in which they are developed.

Shoe-Bag.

FIGURES NOS. 1 AND 2.—These engravings illustrate a handy and pretty receptacle for shoes, slippers, etc., Figure No. 1 showing the bag closed and Figure No. 2 showing it open. The material is canvas, and the lining is Silesia. The outside is cut long enough to fold over and form the cover, which is nicely curved at its edges and held down with a loop passed over a button arranged as pictured. The pockets are formed of a straight section of the canvas lined like the outside. Two box-plaits are formed on the under side about midway between the center and sides, and the section is joined at its sides and lower edges, and also down the center of the plaits, which give the pockets the needed spring. A row of wide velvet ribbon is stitched along the top of the pockets, and the lower edge is decorated with short strips of narrow velvet ribbon of alter-

nating lengths. The outside of the cover is similarly decorated with strips of the narrow velvet ribbon, and the owner's initials or monogram in embroidery or metal may decorate the cover. Any preferred material strong enough for the uses of the article may be selected, crash, linen, towelling, *crétonne*, etc., being much liked. Fancy stitching may be applied as decoration instead of the velvet ribbon, or all the edges may be bound with bright-hued ribbon or braid.

Decorated Shoe-Box.

FIGURE NO. 3.—The ever useful shoe-box —and in this instance a well-dressed one—is here pictured. Of its utility every woman knows, and its admirers are many in number. An ordinary box is lined with pink satin and has pale-blue satin on the outer side, and on the latter are arranged flowers cut out of pink satin and slightly wadded. The middle of the flower is made by a knot stitch of tinsel thread, and the stems are formed in the same way. A cording outlines the box and conceals the sewing. If preferred, the entire box may be covered with sateen, and the flowers may be of the same material. The size for the petals of the flowers on the box is given at Figure No. 4.

NEEDLE-CRAFT.

FIGURE No. 1.—SHOE-BAG—CLOSED.

FIGURE No. 2.—SHOE-BAG—OPEN.

FIGURE No. 3.—DECORATED SHOE-BOX.

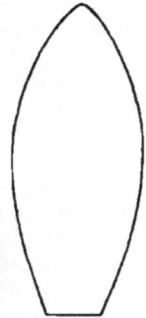

FIGURE No. 4.—SECTION OF FLOWER ON SHOE-BOX.

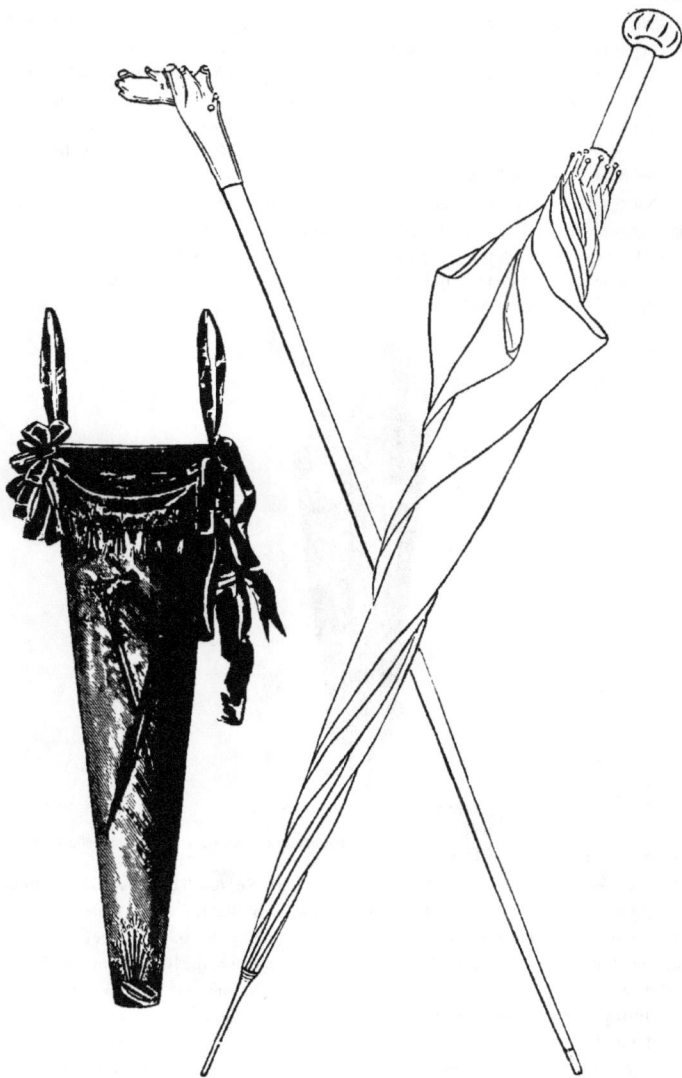

FIGURE NO. 5.—UMBRELLA-
AND-CANE POCKET.

FIGURE NO. 6.—EMBROIDERY DESIGN FOR UMBRELLA-
AND-CANE POCKET.

Section of Flower on Shoe-Box.

FIGURE No. 4.—The design for one petal of the flower on the shoe-box is here shown. Care should be taken that the petals are all of one size ; if not, the effect will be irregular and undesirable.

Umbrella-and-Cane Pocket.

FIGURE No. 5.—The back of this handsome receptacle for the umbrella and walking-cane is made of heavy cardboard, that is covered smoothly on the outside with cloth, linen canvas, crash, felt, Silesia or any preferred mate-

silks, and fancy stitches also decorate the lower part above the band of wide ribbon that neatly completes the end. A long loop of narrow ribbon is fastened to each upper corner, by which to hang up the pocket, and a rosette bow of wider ribbon is attached to the end of the left loop ; while a bow of long loops and ends of ribbon is tacked over the end of the right loop. A cane and umbrella crossing each other are embroidered on the center of the pocket. The outline of this design may be seen in full size at Figure No. 6.

FIGURE No. 7.—UMBRELLA-CASE.

rial, and on the front side with any of the fabrics mentioned or with silk, plush, pongee, etc. The front portion is of fine felt cloth and is cut wider than the back and curved out deeply at the top. It is joined to the back at the sides and lower end, and is faced on the outside to the depth of a wide hem at the top. Along the lower part of the facing are grouped in an ornamental manner fancy stitches done with vari-colored embroidery

Embroidery Design for Umbrella-and-Cane Pocket.

FIGURE No. 6.—This design is embroidered on the umbrella and cane pocket illustrated at Figure No. 5 in this chapter. It is the proper size for the decoration, and may be done in outline or Kensington stitch, as preferred. Wood-brown, dark-blue, black or any preferred color or colors may be used. Usually, the cane will contrast with the umbrella.

Umbrella-Case.

FIGURE No. 7.—This case includes a back portion and two pockets made from jean, felt cloth, heavy canvas, burlaps, reps, or any suitably heavy material. The side edges of the parts are joined and then bordered with bright-colored braid machine-stitched on, the braid being arranged in a similar manner about all the edges. The pockets may be cut separately, but the case will be all the stronger for cutting them in one piece. In either event stitching catches them to place down the middle, and a row of the braid is placed over the fastening to correspond with the finish at the sides. The pockets may be decorated with embroidery done in the South-Kensington outline-stitch, or they may have the owner's monogram embroidered upon them. A loop is fastened at the top of the back at the center, to suspend the case on the wall. Such cases will be found an excellent protection for nice umbrellas, are really very simple in construction, and require but little time to make them.

Lamp-Shades.

A PRETTY shade for a piano lamp that is to stand in a room where the general effect is light and dainty, is of pink satin, bordered with a flounce of pink lace, and trimmed with pink clover-blossoms and delicate green grasses, branched with a few ferns. As the shade is mounted on a wire frame having but few supports between the outer ring and the small one at the top, the satin is lined with thin pink tarlatan to give it a little firmness. The fulness is drawn into a frilled heading, at the smallest portion and the floral decorations are arranged with careless grace, and yet in such a way that no fear of their slipping out of place need be entertained. A pretty gradation of tints which harmonizes with almost all colors seen in draperies, upholsteries, etc., is in three shades of yellow. One which is to shade a table lamp in a white and gold room is of white silk with a fringe of gold-colored silk. An orange shade, with white lace for its garniture, is effective upon an iron lamp, which is to stand in a room furnished in rather dark colors.

Slumber Rolls.

Some of them, which are really very handsome in the hand, seem to lose their beauty when attached to the chairs they are supposed to make comfortable. If not properly adjusted, they are not apt to impart either beauty or comfort. One shaped like a diminutive round bolster is attached to a chair of antique oak as follows: The roll, which is covered only with muslin, is firmly tied to the back of the chair with linen tape, securely fastened at its ends and center. A scarf of India silk, twenty-seven inches wide and a yard and three-quarters long, is then wound in and out about the framework of the chair-back so as to cover the roll in loose, graceful folds. One end of the scarf is hemmed and caught up at its corner so as to form a sort of loop, while the other is bordered with a fringe of spun-silk tassels and falls in a graceful cascade of folds.

Crescent-shaped slumber rolls may be covered to serve as scarfs by allowing considerable extra length at each end of the cover, and width enough to give a graceful fulness.

A pair of oblong cushions hung in saddlebag style over the head-rest may be made very ornamental without extra work if they are covered with flowered silk or crétonne, and tied on with ribbons. The one which hangs over the back need not be filled with anything better than excelsior inside a layer of cotton batting.

CHAPTER XXXII.

INFANT'S CARRIAGE-PILLOW AND BLANKET.

Infant's Carriage-Pillow.

FIGURE No. 1.—This dainty head-rest for Baby while enjoying an afternoon airing in his carriage is made of white Surah, upon which are embroidered graceful sprays of small flowers that look as if they had been just showered on the pillow. The sprays may be merely outlined, or they may be embroidered solidly or worked in the South-Kensington stitch ; or, if desired, the flowers may be made of ribbon. Hand-painting is also effective. A frill of deep lace, headed by a ruche of fringed-out Surah, trims the pillow all around ; and the result is soft and delicate. Of course, the pillow is made of down, feathers or whatever is preferred, put in a case of stout fabric and then covered as pictured. Delicate blue or pink or any other shade of Surah or silk may be used instead of white ; and the lace may be of any preferred variety. The sprays may be made of appliqué ornaments, with good effect.

Sprays in South-Kensington Outline-Stitch.

FIGURES NOS. 2 AND 3.—These pretty sprays decorate the infant's carriage-pillow pictured at Figure No. 1. In this instance they are worked in South-Kensington outline-stitch, but may be solidly embroidered if preferred. The sprays may be embroidered on any article of ornament, with pretty effect.

Figures Nos. 2 and 3 show two of the sprays in outline-stitch, Figure No. 5 shows a spray solidly embroidered in South-Kensington stitch, and Figure No. 4 shows a cluster of blossoms done with ribbon. All these sprays, worked in either manner, are pretty for adorning the pillow represented.

Cluster of Flowers Made of Ribbon.

FIGURE NO. 4.—Very narrow ribbon is used for the flowers, and the stem is done with floss. Each petal is formed of a section of ribbon, and the center is composed of knots of floss. The work is very simple, but requires care to result well. It may be done on cloth, plush, velvet, silk or satin, and results handsomely.

Spray in South-Kensington Stitch.

FIGURE No. 5.—This spray forms one of the bits of adornment on the carriage-pillow pictured at Figure No. 1. It is done in the well-known South-Kensington stitch, and is just as suitable for the adornment of lambrequins, table-scarfs, etc., as for the pillow.

Baby's Blanket.

FIGURE NO. 6.—In the engraving is shown a dainty blanket formed of a square of cream-white camel's-hair cloth powdered with yellow embroidered on it in white. Blue-and-white and pink-and-white are dainty colors for these blankets. Flannel, smooth cloth, eider-down cloth and camel's-hair are the preferred mate-

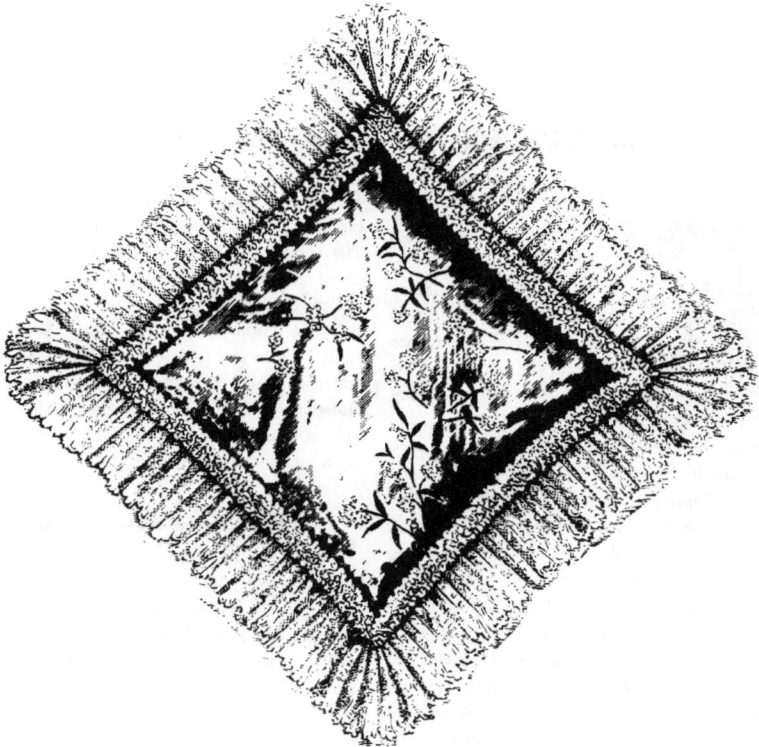

FIGURE NO. 2.

FIGURE NO. 4.—CLUSTER OF
FLOWERS MADE OF RIBBON.

FIGURE NO. 3.
FIGURES NOS. 2 AND 3.—SPRAYS IN SOUTH-
KENSINGTON OUTLINE-STITCH.

FIGURE NO. 5.
FIGURE NO. 5.—SPRAY IN SOUTH-
KENSINGTON STITCH.

may be done in colors to harmonize with the ground, and the ribbon may be of any preferred variety.

Word Decoration for Baby's Blanket.

FIGURE No. 7.—This pretty lettering is for the blanket illustrated below. It may be

FIGURE No. 6.—BABY'S BLANKET.

FIGURE No. 7.—WORD DECORATION FOR BABY'S BLANKET.

The proper size for the word "Baby" to be embroidered on the blanket is given at Figure No. 7, and it may be easily traced. done in outline, Kensington or satin stitch with floss or metal thread, or it may be hand-painted.

CHAPTER XXXIII.

FANCY-WORK APRONS.

FIT companion to the work-basket is a fancy-work apron, and much artistic taste is now expended on this garment to make it a bit of loveliness to the eye and a dressy contribution to the toilette. All kinds of dainty fabrics are used for its construction, and there is no limit to the beautiful effects to be achieved with ribbons, embroidery, lace, etc.

Fancy Apron.

FIGURE NO. 1.—This dainty apron is made of scrim. It is hemmed at the side edges and more deeply at the bottom, the hems being cat-stitched to position. Above the hem at the lower edge threads are drawn crosswise for three rows of ribbon, which are run in and out in the usual way. The ribbon is of a pretty heliotrope shade, and so is the embroidery silk used for the stitching. The top of the apron is gathered and joined to a belt that is extended to form long ties, which are bowed at the back. A row of cat-stitching is made along the top of the belt, and a bow of ribbon wider than that across the bottom of the apron is fastened to the belt near the left side. On the right side of the apron is a handkerchief pocket in patch style; a hem cat-stitched to place finishes the top of the

pocket, and cat-stitching is also used in applying the pocket. Ribbon is run in the pocket just below the hem, and a small bow of similar ribbon is tacked to the center of the pocket. The ribbon may be of any color preferred, and the stitching may be feather, brier, herring-bone, etc., as preferred.

FIGURE NO. 1.—FANCY APRON.

Words to Embroider on Fancy-Work Apron.

FIGURE NO. 2.—These three words may be outlined on any fancy-work apron when plain material is used for its construction.

They are of suitable size, and the Kensington outline-stitch is used. On an apron shaped like that shown at Figure No. 1 the words could be embroidered on one side or about the lower edge. Of course, they are also adapted

bottom, at the sides and across the top, a wide ribbon being inserted in the hem at the top to draw the apron in and to tie about the waist. The hems are held with button-hole stitches of yellow floss; threads are drawn

Fancy Work Apron

FIGURE No. 2.—WORDS TO EMBROIDER ON FANCY-WORK APRON.

to any other style of fancy-work apron and crewels, flosses, silks, etc., may be used for outlining.

Fancy Apron.

FIGURE No. 3.—This apron is pictured as made of scrim. A deep hem is made at the

above the bottom hem to form three rows of squares, which are filled in with long stitches of the floss radiating from the center to the edges. These stitches produce the effect of daisies and are soft and beautiful. Narrow ribbon the color of the embroidery silk is run in to show in the openings at the corners of the squares. The stitches may be shaded blues, heliotrope, pink, scarlet, pale-blue or green. A row of button-hole stitching is also

Fancy Apron.

FIGURE NO. 4.—Linen is the material used for this apron, the simple finish being a deep hem, with the threads drawn and caught in

FIGURE NO. 3.—FANCY APRON.

FIGURE NO. 4.—FANCY APRON.

made across the apron at the top of the squares. Extreme care is needful in drawing the thread to form the regular effect which is so desirable to the good finish of the work.

network fashion. Above this are Greenaway designs done in many colored crewels, while the belt is confined at the back by long ties of écru ribbon. Pongee or Surah silk is often

chosen instead of linen, but the ease with
which the latter may be embroidered goes far
to commend it to the amateur worker not as

Outline Design for Decorating Fancy Apron.

FIGURE No. 5.—Whether the little Romeo
is here urging an invitation to the dance or

FIGURE No. 5.—OUTLINE DESIGN FOR DECORATING FANCY APRON.

yet certain of her success on finer stuffs.
The designs used in embellishing this apron
are illustrated at Figures Nos. 5, 6 and 7.

suggesting a cool and shady retreat, nobody
can say, save the little maid who listens so
intently.　Such designs would be particularly

appropriate for hangings, for linen covers for a baby's couch, or for the mantel drapery in a young girl's especial retreat.

he dances forward to meet his partner. The exact delineation of her gown and bonnet cannot but call forth admiration, and convince

FIGURE NO. 6.—OUTLINE DESIGN FOR DECORATING FANCY APRON.

Outline Design for Decorating Fancy Apron.

FIGURE NO. 6.—This sketch in outline-stitch gives the interested looker-on an opportunity to study the position of the courtier as the lovers of the picturesque how much more possible it is to draw pretty maidens than graceful swains, e'en though the latter merit our especial admiration.

Outline Design for Decorating Fancy Apron.

FIGURE No. 7.—This pretty " treading " of a measure is one of the outline designs that decorates the lower edge of the No. 4 apron.

brought before the mind's eye with very little trouble. Very quaint effects are obtained by choosing tints the reverse of realistic for this kind of work. Very often the entire design is

FIGURE. No. 7.—OUTLINE DESIGN FOR DECORATING FANCY APRON.

It is done in crewels, and to the taste of the worker is left the choice of colors. These designs are given in the full size, so that they can be easily understood and the effect done in one color, and it is really wonderful how much originality of effect may be brought out by such uniformity. Any preferred commingling of tints is, however, in order.

CHAPTER XXXIV.

- SOFA PILLOWS AND CUSHIONS.

HE fashion of having couches and sofas provided with pillows and pillows and pillows, cushions and cushions and cushions, leads to the development of beautiful articles into which the worker introduces whatever style of needlework or variety of painting she is most proficient in doing.

Sofa-Pillow.

FIGURE No. 1.—A square of velvet forms the foundation for the top cover of this beautiful pillow, and is enriched with embroidered ribbons in different colors, arranged to produce a plaided effect. The embroidery on the ribbons consists of crazy-stitches done with many-colored flosses, and produces a brilliant effect. Silk cord borders the visible edges of the ribbon, and two rows of the cord border the edges of the square, being fancifully looped at the corners. The ribbons may be different shades of one color or of several contrasting shades. Two triangular pieces of very wide sash-ribbon, separated by a section of plush, velvet or satin, to which they are united so that all form a square, may be utilized for one side of a cushion or pillow, with

good effect. Handsome brocaded ribbons are effective for this purpose.

Sofa-Pillow.

FIGURE No. 2.—This engraving illustrates an odd-looking but handsome sofa-pillow of garnet plush, old-gold plush and delicate blue satin. The band about the middle is of old-gold plush, edged at both sides with gold-and-garnet silk cord. The corner of blue satin is elaborately embroidered with embroidery silk, done in South-Kensington stitch. Cord borders the top of the embroidered section, and also the opposite end of the pillow. The pillow is shaped like a bag, and at its cord-bordered edge is deeply lined with old-gold satin, and the pillow is then tied closely about at the end of the lining with gold-colored satin ribbon, which is arranged in a rosette of long loops and ends upon the upper side. The result is both rich and elegant. Other colors in the same materials may be as effectively combined, and hand-painting or appliqués may decorate the satin corner, instead of the embroidery pictured.

Sofa-Pillow.

FIGURE No. 3.—The shape of this sofa-pillow is such that one finds it especially suitable to have it perfumed with lavender or violet, the powder being thrown among its feathers or down. The satin cover is of a pale-blue shade, and the velvet portion that apparently the satin underneath, and, as it is drawn in by a broad pale-blue satin ribbon tied in a bow at one side, the likeness to a large sachet

FIGURE No. 1.—SOFA-PILLOW.

overlies it is of very deep crimson, having passion flowers in their blue shades worked upon it. The outlining of the points is done with pale-blue silk cord, and the frill at the top is finished in the same way. The frill shows is preserved. While very decorative and decidedly beautifying to a room, it is well to remember that such cushions cannot be commended for any other purpose than the purely ornamental.

Sofa-Pillow.

FIGURE No. 4.—The brilliant combination of white and gold is achieved in this lovely long stitches across the surface of the pillow, which is like a gleam of sunshine in a pretty room. A frill of inexpensive white lace sur-

FIGURE No. 2.—SOFA-PILLOW.

FIGURE No. 3.—SOFA-PILLOW.

pillow. The material is white India silk, on which the design pictured is stamped and then simply outlined with bright yellow filoselle. Threads of the bright color show in rounds the pillow, adding to its dainty effect. Other colors may be combined in a similar way, and the lace may be of any preferred variety. Sometimes the designs on the pillows are *en appliqué*, but they are not so dainty as that pictured.

Fancy Sofa-Pillow.

FIGURE No. 5.—This engraving illustrates

It is embellished with leaf-sprays and blossoms cut from crétonne and embroidered all over in Kensington stitch, done with colors exactly matching those in the design. The corners of the cushion are covered with corner-

FIGURE No. 4.—SOFA-PILLOW.

of pompons edges the pillow, those at the corners of the pillow and the center-piece being

velvet, plush, satin, cloth, etc., and similarly decorated. A design may be cut from any

FIGURE NO. 6.—SOFA-PILLOW.

FIGURE NO. 7.—FANCY PILLOW.

larger than the others. The entire center-piece may be of crétonne, or it may be of

preferred piece of crétonne and similarly applied, with pretty effect.

Sofa-Pillow.

FIGURE No. 6.—The handsome sofa-pillow here illustrated has a center square of corded square is embellished with oak leaves cut from the velvet and applied with filoselle. It is bordered all round with cord arranged in

FIGURE No. 8.—SOFA-PILLOW.

FIGURE No. 9.—SOFA-PILLOW.

silk and a band-like border of velvet in a very strongly contrasting shade, the silk being pale-gold and the velvet golden brown. The loops at the corners, the middle loops being interlinked by similar loops arranged at the outer corners of the pillow, which is edged all round with cord. The decoration is very effective and very artistic. The back of the pillow shows the shade of the silk. Green velvet may be used with pink or blue or with light golden-brown silk; and if one has artistic ability, the leaves may be tinted in Autumn colorings. Any preferred variety of leaf may be chosen for application.

Fancy Pillow.

FIGURE No. 7.—This exquisite pillow is of dark-green velvet, with its upper corner of *cresson*, forming a decided contrast and sug-

much nicer and be very suitable to have down fill the case.

Appliqué is now much used as a decorative item in preference to hand-painting and embroidery, although these have by no means lost favor in the eyes of art-lovers.

Sofa-Pillow.

FIGURE No. 8.—The dainty sofa-pillow here represented is a charming illustration of this beautiful work, and is made of garnet plush and heliotrope satin. The center is a square formed of two triangles, each made of strips of plush and satin joined together, and

FIGURE No. 10.—FIR-PILLOW.

gesting a scale between the two shades. In the lower corner is carefully applied a beautiful cluster of water-lilies, specimens of manufactured silk-embroidered appliqués, and underneath them in outline-stitch the worker has an opportunity with her needle to portray the water in which they grow. After being made, heavy silk cord in a golden shade is used for outlining the pillow, and a prettily made bow of green satin ribbon is placed in the upper corner to bring out the *cresson* shade as well as add to the beauty of all the rest. By-the-bye, it is well to remember that it will make it

having their seams covered with pale-pink floss in herring-bone stitch. The strips in each triangle are differently arranged, so that a stiff, set appearance will not be produced. The cushion is made octagonal in shape by hexagonal sections of plush and satin arranged alternately all around the square. In each section a flower design is appliquéed, and these may be different in every section or only in the alternating sections, as preferred. If a delicate effect be desired, the flowers may be of velvet or plush, and the stems and leaves may be formed with floss in the South-Kensington stitch. The colors for the cushion may be any two most pleasing to the worker's taste, and may be delicate or brilliant, as preferred.

Sofa-Pillow.

FIGURE NO. 9.—This handsome sofa-pillow

under a large rosette bow of ribbon. The leaves and stems of the sprays are done in the Kensington stitch, while the daisies are worked in a loop stitch. The centers of the daisies are usually done in the well-known knot-stitch. Any desired material may be

FIGURE NO. 11.—INSCRIPTION FOR FIR-PILLOW.

is made of garnet velvet, and is shaped in the usual manner. It is edged all around with garnet-and-gold cord, that is also very ornamentally looped at the corners. On one side is embroidered artistically grouped sprays of daisies, that are seemingly tied to one corner

made into sofa-pillows, and the design may be either painted or embroidered.

Fir-Pillow and Inscription for Decorating It.

FIGURE NOS. 10 AND 11.—A fir-pillow with its delightful woody aroma is a delight to most people. Such a pillow is here illustrated. The cover is of pongee silk in its natural tint and the filling is young cones and twigs, cut with a pair of sharp scissors from the parent bough while they are still filled with the pungent, agreeable odor which they give out so freely after being dried. Upon the cover the inscription "Dreams of the Forest," is worked with brown silk, the words being arranged so as to permit of increasing the decorative effect by the addition of young cones and fir twigs, which are worked in pine green

chenille and appear to have been carelessly scattered over the surface.

FIGURE No. 11.—The words composing this inscription are of the proper size for decorating a cushion and are worked in outline stitch. Embroidery silk, crewels, gilt thread, metal cord or any working material harmonizing with the material made up may be used for them, and this arrangement of the words may be varied to agree with the position of whatever other decoration is wrought upon such a pillow.

A Couple of Palm-Leaf Fans.

THEY form the back of a wall pocket, as novel and pretty as it is useful. Each fan is doubled lengthwise until its outer edges meet. These edges are tacked firmly together to preserve the shape thus produced, and the two fans are placed against each other with their centers meeting, and are held in this position by a tacking at their lower extremities and a string wound tightly about their handles. The front of the pocket is formed

of a piece of pasteboard covered with plush, and the cornucopia shaped openings formed by the folded fans are filled in with puffings of silk. The handle is covered with silk or plush, and all the edges are finished with a thick silk cord. The pocket is suspended by a ribbon bow or a loop of cord, and the appearance is much more attractive than when a single fan forms the back, while the cost is increased only the merest trifle.

The
DELINEATOR
is

A Monthly Magazine of Fashion, Culture and Fine Arts.

E ACH issue contains illustrations and descriptions of Current and Incoming Styles for Ladies, Misses and Children, articles on the newest Dress Fabrics and Novelties in Trimmings, and representations of the latest ideas in Millinery, Lingerie and Fancy-Work.

In addition there are papers by practical writers on the Household and its proper maintenance, and a selection of entertaining and instructive reading on the Elegancies of Life.

Terms for this Publication:

Subscription Price, $1.00, or 5s., per Year. + Single Copies, 15 Cents, or 8½d.

GUARANTEED CIRCULATION, OVER ONE QUARTER OF A MILLION COPIES MONTHLY.

Parties subscribing are requested to particularly specify the number with which they wish the subscription to commence. Subscriptions will not be received for a shorter term than one year, and are always payable in advance. We have no Club Rates, and no Commissions are allowed to any one on Subscriptions sent us. The Postage on the "Delineator" is prepaid by us to any part of the United Kingdom, the United States, Canada or Mexico.

RATES OF POSTAGE TO FOREIGN COUNTRIES:

When the *DELINEATOR* is to be sent from the Publishing Office in New York to any of the following Countries, 35 Cents for Extra Postage must accompany the subscription price of the Magazine: Africa (British Colonies on West Coast), Abyssinia, Argentine Republic, Asia, Austria, Azores, Bahamas, Barbadoes, Belgium, Bermudas, Bolivia, Brazil, British Guiana, Cape Verde, Ceylon, Chili, China (via Hong Kong or San Francisco, Columbia (U. S. of), Costa Rica, Curacao, Egypt, France, Germany, Gold Coast, Great Britain, Guatemala, Hawaiian Kingdom, India, Ireland, Italy, Jamaica, Japan, Madagascar (St. Mary and Tamatave only), Mauritius, Nassau (New Providence), New Caledonia, Newfoundland, Nicaragua, Panama, Paraguay, Persia, Peru, Russia, Sandwich Islands, Servia, Siam, Sierra Leone, Singapore, Spain, Sweden, Switzerland, Trinidad, Uruguay, Venezuela and Zanzibar.

For the following Countries the Extra Rate to be prepaid with each subscription is appended : - Australia, 2s.; Fiji Islands, 2s.; New South Wales, 2s.; New Zealand, 2s.; Accra, 8s.; Africa, West Coast of (except British Colonies), 8s.; Cape Colony (South Africa), 8s.; Natal (British Mail), 8s.; Orange Free State, 8s.; Madagascar (except St. Mary and Tamatave), $1.32; Transvaal, $1.32.

Address:

THE BUTTERICK PUBLISHING CO. (Limited),

171 to 175, Regent Street, London, W.; or 7, 9 and 11 West Thirteenth Street, New York.

CHAPTER XXXV.

TIDIES AND FANCY MATS

RAWN-WORK in all its different varieties is in great favor for chair-scarfs, tidies and all the odd but numerous belongings of a room to which it may be adapted. On scrim the threads are caught and the weaving process arranged by the use of very narrow ribbons specially sold for the purpose, gamut to the deepest shade ; and occasionally they will offer a contrast, pink and blue, *cresson* and shrimp, and orange and brown, being much liked.

Scrim Tidy.

FIGURE No. 1.—A tidy or cover for a cushion. The scrim is drawn at regular intervals, and the ribbon run through is orange satin, the lightest shade being first and a very deep

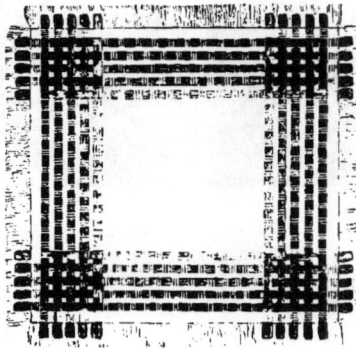

FIGURE No. 1.—SCRIM TIDY.

and which are easily drawn through the eye of a worsted needle. Sometimes all the rows of ribbon will be of one color ; again they will start from the lightest and run the tone being reached in the last row. Where the ribbon ends a loop is arranged, and rests against the fringe formed by fraying the edges of the cover. Such tidies or covers are usu-

...day placed in diamond shape on a cushion the col.. of the ribbon, and in this instance the cushion could be of satin in a light yellow shade.

Scrim Tidy.

FIGURE No. 2. This handsome tidy for a

instance are Autumn foliage, including sumach leaves and blossoms, both of which are described and shown in the required size at Figures Nos. 3 and 4.

Sumach Design for Scrim Tidy.

FIGURE No. 3.—This pretty design forms

FIGURE No. 2.—SCRIM TIDY.

chair or table is made of fine scrim, hemstitched all around. Crossing the center both ways is a narrow section of scrim hemstitched to position, the threads being drawn in the usual way. In each of the large squares thus formed contrasting designs are embroidered with flosses. The designs employed in this

part of the embroidery elaborating the tidy shown at Figure No. 2. The sumach flowers are done in the knot and filling-in stitches. The leaves are worked in South-Kensington stitch, and may be green or may show the brilliant tintings which Autumn gives them, as best liked.

Autumn Leaves for Scrim Tidy.

FIGURE No. 4.—This graceful spray of leaves is worked in South-Kensington stitch are brown, gold and olive, or red, gold and olive. If desired, the entire spray may be in olive tints, to suggest young leaves, and may

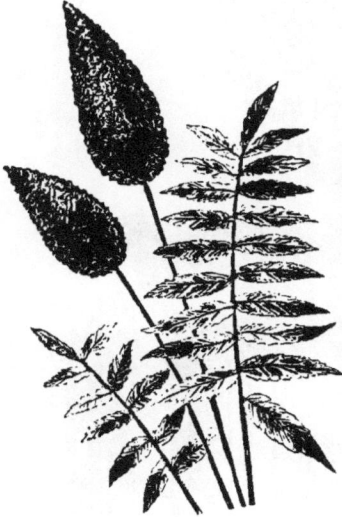

FIGURE No. 3.—SUMACH
DESIGN FOR SCRIM
TIDY.

FIGURE No. 4.—AUTUMN
LEAVES FOR SCRIM
TIDY.

FIGURE No. 5.—FANCY TIDY.

in brilliant flosses or crewels. The colors that blend well and naturally in such leaves be embroidered on plush, velvet, cloth or any fabric.

FIGURE NO. 6.—FANCY MAT.

FIGURE NO. 7.—TIDY, WITH PAINTED JAPANESE CENTER.

which may combine three shades of plush, satin, are comprised in this beautiful item of decoration. The sections are neatly joined by over-and-over stitches on the under side, and the joined portions are bordered all around with some pretty lace, which may be expensive or not as desired. The sections are embroidered with different designs, the center section being more elaborate in its work than the other two. A band of wide ribbon, embroidered in a pretty vine design, crosses the center section diagonally, the embroidery upon this section being done so as to appear to be partly concealed beneath the ribbon.

Fancy Mat.

FIGURE No. 6.—This pretty mat may be used under a lamp, vase, etc. It is of deep-purple velvet and has a border decoration of pansies in purple and gold, with their foliage. The decoration is *en appliqué*, and is one of the manufactured silk appliqués, of which there is a large assortment on the market. Large artificial pansies such as are used in millinery are sometimes employed as a border for such mats. Asters or any flowers that can be arranged to lie flatly may also be used as a border for a fancy mat that is not liable to frequent disarrangement.

Japanese Tidy.

FIGURE No. 7.—The fancy for Japanese art is expressed in a variety of ways and finds many charming exponents in articles of household decoration. An unique specimen of it forms the center of this tidy. This portion of the article can be bought all ready for use, or, if a person have considerable skill with the brush, this design or any other can be reproduced upon silk. Two bands of satin ribbon in contrasting colors are now applied as a border, their edges being joined by differently colored silk in perceptible stitches of any kind. Outside of this is a border of black lace, stitched on in the same way.

White lace may be used instead of black, and ribbons of any desired hue may be selected. Sometimes the centers of purchased tidies are appliquéed upon linen, canvas, etc., and these are less expensive than the painted ones.

Fancy Tidy.

FIGURE No. 8.—A tidy, suitable for the back of a chair or the arm of a sofa, is here illustrated. A square of velvet forms the foundation, although satin, silk, flannel, felt or cloth may be used instead. It is crossed diagonally by two strips of ribbon, one of which should be either blue, orange, red or any other color desired, while the other should be a direct and bright contrast in color. In this instance one is sapphire-blue, and the other is gold color. On the latter are arranged tiny squares of velvet, which are over-stitched in coarse blue silk-floss, the design being clearly illustrated by the engraving. The edges of the yellow strip are fastened down with blue floss in star-stitch, while the blue ribbon is caught in the same way with gold-colored floss. Narrow, lozenge-shaped strips of velvet are arranged crosswise on the blue ribbon, and the embroidery over and around them is done in gold-colored floss. Tiny flat buttons of the satin ribbon in both colors are arranged on the angles of the crossing of the ribbons, and they are also crossed with floss and otherwise decorated as represented. The whole tidy is then bordered with lace, which may be of an antique pattern or of any design preferred.

Antique lace for bordering tidies of silk, satin or blocks of the same lace, comes in pretty patterns and at moderate prices. The blocks are about six inches square, and no two are alike. Two of them, and two satin blocks of the same size ornamented like the large tidy described, would form a handsome tidy if bordered with antique lace. In joining them, the lace and silk blocks come at the diagonally opposite corners.

Fancy Tidy.

FIGURE No. 9.—This dainty piece of work is formed of an oblong section of silk, all the edges of which are fringed out neatly. Inside the fringe the edges are bordered with three

shown in the engraving. The silk is pale blue, the ribbon black, and the stars yellow, while the floral decoration is one of the current manufactured appliqués, representing Marechal Neil roses and their foliage. Scrim forms a pretty background and would be less expensive than silk, and a pretty effect might be produced on it by having purple vel-

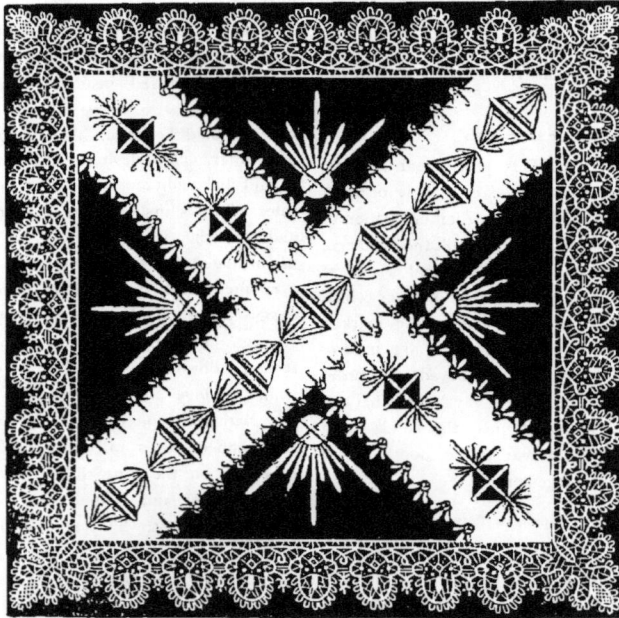

FIGURE No. 8.—FANCY TIDY.

strips of velvet ribbon, which are pointed at one ends and extend the full breadth or width, the base near the lower ends of the lighter strips falling a short distance triangle. These ends are tipped to match the stars bordering the where they are crossed. A cluster of with realistic foliage is appliquéd as

vet ribbon and an appliqué of clustered pansies. Daisies cut from white lamb's-wool cloth might take the place of stars, with pretty effect.

Canvas Tidy.

FIGURE No. 10.—Tidies are greatly diversified in material and pattern, and certainly reward the ingenious maker by their beauty

and usefulness. The one illustrated is composed of white Java canvas and two colors

Though the combined effect of the colors is
quite Oriental, yet the design is of the

FIGURE NO. 9.—FANCY TIDY.

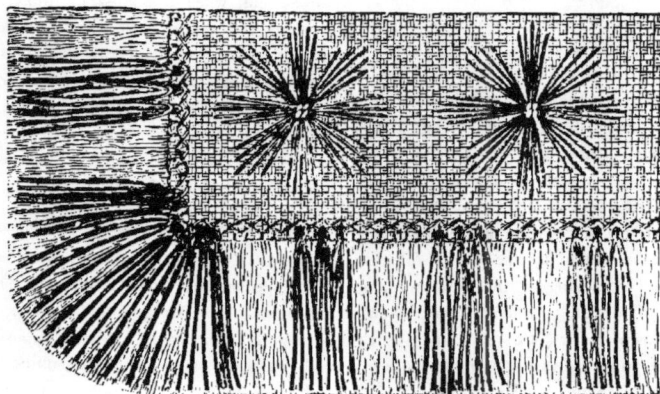

FIGURE NO. 10.—CANVAS TIDY.

worsted—cardinal and golden-yellow.

simplest character, being cardinal marguerites

or daisies with yellow hearts. A reference to the engraving will best explain how they are worked, as all the threads of the canvas are fully delineated and may be easily counted. The design is of the proper proportions and size, and the fringe of the required length. The tidy may be made as large as desired, and when the marguerites are worked, the margin of the canvas is ravelled to form a fringe, the edge remaining being then over cast in button-hole stitch below a narrow cross-stitch design. Cardinal threads are next caught at regular intervals through the edge with a crochet-hook and firmly knotted, after which the fringe is "evened" along the ends.

Canvas Tidy and Decoration with Diagram for Colors.

FIGURES NOS. 11, 12 AND 13.—Something very pretty in the way of tidies is here represented, and full instructions as to the colors to be used accompany the illustration of the article. As the tidy is designed principally for the backs of large chairs, arms of sofas, etc., it is ingeniously cut in a half-square of the triangle shape. The bias edge is plainly hemmed so as to make the tidy look as if folded under, and the edges are finished with a fringe of worsted, each tassel being drawn in by three stitches and then cut off at an even and desirable length. The extra canvas under the fringe is then cut or ravelled away. The butterfly is done with single zephyr, in the shades indicated by the line of blocks, and named according to the corresponding blocks in the design. To make it very showy four threads of canvas are taken up in each stitch, instead of the two seen in the pattern, which is given in the usual canvas stitch. If silk is used, then the design had better be done in the usual stitch so as to make it appear thick enough. An odd fancy in mak-

ing a square tidy is to work a large butterfly in one corner, and one or more smaller ones flying downward or upward from it. The butterfly may also be used as a center-piece only, with a fringe of the same colors about the edge. Pearl, drab, or écru canvas is the prettiest for a butterfly tidy. The design will be found very neat upon collar, cuff, glove or jewel boxes.

Tidies of Satin and Lace.

FIGURES NOS. 14 AND 15.—The most troublesome portions of the tidies represented are the satin blocks, which should be decorated as represented either by embroidery or painting, whichever is preferred. The rest of the work is easy enough, as it consists simply in joining blocks of antique lace to those of satin and bordering the edges with a frill of lace to match. These blocks and the edging may be found in almost any fancy-goods store, and are very pretty when formed into a tidy, but are anything else when seen on the counters. The blocks and lace are loosely woven of what looks like unbleached linen thread, but, when combined in tidies or on curtains for windows with satin or batiste, they are very tasteful indeed. The tidies illustrated may be used for a sofa or a large chair; the large one being for the back and the other for the arm. Pale-blue, navy-blue, rose-color and cardinal are the shades of satin usually selected to combine with the lace.

Marguerite Tidy and Sections Composing It.

FIGURES NOS. 16, 17, 18 AND 19.—Among pretty specimens of home fancy-work the tidy known as "The Marguerite" is particularly noticeable. One would scarcely suppose that such common materials as serpentine braid and a few bits of silk would, when properly arranged, form so charming a tidy; yet the result must be seen before its loveliness can be fully realized. Figure No. 16 shows the

FIGURE NO. 11.—BUTTERFLY DESIGN FOR TIDY.

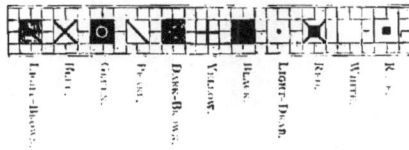

FIGURE NO. 12.—DIAGRAM FOR COLORS.

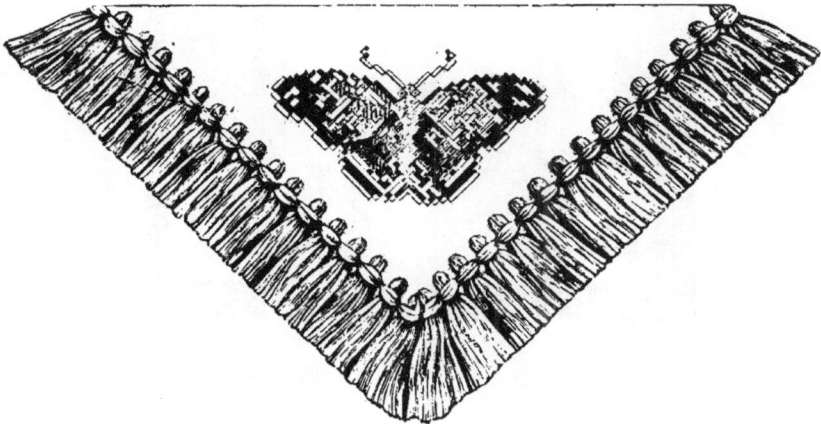

FIGURE NO. 13.—DESIGN FOR TIDY.

appearance of a portion of a tidy when finished, though on a very diminutive scale; for as many marguerites as are necessary to daisies are joined, which is one of the most important details. The foundation is made of stiff muslin, and cut just the size indi-

FIGURE NO. 14.—TIDY OF SATIN AND LACE.

FIGURE NO. 15.—TIDY OF SATIN AND LACE.

obtain the desired size must be joined when making the tidy. The engraving, however, serves to explain the manner in which the cated by Figure No. 17, which also shows how the wrong side of the flower looks while undergoing the process of its formation. It will be noticed at **Figure No. 18**, that, when the braid is sewed on, the inner points are drawn closely enough together to prevent curling over too far; and it would probably be a good idea to gather the braid before applying it to the foundation. After the two rows are sewed on, a button-mould is covered

yet tidies of this description may be made of any color the braid is found in. If care is taken to make them substantially, "Marguerite tidies" may be washed as easily as a piece of muslin. Figure No. 19 shows a single daisy when completed, and ready to join to others already made. In connecting the points care

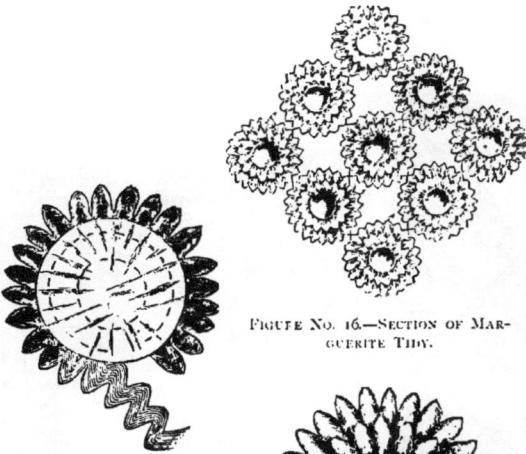

FIGURE No. 16.—SECTION OF MAR-GUERITE TIDY.

FIGURE No. 17.

FIGURE No. 19.

FIGURE No. 18.

FIGURES NOS. 17, 18 AND 19.—METHOD OF MAKING MARGUERITES.

with yellow or brown silk to form the center of each, and is joined to the muslin foundation, so that the inner points of the second row are concealed by it. If preferred, a worsted center may be made, or the yellow worsted buttons used by upholsterers may be substituted. Although white marguerites with the centers described are the truest to Nature.

should be taken to do it very thoroughly, as such articles are liable to be pretty roughly treated, especially if they adorn chairs and sofas that are in daily use.

Damask Tidy.

FIGURES NOS. 20 AND 21.—The tidy illustrated by Figure No. 20 is probably one of the prettiest in vogue, while also novel in construction. The block shown by Figure No. 21 is an enlarged representation of those seen in the tidy, and is calculated to show the method of making, and also the general effect. Stair damask is the material for the foundation, and as it has a light and a dark side, the former should be chosen for the surface, because it will throw up the colors of the worsteds used in the embroidery in a better light. When the tidy is worked in the blocks illustrated, the embroidery of the lines is done in an over-

the bars may be worked with one color and the leaves with alternate green, brown and orange or scarlet, to represent Autumn tints; or the bars may be of solid color and the leaves of shaded worsted in one color or in the tints just mentioned. Both large and small tidies may be made in this way. Covers for furniture or hassocks may also be elaborated by this process if a lady has leisure and patience, thus forming a pretty decoration at a moderate expense. Any canvas may be used in

FIGURE NO. 20.—DAMASK TIDY.

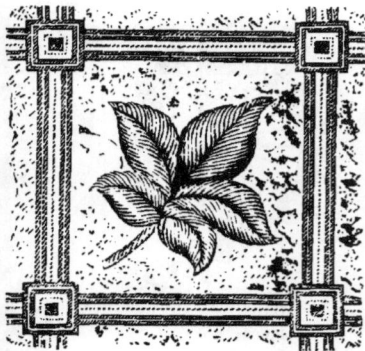

FIGURE NO. 21.—SECTION OF TIDY.

hand stitch as pictured in the engraving of the single block. In making the leaf it would be better to put a coarse filling through it before overlaying it with the smooth stitches. The latter should commence at the center of each portion so as to form the veining of the leaf. Sometimes these tidies are worked all in one color, and again several tints are introduced, or shaded worsteds are used. For instance, the embroidery may be done in brown, blue, scarlet, purple or crimson; or

this manner, except such as generally forms the foundation of slippers and cushions, when the groundwork is formed of a filling of worsted.

In making the pattern the lines should extend to within about two inches of each edge, and when the embroidery is finished this spare margin should be ravelled to form a fringe, a tiny overcasting holding the thread firmly at the top of the fringe. If prepared for delicate tidies the bars and leaves may be made of silk, with a very pretty effect; or if a still more delicate article be desired, the tidy may be made of white net, and the bars and leaves darned in with floss of various tints or all white. White Swiss, embroidered with white in similar designs, is pleasing when laid over dark or delicately colored upholstering.

Chair Tidy.

FIGURE No. 22.—This pretty tidy for chair or sofa is made of an oblong section of garnet

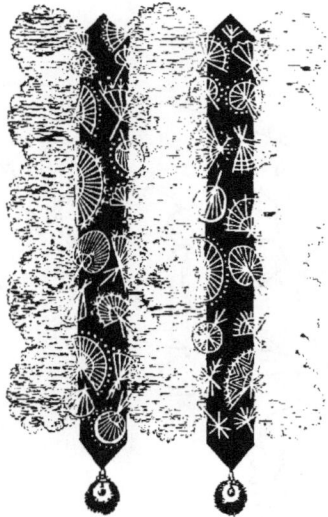

FIGURE NO. 22.—CHAIR TIDY.

felt cloth. The edges are scolloped and pinked, and down each side of the center is a band of wide velvet ribbon applied with fancy stitches of floss in a variety of colors, the stitches being so arranged as to outline all sorts of fancy shapes in fans. The ends of the bands are finished in points, which come between the scollops in the ends, the lower ends of the bands being extended quite a

little below the cloth and tipped with fancy chenille ornaments. The cloth may be of any preferred color, and so may the velvet ribbon; and any desired style of ornament may be added to the ends of the bands.

Fancy Tidy.

FIGURE No. 23.—The center of this dainty tidy is an oblong section of velvet with the corners cut off neatly; and it is handsomely decorated with an embroidery design of fine

FIGURE No. 23.—FANCY TIDY.

flowers, the flowers being made of narrow ribbon and the leaves, etc., worked with filoselle. It is bordered all round with wide fancy ribbon, and a decoration of wide lace is added to the outer margin of the ribbon. The center may be of wide ribbon, plush, velvet or satin, as preferred; and the ribbon bordering it may be of any color that will contrast agreeably with it.

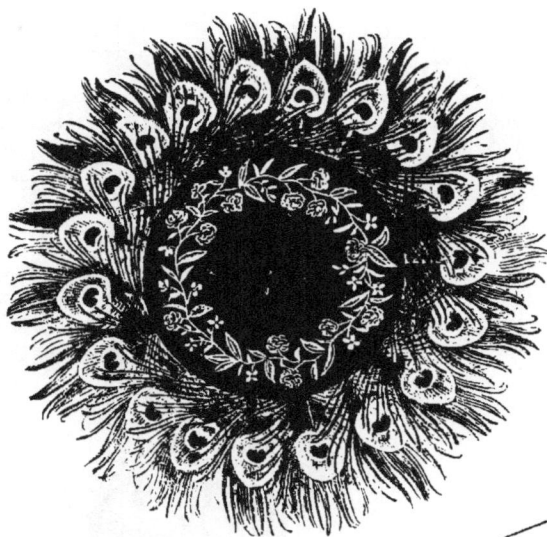
FIGURE NO. 24.—FANCY MAT.

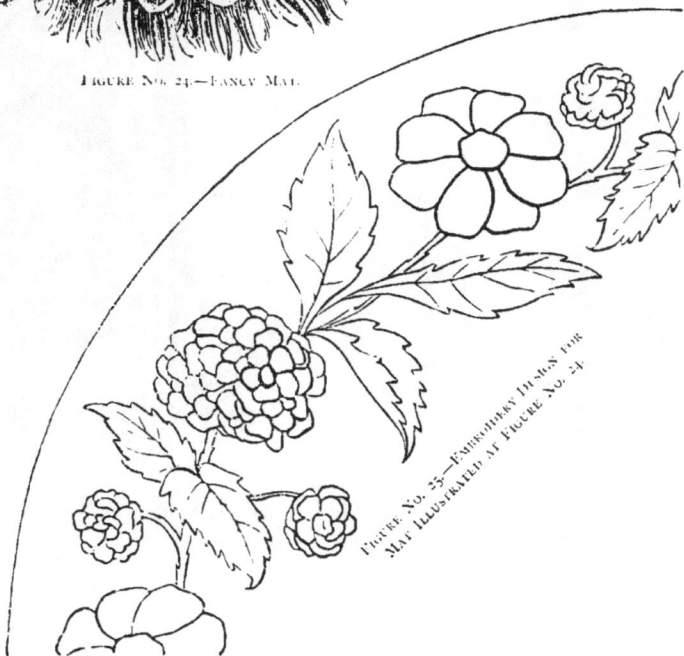
FIGURE NO. 25.—EMBROIDERY DESIGNS FOR
MAT ILLUSTRATED AT FIGURE NO. 24.

Fancy Mat.

FIGURE No. 24.—A use for the peacock here suggests itself. Two pieces of pasteboard are cut the proper shape, and each is covered with purple velvet, the under one, however, not being decorated. The upper portion is embroidered in silks, the colors being greens, golds and browns. Then with much care the feathers are fastened between the mats as pictured, and the one perfect mat is achieved. Glue or stitches will be found the surest way of holding the feathers, which should be fastened to the under mat before the upper one is added, and care must be taken not to soil the velvet. A section of the embroidery design used in decorating the mat is given at Figure No. 25.

Embroidery Design for Mat.

FIGURE No. 25.—A quarter of the design embroidered on the peacock-trimmed mat is here given, so that the exact idea may be gotten and the worker draw her own design if she wishes.

A Dainty Mat.

THOSE who carefully study effect in house decorations know that lack of harmony in grouping is the cause of most of the failures attending the efforts of many who are obliged to confess that with all wished for means at hand, they cannot make their apartments appear tastefully furnished. A cabinet or a fancy table that is overloaded with the choicest specimens of Keramic art is not decorative, and it does not display its beautiful burden to good advantage. A china vase, a delicate statuette, or a pretty easel supporting a photograph or an etching, sometimes has its beauty entirely obscured by being placed in too close proximity to larger and inharmonious objects. As a rule, all dark woods are unfriendly to objects of art which are dark or neutral in tone, or which have not sufficient surface to throw the dark background into obscurity; and this is the reason why "a dainty mat" is always appreciated. One which adds to the artistic effect of a low round vase with a short and narrow neck, is formed of a square of very yellow plush, bordered with lace, that is quite oriental in effect. The plush is a scrap about eight inches square left from a cushion, and the border is simply a piece of linen lace, neither very fine, nor very coarse. It has an open, regular design in which silver, gold, copper and electric blue metallic cords are run, their insertion being guided by the design of the lace and as much being run in as the openings permit. The lace is laid flatly about the plush, with its edges extending a little beyond, and its selvage after being sewed to position is overlaid with a row of the metal cord. The corners are neatly and uniformly turned and securely tacked, and the effect is very attractive. When placed in position beneath the vase only enough of the yellow plush is visible to form a narrow rim outside the cloudy gray which is the color of the vase at its base. The lace shows the brilliant metallic tints to good advantage, and possesses an air of special richness that well repays the maker for having expended a few cents for the remnant and carefully saved the odds and ends of metallic cord remaining after making a piano cover.

A Common Mistake.

IN selecting fringe for the ornamentation of
any article having many curves or angles, it is
a mistake to choose that which is composed
of thick, heavy strands, although at first
thought such varieties seem most desirable on
account of their fluffiness. The strands separate and fall apart if applied otherwise than
in a straight line, and consequently a fringe
with netted or latticed work for the greater
part of its depth can be used to much better
advantage. Such fringe may seem to be
sparsely tasselled as it is held in the hand,
but in its proper place it is much more effective than the heavier varieties. Very often a
fringe having a deep, open heading above a
row of tassels may be arranged to overhang
(drape, the upholsterers call it) a fringe that
is composed of heavy single strands. Such a
combination gives the effect of sufficient body,
with an airiness and grace which could not be
developed with the heavier fringe alone.

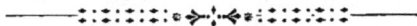

CHAPTER XXXVI.

FANCY TOWELS AND SPLASHERS.

Decorated Towel.

FIGURE No. 1.—As a cover for towels that are to hang upon a rack after being used, or even as a scarf for tables, chairs, *chiffonniers*, etc., the towel here illustrated is at once handsome and convenient. It may be of damask, Turkish towelling or any fabric that will fringe out nicely. The bird may be of any color or colors desired, its correct size being illustrated at Figure No. 5. A cream-colored damask towel is very effective decorated in this way.

Fringe of Decorated Towel.

FIGURE No. 2.—The effect of the fringe on the towel illustrated at Figure No. 1 is beautifully represented by this engraving. The strands are separated at wide and narrow intervals alternately, and are knotted as described at Figure No. 3. When the strands have been divided at the last wide interval, they are tied in ordinary knots, instead of with the thread, and the tassels produced below the last knotting are full and heavy. The fancy stitches in the upper wide depth of strands may be of worsted or silk floss, and are worked in the manner so clearly illustrated at Figure No. 4.

Drawn-Work for Decorated Towel.

FIGURE No. 3.—This engraving very clearly illustrates the method of knotting the threads in the first row or heading of the fringe on the towel. The fringe threads are separated into strands, having equal numbers of threads, which are knotted by a single thread from a needle. These strands are also divided into halves, each half from each strand being knotted in a similar manner to the nearest half of the adjacent bunch of threads.

Ornamental Design in South-Kensington Outline Stitch.

FIGURE No. 4.—This design is done in the South-Kensington outline stitch, and is pretty for borders or headings to towel fringes, or for embroidery, edging inserted strips in table-covers, scarfs, lambrequins, etc.

Bird in South-Kensington Stitch.

FIGURE No. 5.—This lovely bird may be of one or many colors, and is done in the well-known South-Kensington stitch with worsted, linen or silk flosses. The butterfly may be of brilliant hues, and the bough of olive green. The bird is of the proper size for towels, scarfs, lambrequins, etc.

Designs for Feather-Stitching.

FIGURES Nos. 6 AND 7.—These two designs are very pretty for fastening the edges of

ribbons or strips of contrasting fabric to position, or for outlining borders, hemming flannels
and embellishing fancy-work generally. It is

will show how handsome a plain Turkish
towel may be made with coarse linen thread
and bright floss, either linen or woollen. To

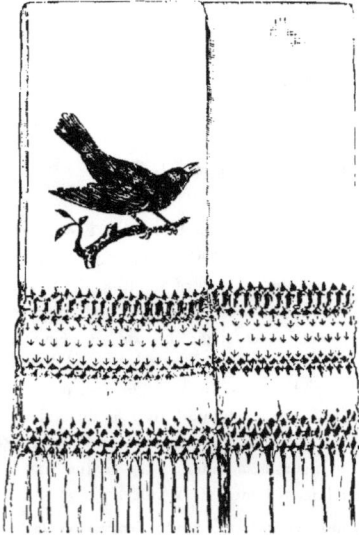

FIGURE No. 1.—DECORATED TOWEL.

FIGURE No. 2.—FRINGE OF DECORATED TOWEL.

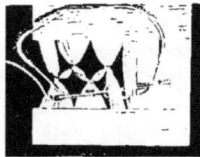

FIGURE No. 3.—DRAWN-WORK FOR DECORATED
TOWEL.

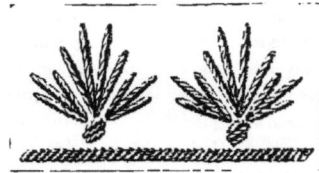

FIGURE No. 4.—ORNAMENTAL DESIGN IN
SOUTH-KENSINGTON OUTLINE-STITCH.

done by the chain-stitch movement, and is
very simple.

Embroidered Turkish Towel.

FIGURE No. 8.—A reference to this figure

form the fringe, unbleached coarse linen
thread is drawn in as illustrated, the loops
serving to confine the threads to the towel,
and knots securing them in fringe form at the

end. Although of necessity the design for the darning in of the colored floss as well as the fringe, is quite small, it will serve as a handsomely arranged. All of these tints may be mingled in the fringe as well, if preferred to the unbleached thread.

FIGURE NO. 5.—BIRD IN SOUTH-KENSINGTON STITCH.

FIGURES NOS. 6 AND 7.—DESIGNS FOR FEATHER-STITCHING.

guide to the worker. The colors generally employed are scarlet, bright-blue, yellow and black, which are ornamental in effect when

Lace Splasher.

FIGURE NO. 9.—This dainty adjunct is made of four contrasting squares of antique lace carefully sewed together so that they may lie perfectly flat, and is to be placed behind the receptacle for waste water. A finish is given by a border of antique lace arranged without any fulness, each corner being cut so that no gathers will be necessitated. When the square is completed it is placed over another, somewhat larger, of bright Turkey-red, and the two are firmly tacked to position. If the Turkey-red is not in harmony with the room, material of any other shade may be

blind-stitched to position; the upper edge of the band concealing the ends of appliquéed selections from Nature's garden. These selections comprise cat-tails in their rich brown color, matured mullen blooms and leaves in their queer green and yellow hues, and sumach leaves in the glowing tints of Autumn coloring. These may be embroidered in crewels or flosses to obtain the proper tinting, or only those with the varying colors need be embroidered. Damask and other handsome

FIGURE No. 8.—EMBROIDERED TURKISH TOWEL.

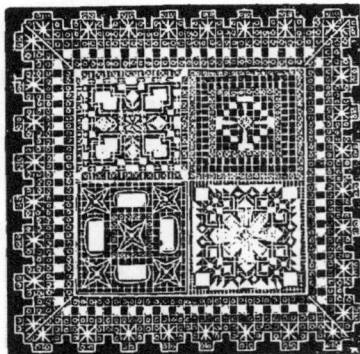

FIGURE No. 9.—LACE SPLASHER.

substituted; but, being a healthy tone and one that does not fade soon, it is often preferred.

Fancy Towel-Cover.

FIGURE No. 10.—A tastefully decorated towel-cover is illustrated in this engraving. It consists of a linen towel of a diagonal pattern, with heavy tassel-fringe upon the ends. Above the fringe its ends are crossed by a broad band of Turkish towelling, that is neatly

towels may be elaborated in this way. The Turkish towelling may be omitted in favor of contrasting silk, velvet, satin or embroidered felt cloth, etc., when momie cloth or other fine material forms the foundation. When canvas, silk, velvet, felt-cloth, plush or Turkish towelling is used for the formation, they will be decorated with beautiful worsted fringes, appliquées or embroidery, as preferred. A lining of Silesia, silk or satin will usually be added to very handsome articles of this kind.

Kitchen Splasher.

FIGURE No. 11.—A section of enamelled, splasher, which will be useful in protecting the wainscoting or wall at the kitchen sink.

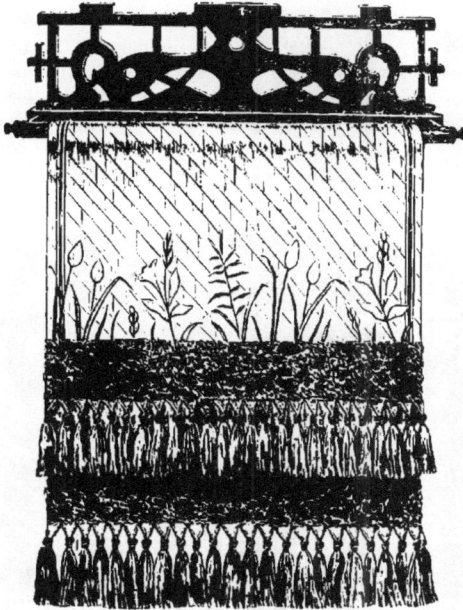

FIGURE No. 110.—FANCY TOWEL-COVER.

FIGURE No. 11.—KITCHEN SPLASHER.

marbled oil-cloth was used for making this   Its edges are pinked and it is fastened to place at the top by three large brass-headed nails. The utensils pictured upon it may be outlined with embroidery cotton or painted, as preferred. When the splasher is soiled, a careful wiping with a soft cloth will freshen it.

Linen-and-Lace Splasher.

FIGURE No. 12.—This splasher has a center-piece of coarse linen, with cat-tails and their foliage worked upon it in crewels. Fitted around this as illustrated are twelve

Embroidery Design for Splasher.

FIGURE No. 13.—This design is worked on the center-piece of the splasher illustrated at Figure No. 12. It may be done in browns entirely, though a better effect is obtained if browns and greens are used. Unless one is used to working in crewels, it would perhaps be wise to present the design in outline-stitch.

The practical value of fancy work lies in the ability of the worker to make her work attract-

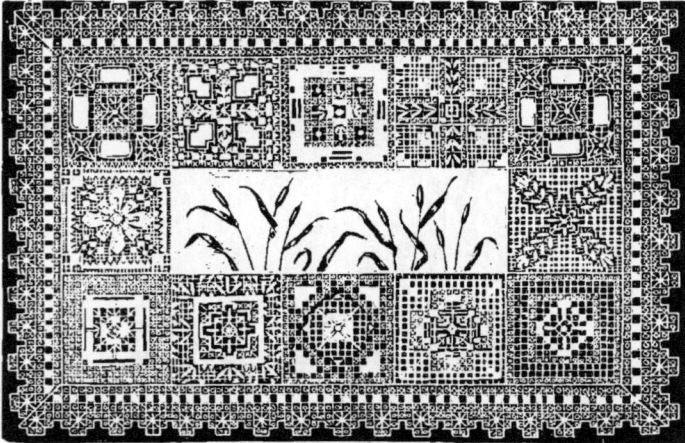

FIGURE No. 12.—LINEN-AND-LACE SPLASHER.

squares of antique lace, each in contrast with the other. The border is of antique lace, and the whole, when finished, is laid against the background of Turkey-red. Small brass tacks may be used for the fastening to the wall, or the heads of ordinary tacks may be covered with a bit of Turkey-red. If preferred, scrim may be substituted for linen, the effect being equally good and many finding it easier to work upon. This splasher is to be placed back of the washstand.

ive without impairing its usefulness for the purpose it is designed to serve. Dotted Swiss muslin decorated with long, overwrought stitches in zephyr or crewel serves many practical and pretty purposes, some of which are here illustrated.

Splasher, to Fasten Back of a Washstand.

FIGURE No. 14.—This splasher is made of zephyr-decorated, dotted Swiss, laid over pink, blue, red or lavender cambric, and bordered with lace. The bows match the tint of the cambric and cover the tacks holding the splasher to the wall. A border of plain, plaited Swiss, with or without a lace-finished edge, may be used in place of the lace frill here seen.

Design, in Full Size, for Splasher Illustrated at Figure No. 14.

FIGURE NO. 15.—This engraving shows

similarly to the other, but in a different design, and with plaited Swiss about the edges, and worsted cord and balls in place of bows. Lace, either gathered or plaited, may be used for the border.

Design, in Full Size for Splasher, Illustrated at Figure No. 16.

FIGURE NO. 17.—This design is more intricate than the other, but is easily followed.

FIGURE NO. 13.—EMBROIDERY DESIGN FOR SPLASHER.

the method of embellishing Swiss for the purpose mentioned. Single zephyr is used for the lines and to otherwise decorate the muslin. Blue, red, olive, pink, brown, lavender or any other tint preferred may be represented by the worsted.

Splasher, to Fasten Back of a Washstand.

FIGURE NO. 16.—This splasher is made

The dots upon the Swiss are closer and smaller than in the other, and the material is well covered by the design.

Fancy Bath-Towel Holder.

FIGURE NO. 18.—This holder is made of a length of wide velvet ribbon that is passed through three rings and then doubled, two of the rings being placed in the folds, while the third comes where the ends are joined and is used to suspend the holder. Through each of

tiny rings sewed all over it in a simple figure design. Wooden rings of the kind illustrated

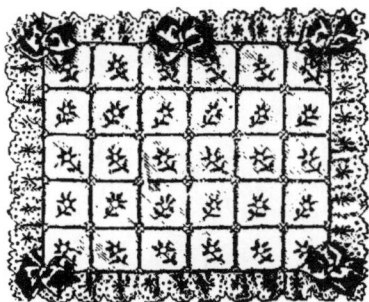

FIGURE NO. 14.—SPLASHER, TO FASTEN BACK OF A WASHSTAND.

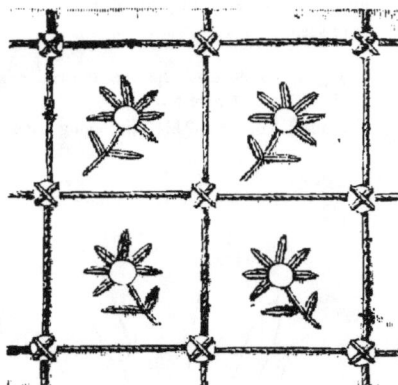

FIGURE NO. 15.—DESIGN, IN FULL SIZE, FOR SPLASHER ILLUSTRATED AT FIGURE NO. 14.

FIGURE NO. 16.—SPLASHER, TO FASTEN BACK OF A WASHSTAND.

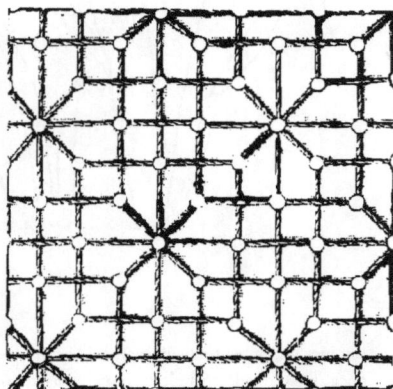

FIGURE NO. 17.—DESIGN, IN FULL SIZE, FOR SPLASHER ILLUSTRATED AT FIGURE NO. 16.

the other rings a fancy bath-towel is drawn to fall gracefully. The ribbon is decorated with

are obtainable for a small sum and may be utilized in a variety of practical and pretty ways about the lavatory. Four of them, hung in a row, will hold several towels, and where the ablutions of two or more persons are performed, the rings holding the special towels of each may be marked with initials done in fancy-headed tacks or nails. If metal rings are may be utilized to good advantage where space is limited. Besides holding bath-towels, a wash-bag, shoe-bag and similar articles may be suspended from it; and, if arranged to hang at different lengths, no one article will infringe upon another. A practical hint, not

FIGURE No. 18.—FANCY BATH-TOWEL HOLDER.

used, it is advisable to crochet over them with cord. A strip of linen, ornamented with outline stitching, or without any decoration, may take the place of ribbon.

A ring larger than those illustrated, with several hooks or screw-eyes fastened in it, misplaced in this connection, is as follows: use round cord for suspending any receptacle that is to receive much weight. Cord of this description will bear the strain imposed upon it much longer than tape, braid or any flatly woven material.

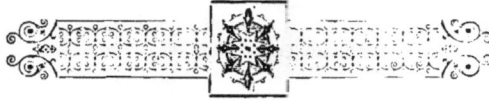

CHAPTER XXXVII.

FANCY PILLOW AND SHEET COVERS—GOWNS AND GOWN CASES.

EXTREME daintiness in the dressing of one's couch is always requisite to a person of refined instincts, and suggestions for pretty covers for pillows and for sheet-shams are always appreciated. This chapter contains several designs which are as practical as they are pretty.

Fancy Pillow-Cover.

FIGURE No. 1.—A pillow-cover matching the sheet sham on the following page is here shown, the materials employed being sheer white lawn and rose-colored satin. If preferred, pale blue, scarlet or any color liked could take the place of the rose; but, somehow, it seems especially suitable, while the blue belongs to the cradle of a wee baby.

Fancy Sheet-Sham.

FIGURE No. 2.—A sheet-sham of very sheer lawn, intended for ornament, has its use in a household where the head of it is interested in art at home. This one is finished around the edge with a deep border of antique lace, and its beauties are brought out by an intermingling of Kursheedt's Standard satin quilting of rose color. Each point of the lace is tied over the silk by a rose-colored ribbon,

FIGURE No. 1.—FANCY PILLOW-COVER.

and the whole air is as dainty and fresh as the Spring roses it should herald.

Fancy Pillow-Sham.

FIGURE NO. 3.—This engraving illustrates a square is a row of embroidered insertion, and bordering this is a row of deep, fine embroidered edging. The centers of the two pillow-shams may differ, but the borders of

FIGURE NO. 2.—FANCY SHEET-SHAM.

Fancy Pillow-Sham.

FIGURE No. 4.—The center of this beautiful pillow-sham is made of scraps of all kinds
lace edging is added, being slightly fulled in
the corners. The edge decoration may be of
any preferred kind of lace and may or may

FIGURE No. 4.—FANCY PILLOW-SHAM.

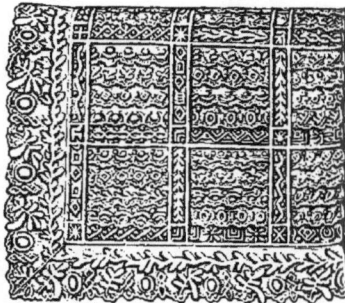

FIGURE No. 5.—PILLOW-SHAM.

of lace edgings and insertions put together in
crazy patchwork fashion; around the square
is a row of insertion, and then a row of pretty
not match the bordering row of insertion.
Italian lace is inexpensive and very dainty
for edge decorations to shams and also to

spreads, which may be similarly made up. The two shams and the spread may show entirely different scraps and different arrangements of them, but the edge finish of all should be alike. Torchon, Medici and all joined to form squares, the sides of which are bordered with insertion. Samples of edging or insertion, or pieces left from dresses or underwear, may be thus utilized, and shams made in this way will launder

FIGURE No. 6.—NIGHT-GOWN CASE.

kinds of linen and cotton laces may be used.

better than the "crazy" style illustrated in this chapter.

Pillow-Sham.

FIGURE No. 5.—This handsome sham is made of samples of embroidered edging and insertion joined together, and has a border formed of a row of edging. The pieces of edging are almost all of equal size and are

Night-Gown Case.

FIGURE No. 6.—This pretty receptacle for *robes de nuit* when not being worn is made of fine linen shaped as illustrated and having two receptacles for the gowns. Each is hemstitched all around, and then the entire case is finished with antique lace, sufficient fulness being allowed at each corner so that it will not draw. On the one pocket is embroidered in white the welcome wish "Pleasant Dreams," while on the other is a band of on the gown-case. It may be done in white or colored cottons, crewels or silks, the choice depending entirely on the material used for the case. Silver and gold tinsel thread are especially effective for embroidery or outline

FIGURE NO. 7.—EMBROIDERED MOTTO.

musicians who, from the energy they infuse into their work, would hint that one must awaken and be up for it is no longer time to court the drowsy god. Of pongee or scrim, this case would be pretty and would not be more difficult to work upon than the linen.

Embroidered Motto.

FIGURE NO. 7.—An illustration is here given, in its proper size, of the desirable wish work upon dark backgrounds. As a rule, however, the preferred material for the making of gown-cases will be bright in color, though dark fabrics may be used if preferred.

Outline Work in Full Size for Gown-Case, as Illustrated at Figure No. 6.

FIGURES NOS. 8, 9, 10 AND 11.—This funny little quartette of musicians is embroidered in outline-stitch, as illustrated on the gown-case. They may, however, be embroidered or sufficient individuality to be shown separately. The expression on each face is capital, and

FIGURE No. 8.—PART OF OUTLINE WORK IN FULL SIZE FOR GOWN-CASE.

done in pen-and-ink, and they may be together at their enjoyable task or may have handy maidens can easily see how they may be utilized upon *serviettes*, tea-cloths, towels or *menus.* The last, of course, would be done with pen-and-ink.

done by their home relatives, and the results are often elaborate and beautiful. The work

FIGURE NO. 9.—PART OF OUTLINE WORK IN FULL SIZE FOR GOWN-CASE.

The decoration of the sleeping-gowns of the male members of the family is generally is very simple, and with pretty designs to follow is not in the least arduous.

In this chapter are also shown designs and most effective in the catalogue of stitches, that are pretty and graceful for specified and one that is not injured by laundering. portions of

FIGURE No. 10.—PART OF OUTLINE WORK IN FULL SIZE FOR GOWN-CASE.

portions of these garments of the bed-chamber. The stitch is the South-Kensington outline-stitch, one of the simplest

Colored wash cottons on cotton goods, worsteds on wool goods and wash silks and fadeless etching silks on silk textures are used for the embroidery, and any preferred color or colors may be chosen. Sometimes show all the natural colors carefully blended. Blues and reds are especially liked for

FIGURE NO 11.—PART OF OUTLINE WORK IN FULL SIZE FOR GOWN CASE.

the entire design is done in one color, and oftentimes several desirable shades are used, with very good effect. Floral designs often monochromatic effects, as they are less likely to fade by the frequent laundering than the more delicate colors.

Gentlemen's Night-Shirt, and Designs for Embroidering It.

FIGURES NOS. 12, 13, 14, 15 AND 16.—This shirt is made of fine cambric. Its collar is A patch pocket is applied on the left breast and the design used in its decoration is portrayed at Figure No. 15. The cuffs are ornamented with the design shown at Figure

FIGURE NO. 12.—GENTLEMEN'S NIGHT-SHIRT.

FIGURE NO. 13.—DESIGN FOR EMBROIDERING COLLAR.

in rolling style and is decorated with embroidery in the design shown at Figure No. 13. The applied lap down the closing is elaborated by the design shown at Figure No. 16.

No. 14, and are moderately deep. The designs are all pictured in the correct sizes for the parts they are to decorate, and may be traced on thin paper, which may be basted

FIGURE No. 14.—DESIGN FOR EMBROIDERING CUFF.

FIGURE No. 15.—DESIGN FOR
EMBROIDERING POCKET.

FIGURE No. 16.—DESIGN FOR
EMBROIDERING LAP.

on the parts to be decorated and the design worked through the paper. The pocket, along the edges of the collar. A very nice pattern for night-shirts is No. 2479, price **1s.**

FIGURE No. 17.—SACHET SHIRT-CASE, CLOSED.

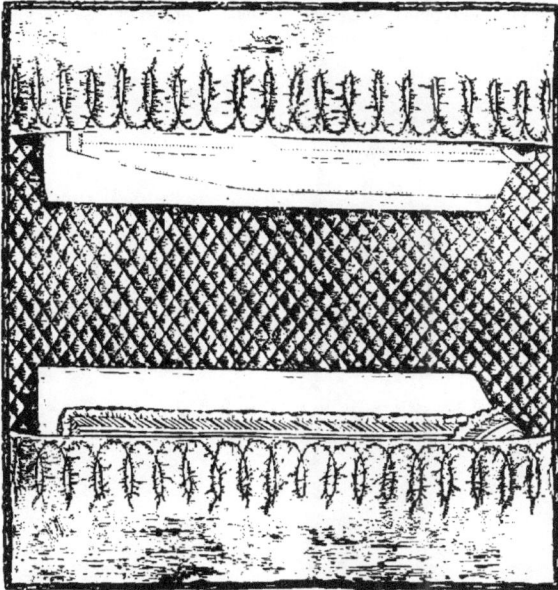

FIGURE No. 18.—SACHET SHIRT-CASE, OPEN

lap and cuffs are stitched to position at their edges, and a row of stitching is also seen or 25 cents. It is in eight sizes for gentlemen, from twenty-eight to forty-six inches, breast measure, and is illustrated in our Catalogues for the season. The upper part of the back is a smooth-fitting yoke. If desired the shapes here shown for the cuffs and pocket may be substituted for those provided in the pattern.

Sachet Shirt-Case.

FIGURES No. 17 AND 18.—These engravings illustrate a handsome receptacle for a gentleman's day and night shirts. The case is made of satin and lined with quilted satin evenly wadded, the cotton being thoroughly sprinkled with some favorite *sachet* powder. The pockets are sections of satin of suitable width, similarly lined, and are decorated with a simple design done with embroidery silks.

Figure No. 17 shows the case closed and decorated with a spray of strawberry vine *en appliqué*, which shows the progress of the fruit from the frail blossom to the luscious ripe berry. The spray is a selection from Kursheedt's Standard floral *appliqués*, and is very graceful and rich in coloring. Figure No. 18 shows the case open and the mode of arranging the shirts. The edges of the case are bound with velvet ribbon. Plush, velvet, silk, Surah, pongee or any preferred material may be used for such cases, and the colors may be selected according to taste. The lining will often contrast with the outside, but the pockets will usually be of the same color as the lining. Any decoration preferred may be added to the outside, the monogram or initials of the owner being very effective.

CHAPTER XXXVIII.

FANCY BAGS.

HE ingenious woman who seeks to decorate her home and make some of the dainty little attributes in vogue for her own personal use, soon finds of how much value is each scrap of bright ribbon, each twist of gay-colored silk and each of the so-called odds and ends. The time always comes when they may be used, and never were they more desirable than in these days of striving after Oriental effects and strange minglings of coloring. Not only does one wish to have the work beautiful, but also to have it in a proper casing; and as everything antique in shape or odd in design is specially desirable, it is easy to understand why fancy bags for holding work, opera-glasses, cards, etc., are pronounced "too lovely." A little care in combining the colors, and much care in making the stitches even, are the principal requisites needed toward making such articles a success.

Work-Bag.

FIGURE No. 1.—The bag illustrated is made of strips of different colored ribbon, joined together by an over-and-over seam and then ornamented on the right side with feather-stitching in gold floss. All the seams are completely joined, save one, which is left open in the middle for a suitable distance, to allow the work to pass in and out. The ends are drawn together, and a full silk tassel of yellow silk finishes each. The sliding rings are of ivory and may be obtained at any saddler's. While a very rich effect is obtained if parti-colored ribbons are used, still, if desired, only two shades need be employed, good contrasts being obtained with pink and *grenat*, blue and lemon, bronze and deep scarlet, or lavender and orange. Satin, grosgrain or any quality of ribbon may be used, while, for greater elegance, gold or silver slides may be gotten, instead of the ivory ones. If a mourning bag is wanted, black and purple satin ribbon may be used, with black silk and jet tassels finishing the ends and the rings formed of ebony.

Detail of Stitches Used in Figure No. 1.

FIGURES NOS. 2 AND 3.—Illustrations are here given of the method of joining the ribbon for the bag together in the usual over-and-over seam, and also of the feather-stitch that serves to ornament the strips. As a specially decorative result is attained by the use of bright yellow floss, it is oftenest chosen for this purpose. If desired, a single row of the feather-stitching only may be employed, in which case it should be immediately between the two strips.

Knitting-Bag.

FIGURE No. 4.—As a receptacle for the ball of knitting wool or silk this bag is most useful; it is also an artistic ornament to hang over a chair or on the corner of the work-

pretty lining. The revers or lap is elaborated by embroidered floral sprays and a row of imitation old coins about the edges. The lower end of the bag is plaited in along the fold and finished with loops and ends of cord tipped with large plush pompons. The coins may be replaced by any preferred style of drop ornaments, or the edge may be left plain.

Such bags may be as beautiful as the most fastidious taste requires and may be made of

FIGURE No. 1.—WORK-BAG.

FIGURE No. 2.—OVER-AND-OVER STITCH USED IN THE WORK-BAG SHOWN AT No. 1

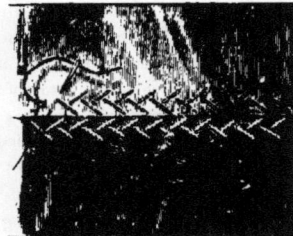

FIGURE No. 3.—FEATHER-STITCH USED IN THE WORK-BAG SHOWN AT No. 1.

table when otherwise not in use. It is formed of a straight piece of silk lined with a contrasting color, folded double, crosswise, and joined at the sides. Two deep slashes are made from the top down for several inches in the front of the bag, the slashes starting from the same point in the edge and diverging in V shape. The point or V thus formed is turned over on the outside, and the rest of the way round the bag is shirred in on ribbon in a line with the top of the revers. The corners above the latter are plaited and caught down back of the revers, effectively displaying the

silk, velvet, plush, etc.; embroidery, hand-painting, appliquées and all sorts of ornamental work may embellish them, and individual taste may decide as to the colors.

Nile or bright green, with pale pink for lining; crimson with white, pearl, lemon or pale blue; two shades of green; gold with violet or lavender; gray with crimson, heliotrope or pale blue; bronze with olive, cream, gold or apple green; two shades of any one color; black with heliotrope, orange, scarlet, lavender or bright green are all fashionable combinations.

Opera-Glass Bag.

FIGURE No. 5.—This pretty bag for holding opera-glasses is made of olive plush. The bottom is shaped like the large part of lining of deep crimson satin. A casing is made, and strings of crimson satin ribbon are run in, so that they draw easily. On the front is embroidered in pale olive crewels a

FIGURE No. 4.—KNITTING-BAG.

the glass, and is stiffened with pasteboard. The bag part is formed of two pieces properly shaped and carefully seamed at each side; and a perfectly smooth effect is given by the decidedly Japanese study of storks. Velvet or plush may be employed for the outer part of a bag of this description, while silk or satin may be used for the lining. The decoration is a matter of individual taste, it being probable that when the bag is to have much usage, it will not be considered necessary.

Designs for Embroidery on Opera-Glass Bag.

FIGURES NOS. 6 AND 7.—These designs,

stripes upon large pieces of work, they will be found desirable, and may, of course, be in any coloring the worker prefers.

Opera-Glass Bag and Designs for Embroidering It.

FIGURES NOS. 8, 9 AND 10.—This hand-

FIGURE NO. 5.—OPERA-GLASS BAG.

which are pulled through openings finished at the side seams and tied in bows. The deco-

dery designs being given at Figures Nos. 9 and 10. Any preferred colors and materials

FIGURE NO. 8.—OPERA-GLASS BAG.

FIGURE NO. 9.

FIGURES NOS. 9 AND 10.—DESIGNS FOR EMBROIDERING OPERA-GLASS BAG.

ration is worked in South-Kensington stitch in brilliant colors, the correct sizes of embroi-

may be chosen for the bag, and, if preferred, the designs may be painted to resemble Kensington embroidery, with good effect. The ribbons usually match the outside in color, and may have a fancy or a plain edge.

Ladies' Hand-Bag.

FIGURE No. 11.—This pretty bag is shaped from pasteboard. Two sections of the contrasting material. This portion forms the front of the bag, and is embroidered or hand-painted in some pretty design, the initial letters or monogram of the owner being embroidered just above the design, at one side. The parts are joined together by a puff of the

FIGURE NO. 11.—LADIES' HAND-BAG.

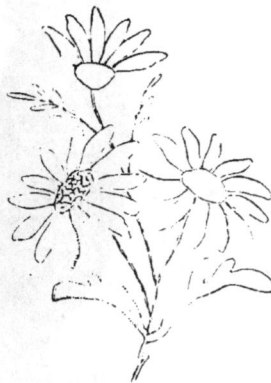

FIGURE NO. 12.—SPRAY OF DAISIES FOR EMBROIDERY.

the shape of the larger portions are cut and are covered on the outside with velvet, plush or whatever material may be chosen, and on the inside with silk, satin or some contrasting fabric. Upon the lower part of one portion is arranged a piece of pasteboard curved at the top, as pictured, and covered smoothly with contrasting material, and the seaming of the puff and also the top of the bag are decorated with a row of silk cord arranged in clusters of loops in the upper corners. The suspending ties or handle are of wide ribbon bowed artistically, but may be of cord, if it be preferred. The exact size of each of the daisy sprays is pictured at Figure No. 12. Two of the sprays arranged with their lower ends crossing form the design used in this instance, but the disposal may be made in any way preferred.

size for decorating the hand-bag shown at Figure No. 11. It may also be used to ornament any article of fancy work, with good effect.

FIGURE No. 13.—FANCY BAG.

FIGURE No. 14.—SHOPPING-BAG.

Spray of Daisies for Embroidery.

FIGURE No. 12.—This graceful spray of golden-hearted daisies may be worked in either the Kensington or satin stitch, the centers of the daisies being usually done in knot stitch. The design is shown in the proper

Fancy Bag.

FIGURE No. 13.—To hang over a chair, sofa, etc., this is a handsome and dainty bag. The materials are pale gold China-silk and crimson velvet, the velvet being set in in diamond shape at the bottom, thus forming a triangle on each side. A row of fancy ribbon is applied with fancy stitches in vari-colored flosses along the sides of the velvet and drawn in with crimson ribbons inserted in the hem. Of course, other colors and other materials may be chosen to please the

FIGURE NO. 15.—WORK-BAG.

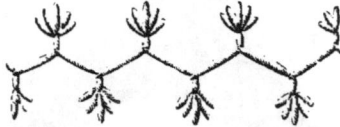

FIGURE NO. 16.

FIGURE NO. 17.

FIGURE NO. 18.

FIGURES NOS. 16, 17 AND 18.—FANCY STITCHES FOR WORK-BAG.

piece, the ribbons being crossed at the center of the bag and finished in pretty points, and the appliqué stitches being continued about the points. The top of the bag is hemmed taste; and the decoration may be as elaborate as desired, but the effect of the present combination is dainty and elegant, and will often be duplicated.

Shopping-Bag.

FIGURE NO. 14.—This stylish shopping-

mounted over a properly shaped section of pasteboard. Black velvet, sewed on flatly,

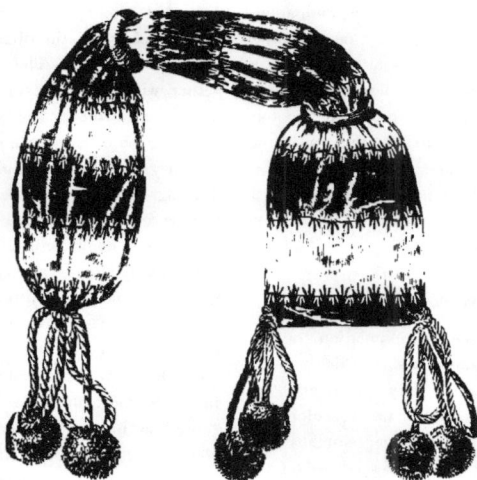

FIGURE NO. 19.—WORK-BAG.

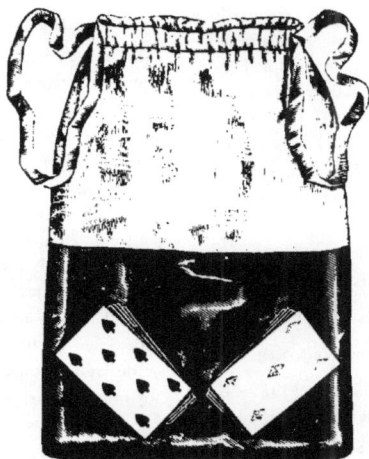

FIGURE NO. 20.—BAG FOR PLAYING-CARDS.

bag is made of pieces of plush and silk of contrasting colors, joined together and

conceals the seams of the pieces, and is embroidered in a narrow vine pattern with bright-colored silks. The monogram is deftly worked on one of the silk pieces, and appropriate embroidered designs are on the other sections. The upper portion of the bag is formed of silk of the same color as the darker plush. Drawing-strings close it at the top, and cords of twisted silk, attached near the corners, afford a handle. Scarlet and olive, dark-blue and gold, brown and orange, acajou and cardinal would be particularly pretty comminglings for such a bag.

Work-Bag.

FIGURE No. 15.—The foundation of this beautiful bag is a fancy basket, which may be oval or round and of any preferred size. Ribbons of different widths in two colors are joined by fine over-and-over stitches, and arranged so that a wide row comes on top and the narrowest width at the bottom. The narrowest ribbon is velvet; it is sewed plainly to the basket inside the edge. Along the joinings of the ribbons are made fancy stitches, which are clearly pictured at Figures Nos. 16, 17 and 18. A narrow ribbon is sewed underneath to the top row at the center to form a casing, in which draw-ribbons are inserted, the ribbon standing in a pretty frill above the casing. A Roman effect may be produced with the ribbons, as each row may be of a different color, or only two colors or two different kinds of ribbon may be used.

Fancy Stitches for Work-Bag.

FIGURES Nos. 16, 17, and 18.—These stitches are used to decorate the work-bag pictured at Figure No. 15, and may be done in different colors, several shades combining well in each. Of course the stitches will also be found useful for other articles of decoration and utility.

Work-Bag.

FIGURE No. 19.—This pretty bag is made of strips of wide satin ribbon in two strongly contrasting shades. The strips are sewed together with over-and-over stitches, and decorated at each side of the seams with feather, herring-bone or cat stitching done with flosses of pretty colors. One end is furnished with drawing cords, which are tipped with large worsted balls, so that the bag may be opened and closed conveniently. The other end is permanently closed; and each corner is decorated with prettily knotted cord, also tipped with balls. The cords may be replaced by ribbons, if desired. The rings may be of bone, horn or metal, and may be plain or fancy, to meet the taste. Purple and gold, garnet and blue or pink, dark-green and pale-blue or pink, scarlet and black, dark blue and canary, are all pretty combinations for such bags.

Bag for Playing-Cards.

FIGURE No. 20.—The engraving illustrates a pretty receptacle for playing-cards. It is formed of two strips of wide ribbon—plain and watered—joined together at their long edges and sewed to form a bag. The top is turned under for a hem in which are run ribbons to draw it together. The cards are cut from white flannel, carefully gummed on and decorated with spades or diamonds of black or scarlet flannel, also gummed on. The other lines are done in outline stitch or with a pen or brush. The ribbons may be scarlet and black or scarlet and white or of any other shades preferred.

Fancy Bag, and Stitches Used in Its Decoration.

FIGURES Nos. 21, 22 and 23.—Ribbon is so pretty for making fancy bags and its use simplifies the work of making so greatly that it is not strange it is usually selected. Ribbon in three widths was chosen for this dainty bag. The widest was used for the bag proper, and the side edges are seamed together in the usual fashion, the top being turned in and finished to form a casing in which are run narrow ribbons that draw in opposite direc-

this ribbon and the bolting-cloth are held in place by fancy stitches, which are accurately illustrated at Figures Nos. 22 and 23. Figure No. 22 shows the arrangement of the stitches upon the narrow ribbon at the top of the bolting cloth, and Figure No 23 illustrates an equally pretty variety of stitches which fol-

FIGURE NO. 21.—FANCY BAG.

FIGURE NO. 22.—FANCY STITCH.

FIGURE NO. 23.—FANCY STITCH.

tions to close the opening and form pretty loops for suspending it. The lower half of the bag below the drawing-strings is overlaid with silk bolting-cloth upon which an exquisite floral design is painted, and about the top of the bolting-cloth is arranged a narrow ribbon, which covers its upper edges. Both

low the lower and side edges. The narrower ribbons may be alike in tint and different from the wider, or they may be of two shades and the wider of a third shade in any color that presents agreeable gradations in its hue. The bolting-cloth may be omitted and the floral design painted or embroidered. Such a bag will not only prove ornamental in a beau-   duster or a piece of soft cheese-cloth, such as

FIGURE NO. 25.

FIGURE NO. 26.

FIGURE NO. 27.

FIGURE NO. 28.

FIGURES NOS. 24, 25, 26, 27, 28, 29
AND 30.—FANCY BAG, AND METHOD
OF MAKING RING DECORATION.

FIGURE NO. 29.

FIGURE NO. 30.

tifully furnished room, but it will also form a   is reserved for use upon bric-a-brac and pol-
convenient receptacle for a tiny fluffy feather-   ished surfaces.

Satin, plush, velvet, etc., may be used for the bag, but where too many raw edges have to be finished, the result is less apt to be entirely satisfactory.

Fancy Bag, and Method of Making the Ring Decoration Shown Upon It.

FIGURES NOS. 24, 25, 26, 27, 28, 29 AND 30.—The bag illustrated at Figure No. 24 is made of satin, and its construction is so simple that only the briefest explanation is necessary. The top is turned in and arranged to form a frill heading above a casing in which are run ribbons that pull in opposite directions, to draw it up to the proper size and form loops to hang it by. For about two thirds of the depth from the lower edge the bag is covered with a network of rings, covered in this instance with embroidery silk shading from deepest to palest green, the shading being done so as to bring the palest tint at the center, and to the lower rings are attached tiny tassels which form a pretty fringe for the lower edge. The method of making this network is as follows.

Fasten the silk about the ring, as represented by Figure No. 25. With a crochet hook catch the worsted, as shown by Figure No. 26; draw the worsted under the ring, and throw the silk over the needle as shown by Figure No. 27; and crochet the loop off the needle as shown by Figure No. 28. Make single crochet stitches in the same manner all round the ring, until the latter is well covered. An illustration of the ring partly covered may be seen at Figure No. 29. The ring entirely covered is shown at Figure No. 30. When the required number of rings are covered, they are sewed together to form the network decorating the bag. Care should be taken to make the crochetted stitches even and close togther. A very elegant effect may be obtained by commencing with the lightest shade of the selected color and grading the rows to the very darkest. For instance, taking the gold shades, begin with white and shade down to the deepest orange; for the red shades, begin with the lightest pink and grade down to the deepest crimson; in blue, purple, green and gray the same method of shading may be pursued. Shading from light to dark is more effective than from dark to light, but either method may be followed. If the material for covering has to be purchased, it will probably be well to know that in shading from light to dark that the second shade will need to be double the amount of the first, the third three times that of the first, the fourth four times that of the first amount, and so on. Brass rings of any preferred size may be used, but they should all be alike. Small rings may be covered with embroidery silks or flosses, but for large rings this would be a very expensive covering, so crewels, zephyrs, worsteds, Saxony yarns, chenilles or any of the thick embroidery goods may be used. For brackets or small lambrequins, the small rings are prettiest. Rings may be made of ordinary thick wire, if the rings cannot be readily purchased; but care should be taken to have them perfect in shape, otherwise they will not look well. The tassels may be made at home, but, as they are not expensive, they are generally purchased. Fringes formed of rings covered in this way are very effective, and in another chapter one forming a lambrequin is illustrated.

Window Curtains.

A ROOM in which the walls and ceiling are
very light or somewhat crude in tint, is soft-
ened and improved by dark window curtains,
but lace, Madras, scrim or muslin curtains
are usually preferred for apartments which
do not require toning down, the choice of
materials being regulated by the style and the
uses of the room and the taste of the furnisher. With any of these curtains, shades of
some agreeable tint may be used, those of
cream color being universally liked because
they harmonize with any other hue and admit
plenty of light. Cream-white lace curtains
are usually most satisfactory in all except
very expensive grades. To the latter class
the pure white tint often adds a charm not
attainable when the slightest variation from
it is visible. India silk, both plain and figured, is used for curtaining vestibules and
halls which have glass lights. All shades
of gold and écru and some shades of red are
among those usually preferred. Blue, except as a figure upon gold or écru has not
many admirers.

CHAPTER XXXIX.

Fancy and Useful Articles Suitable for Gifts to Gentlemen.

THE question what are suitable gifts for a lady to present to a gentleman, receives several pleasing answers in this chapter. All the articles illustrated are useful and ornamental, and are easily made by deft fingers moving to the music of happy thoughts.

illustrate a handy receptacle for correspondence, postage stamps, cards, etc., made of plush and satin. Figure No. 2 shows the book closed, and Figure No. 1 shows it open, with the correct arrangement of pockets. The outside is formed of a piece of plush measuring seven inches and a-quarter across

FIGURE No. 1.—GENTLEMEN'S POCKET LETTER-BOOK—OPEN.

Gentlemen's Pocket Letter-Book.

FIGURES NOS. 1 AND 2.—These engravings

the top and bottom and six inches at the ends. It is lined with satin, and to one end is joined

a piece of satin, of the depth of the end
and about three inches wide, for a pocket.
Between the ends of this pocket and the outside are inserted gore-like pieces, that are
folded in plaits to give a desirable width to
the pocket. To the opposite side is joined a
section of the same depth and about two
inches wide, that is cut out in fancy outline at

position. The outside of the book is embellished with embroidered storks done in South-
Kensington stitch. The exact size of the
design is pictured at Figure No. 3. Any
other ornamentation may take the place of
that represented, and the material may be of
any color or colors and of any variety preferred.

FIGURE No. 2.—GENTLEMEN'S POCKET
LETTER-BOOK—CLOSED.

FIGURE No. 3.—DESIGN IN SOUTH-KENSINGTON STITCH,
FOR GENTLEMEN'S POCKET LETTER-BOOK.

the top. A section, three inches wide and
five inches and a-half deep, is inserted between the outside portion and this section, to
which latter it is stitched to form two com-
partments, one for postage stamps and the
other for visiting cards, the inner pocket
being utilized for miscellaneous cards, etc.
The pockets are all finished with a row of narrow ribbon seamed to the edge and then
turned over and machine-stitched flatly to

Design in South-Kensington Stitch, for Gentle-men's Pocket Letter-Book.

FIGURE No. 3.—This design is of the exact
size suitable for embellishing the letter-book
pictured at Figures Nos. 1 and 2. The colors
may be in accordance with the plumage of the
bird, or of any variety preferred.

Cigar-Case.

FIGURES Nos. 4 AND 5.—The outside of
this case is of figured Ottoman and the inside

of plain Ottoman, and the edges are all bound with kid, machine-stitched on.

FIGURE No. 4 shows the case closed, and on it are fastened three silver initials.

decorated with fancy stitches in vari-colored embroidery silks and stitched to the case at intervals to form pockets, each large enough to hold a cigar without slipping. The outside

FIGURE No. 4.—CIGAR-CASE, CLOSED.

FIGURE No. 5.—CIGAR CASE, OPEN.

FIGURE No. 5 shows the case open and the arrangement of the pockets for the cigars. The pockets are formed of a strip of silk bound at the upper and lower edges with kid, of such cases may be of kid, leather, silk, velvet, plush, reps, etc., and the inside will usually be of silk. The binding may be ribbon, silk braid, etc., as preferred. Sometimes the pockets will be formed of a strip of strong ribbon. Of course, a monogram may be used instead of the initials, if preferred.

for holding the variety of cards just at present in fashion. With a change in the size, the case may be duplicated to correspond. It is

FIGURE NO. 6.—GENTLEMEN'S CARD-CASE, CLOSED.

FIGURE NO. 7.—GENTLEMEN'S CARD-CASE, OPEN.

Gentlemen's Card-Case.

FIGURES NOS. 6 AND 7.—These two engravings illustrate a card-case of a proper size made of kid, and is lined with satin after the designs have been embroidered upon it in South-Kensington stitch. The smaller engraving shows the case closed and with the design side uppermost. The other side may be plain or may have the initials or a monogram upon it. The larger engraving shows

Gentlemen's Shaving-Book, Embroidery and Initial.

FIGURES NOS. 8, 9 AND 10.—These engravings illustrate a shaving-book formed

FIGURE NO. 9.—SAMPLE OF EMBROIDERY.

FIGURE NO. 8.—GENTLEMEN'S SHAVING-BOOK.

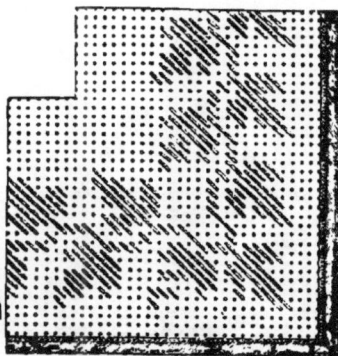

FIGURE NO. 10.—STYLE OF INITIAL.

the interior of the case. Two sections are lined, embroidered and added as illustrated to form pockets, the hollowing spaces being left so as to withdraw the cards with ease. Brown, black and drab kid, with linings of blue, red or lavender, are usually selected. The designs may be done in any preferred color.

of perforated card board, tissue paper of various colors, silk floss and gros-grain ribbon. Six or eight inches square is about the proper size for a book of this kind, and Figure No. 9 illustrates the full size of the embroidery and also shows the number and manner of making the stitches, as well as the method of turning the corner of the embroidery, and also the proportionate width of the binding. The latter, however, should not be applied till the initial represented by Figure No. 10, or any other letter desired, has been added, and the under side of the cover has been lined to conceal the wrong side of

bow, and at one corner a long ribbon is fastened under a bow, and, after its ends are tied in another bow, the loop thus formed is used to suspend the book at one side of the mirror. Other ribbons are fastened to the front edges of the book, and may be left loosely hanging, as illustrated, or tied in a

FIGURE NO. 11.—SHAVING-PAPER CASE.

FIGURE NO. 12.—DESIGN ON SHAVING-PAPER CASE.

the embroidery. After two covers have been made and bound, a number of sheets of tissue paper of mixed shades and colors are cut a trifle smaller than the covers and inserted between them ; the covers are then secured to the paper and each other, by ribbon passed through slits cut at each back corner of the paper, and tacked to the binding at the inside of the cover. Each ribbon is tied into a natty

bow to close the book. Any bright color may be selected for this book, and if preferred the embroidery may be of shaded floss, the binding and ribbons matching the darkest or the medium tint as desired. Worsted may be used instead of silk floss, and is chosen by many in preference, as it always makes the embroidery appear more massive. Plain white perforated-board is illustrated, but silver, gilt or tinted card-board makes very handsome books, when the colors are carefully selected. A quiet but charming contrast would result from the use of *café-au-lait* card-board embroidered, lined and bound with the darkest shade of the same tint, or of drab card-board with the deepest gray trimmings. Blue or cardinal-red would make very showy trimmings.

Shaving-Paper Case.

FIGURE No. 11.—Outside the paper that is

pended. Colored papers may be used if desired, but white ones are always in good taste.

Design on Shaving-Paper Case.

FIGURE No. 12.—The design on the shaving-paper case is here given, and as it is only outlined, etching or painting may be the method used.

Tobacco-Pouch.

FIGURE No. 13.—This article will be a most acceptable and graceful Christmas gift to

FIGURE No. 13.—TOBACCO-POUCH.

FIGURE No. 14.—SPRING LAP-ROBE.

to be used is a sheet of parchment-like paper upon which is written in indelible ink and large letters that which the owner is supposed to desire, "a clean shave." Above this is a smaller cover of écru silk folded over and laced down each side with an olive green cord, which is tied at the termination in loops and ends, the latter being tipped with pompons. Similar pompons are across the edge in front, and upon this portion are cleverly outlined the shaving utensils. A ribbon is drawn through the shaving paper and the eyelets of the case holding the paper, making a loop by which the pretty holder may be sus-

father or brother or to a man friend who is a lover of the weed. Four sections of chamois are comprised in the main portion of the pouch, two sections forming the sides and the other two the front and back. A cording of silk provides a decorative finish for the seams, and a bunch of narrow ribbon loops is caught to the bottom of the pouch at the center. The pouch is deepened by a straight section of silk sewed to its top, and is also lined with silk. A little above the seaming of the silk section to the pouch the lining and outside are sewed together to form a casing, in which are run ribbons that are pulled through openings made in the outside portion at the sides, to draw the pouch up closely. The pouch may be hung by the draw ribbons to the smoker's table, which it will ornament handsomely, and the initials of the recipient may be embroidered solidly or outlined on the pouch, or metal letters may be fastened on, as preferred. Three pipes, crossed and worked in outline stitch, decorate the front.

Spring Lap-Robe.

FIGURE No. 14.—This pretty lap-robe is of light-brown felt, lined with dark cardinal flannel. The two materials are of the same size and the edges are turned in and then stitched together. A short distance from the edge a band of deep cardinal felt is applied with yellow crewel, and on the border is embroidered with crewels in outline stitch a floral pattern. If desired, the initial of the owner or his favorite horse's name may be embroidered in the center of the robe. If one lacks time, the band may be applied to the robe unornamented. Many are seen done in this way, and the effect is still pleasing.

Shells of the Ocean.

IT was a happy thought that directed their use, for they were extremely delicate, some of them being transparent and of a pale golden tint, suffused with a roseate hue, while others showed a pearly lining, and were beautifully crenellated about their edges. None of them were larger than a silver quarter of a dollar, and from this size they decreased to the dimensions of one's finger nail. They had been gathered from various sources,— some from the Florida coast, a few had been picked out of the *débris* strewn by the tide upon the sands around Plymouth; others had been brought back by travellers beyond seas, and a few had been purchased because of their special beauty, and their affinity with those already in possession. They had lain a long time in a box out of sight, though not out of mind, when the occasion for utilizing them arose, because, though they might have been made up into stiff-looking counterfeits of blossoms and foliage, the owner's sense of the fitness of things rebelled against such a disposal. But when she had a little portfolio containing etchings of marine views to place where it would be accessible to inspection, she saw her opportunity and improved it. For a much smaller sum than she would have had to expend for material, had she fallen into the "marine bouquet" folly, she purchased a pretty brass easel, well made and securely mounted, though very airy looking. A piece of pale gold India silk cost but a trifle more, and this she made into a scarf and fringed it with her sea-shells, stringing them on strong silk, graduating them so that the largest shells of each strand came first, and regulating the arrangement to bring a tiny shell at the extremity. One end of the scarf was allowed to fall over a corner of the easel, the other to droop from the little stand which supported it, and on the lower shelf of the stand were placed some bits of coral and curious submarine growths. Who could fail to appreciate the harmony of the entire arrangement?

CHAPTER XL.

METHOD OF MAKING A HAMMOCK OR TENNIS-NET.

THE pleasant, not to say luxurious, feeling one enjoys while swaying to and fro in a well-made hammock swung under the "shady roof" of some friendly tree, or within some bower where "quiet reigns supreme," is one of the strongest arguments in favor of this unpretentious-looking yet most delightful medium of pleasing repose. Persons accustomed to travel, and those who seek rest and enjoyment at rural and sea-side resorts, usually carry their own hammocks with them, and find they are almost indispensable articles of comfort when tired Nature asserts herself and demands attention. The majority of hammocks purchased are very weighty, and this fault proves very often a reason for not carrying them with the travelling paraphernalia. Light ones may also be purchased; but they are, as a rule, more expensive than the general purse can afford. Light, pretty ones can, however, be made at home, with but slight expense, and we have endeavored to assist our patrons in making one of the simplest, lightest and prettiest articles of this kind.

Hammock.

FIGURE NO. 1.—This engraving illustrates the hammock under consideration, the article being small in bulk and light in weight, although it is of the dimensions required for use by persons of all sizes and weights. The cord employed in making is of the soft cotton variety, this being the best for hammocks that are to be carried about from place to place, as it is very light and also very strong. The hammock is very easy to construct; and by carefully following the succeeding directions, any person, either old or young, will, in a very short time gain a thorough knowledge of how to make a hammock.

Wedge or Mesh-Stick.

FIGURE NO. 2.—This engraving illustrates the wedge or mesh-stick to be used in forming the meshes. The wedge may be purchased in any hardware store, or in any place where fishermen's nets, etc., can be bought. It can, however, be easily made at home, where there are handy boys. Take a smooth piece of hard wood about eight or ten inches in length, an inch and a-half in width, and about three-quarters of an inch in thickness; and have it beveled or planed off toward one long edge, so that this edge will be about an eighth of an inch in thickness, leaving the heavier edge of the wedge from three-eighths to half an inch in thickness. All sharp angles should be smoothly rounded off, and then you have your wedge or mesh-stick, just as complete and suitable as if you purchased it.

Needle or Shuttle, Unwound.

FIGURE No. 3.—The needle or shuttle required in weaving the hammock is here illustrated. It is similar to that used by fishermen in making nets, and may be purchased wherever the wedge can be procured, or it may be made at home if a little ingenuity be exercised. Take a

be made as follows : Take a similar piece of wood and cut out each end in a deep curve or heel, making the curve sufficiently deep to retain the cord nicely. Wind the cord straight up and down about this, and the shuttle is ready for work.

Shuttle, Wound.

FIGURE No. 4.—The shuttle is here shown with the cord properly wound on it. In winding the cord on, hold the shuttle in the left

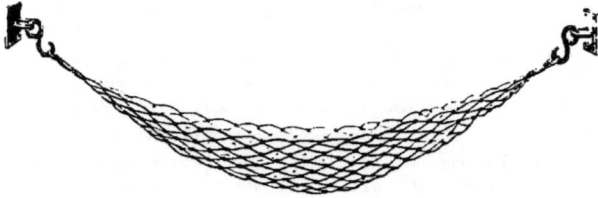

FIGURE No. 1.—HAMMOCK.

FIGURE No. 2.—WEDGE OR MESH-STICK.

FIGURE No. 3.—NEEDLE OR SHUTTLE, UNWOUND.

FIGURE No. 4.—SHUTTLE, WOUND.

smooth piece of hard wood about ten or eleven inches long, a little less than an inch wide, and only thick enough to be supple but not to break. At one end cut it out so as to form a deep curve or heel to catch the cord, and shape the other end off to a long point, thus producing a tongue or olive point. About an inch and a quarter below the point, cut away the wood about an eighth of an inch from each side of the center, for three or four inches down, to form a prong or tooth, about which the cord is to be wound. The illustration shows the shape of the shuttle clearly. A simpler shuttle, not quite so convenient, may

hand and wind the cord over and under, twisting it once about the prong at each turn. The shuttle should be held loosely and in the one position while winding, so as not to twist the cord, which should be wound on tightly so that it will not slip off during the weaving. When the shuttle is wound, then commence as follows : Tie, hang or otherwise fasten a hook to a tree, table, post, door, or any article staunch enough to resist the strength of the worker. Tie the cord around the wedge in an ordinary knot, making the knot at the top or thinnest edge of the wedge, as shown by Diagram No. 1. Slip the loop thus formed off the wedge, and throw it over the hook, placing the knot at the hook. Then take the wedge in the left hand, and hold the thickest edge *toward* you. Bring the cord from the loop on the hook *over* the wedge ; carry the shuttle the loop so that the knot at the hook will not slip away from the hook. Place the thumb close to the end of the loop, holding the cord drawn through the loop down tightly ; now throw the cord up over the loop, and pass the

DIAGRAM No. 1.

DIAGRAM No. 2.

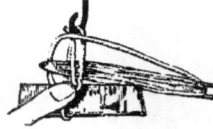

DIAGRAM No. 3.

DIAGRAM No. 4.

DIAGRAM No. 5.

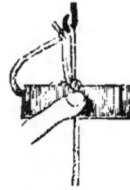

DIAGRAM No. 6.

DIAGRAM No. 7.

DIAGRAM No. 8.

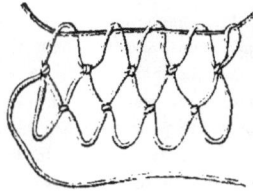

DIAGRAM No. 9.

up underneath, and pass it through the loop on the hook ; pull the cord tightly, so that the sides of the loop through which the shuttle passes will be straight and tight, and the end of the loop even with the top of the wedge, as shown by Diagram No. 2 ; holding the end of shuttle under the loop hung on the hook, taking up both threads of the loop, as shown by Diagram No. 3. Pull the shuttle through, carrying it downward and holding the thumb close to the loop, as shown by Diagram No. 4 : take hold of the cord and pull it as tightly as possible, still holding the thumb in the position directed, so that the cord will not slip. This produces the knot illustrated by Diagram No. 5. The thumb must be pressed firmly over the cord, and the cord drawn as tightly as possible, so that a slip knot will not be produced. Now slip this loop off the wedge, and carry the cord *over* the wedge, placing the top of the wedge close to the knot last formed, as shown by Diagram No. 6. Then carry the shuttle up underneath, and pass it up through the loop last removed from the wedge, as shown by Diagram No. 7; carry the shuttle downward over the wedge, also allowing the wedge to slip downward; pull the cord tightly so as to draw the loop down straight and tight, and bring it close to the top of the wedge, as shown by Diagram No. 8; then place the thumb close to the end of the loop, and press it closely over the cord, as previously directed. Then throw the cord up over the loop, pass the shuttle under the loop drawn down, taking up both sides of the loop; then carry the shuttle downward over the wedge, and pull the cord tightly to make another knot, always holding the thumb closely till the knot is made. Now slip this loop off the wedge, and continue in the same manner to make knots and loops till the required width of the hammock is obtained. In calculating the width for the hammock, it will be well to remember that the number of knots will be double the number of meshes in the width of the hammock; thus: if the hammock is to be forty-six meshes wide, which is a nice, comfortable width for a hammock to be used by large persons, make ninety-two knots in the way directed above. A child's hammock may be from twenty-five to thirty-five meshes wide; and, to obtain this width, make double the number of knots. As the chain of knots increases, the loop on the hook may be taken off and one of the loops nearer the worker thrown on, so that the worker may weave her hammock with perfect ease.

When the desired width is obtained, take off the loop on the hook and also the one on the wedge but do not break or cut the cord. Take a piece of cord about half a yard or more in length, and pass it in and out through one of either of the two rows of loops or meshes made, as shown by Diagram No. 9. Then tie the ends of the cord thus run through, together in a knot, and place this loop of cord over the hook, as shown by Diagram No. 10. Then take the shuttle and wedge in hand; pass the cord over the wedge; carry the shuttle up underneath, and pass it up through the mesh nearest the working-cord, as shown by Diagram No. 10. Carry the shuttle downward, over the wedge, pulling the cord tightly so as to draw the loop down tightly, and bring it close to the top of the wedge; throw the cord up over the loop and pass the shuttle under the loop, as shown by Diagram No. 11, holding the thumb and drawing the cord in the same way as above directed for making the meshes. Keep this loop on the wedge, and take up the next and each succeeding mesh in the same way, holding a convenient number of loops on the wedge, as shown by Diagram No. 12. This retaining of the loops or meshes on the wedge is only to secure a pretty regularity in their size, and also avoids entanglement. When a convenient number of meshes have been taken up in this way—and extreme care must be taken not to skip any—take the wedge in the right hand, and with the left take hold of the first loop or mesh to the *left* on the wedge, and pull all except the *last* loop off; continue to take up the remaining meshes in the same way till all have been taken up. Then proceed to make the next row of meshes in the same manner, and continue knotting and mesh-making till the desired length is obtained. A large-sized hammock, or one forty-six meshes wide, should be about seven or eight feet in length. As the hammock lengthens, the cord on the hook may be end of the net made, out smoothly. Take the end of the cord cut off, and tie it so as to make a long loop; throw the loop over the hook, and hold one end of the net straight across, in front of you. Pass the shuttle

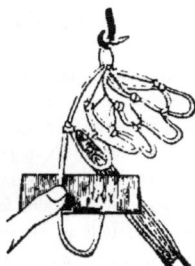

DIAGRAM NO. 10.

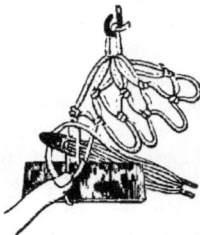

DIAGRAM NO. 11.

DIAGRAM NO. 12.

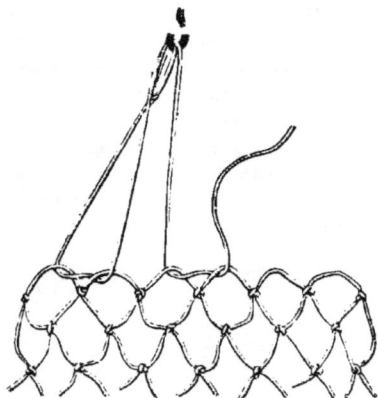

DIAGRAM NO. 13.

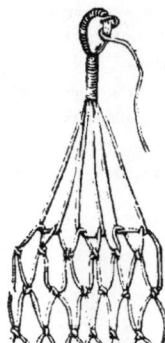

DIAGRAM NO. 14.

DIAGRAMS NOS. 1 TO 14.—METHOD OF MAKING A HAMMOCK.

taken out and run through a row of meshes nearer the weaver, so that she will not have to change her position. This cord is simply to hold the net on the hook, and should be removed when the net is completed.

When the required length for the hammock is obtained, cut the cord off, and draw each through the first mesh at the left side of this end, from underneath, and also through the next mesh in the same manner; then throw the cord over the hook and carry it down again; take up the next two meshes in the same manner and again throw the cord over the hook, as shown by Diagram No. 13; continuing in this way till all the meshes in this end are taken up, to form the guys. The length of the guys from the end of the net to the hook should be about three feet or one yard in a hammock seven feet long. Now wind the cord tightly about the guys far enough below the hook to leave a ring large enough to suspend the hammock, winding the cord closely for several inches; then lift the ring off the hook and wind the cord about it in same way, the method being illustrated by Diagram No. 14. Finish the remaining end of the net in this manner, and the hammock is then completed.

Ladies residing in or near the city can without any difficulty procure steel or iron rings for the hammock, instead of making the cord rings; which, of course, are not so durable. When metal rings are used, hang the ring to be fastened on, upon the hook, and run the guys through it instead of on the hook, and wind the cord about the guys for several inches.

Two, three or more colors may be introduced in hammocks of this style, and the result will be very pretty. Red, white and blue; cream, *écru* and brown; *écru*, red and brown; blue, yellow and red or brown, are all suitable combinations for articles of this kind. The cord may be light or heavy in weight, according to the strength required, and may be purchased by the hank or pound; the price asked for it being small, and the cost of a hammock therefore being proportionately trifling.

The same implements and the same variety of stitch are essential in making a tennis net, and such work can be taught to young men and boys with strong hands, who can make very durable nets for this fascinating game. Of course after the dimensions requisite for a tennis net are obtained, the ends are stretched instead of being drawn up as for a hammock and are provided with cords to attach them to posts.

Hammocks and tennis nets, gilded or bronzed with liquid or dry gilding or bronzing are now utilized as house decorations, and aside from their intrinsic beauty they are valued because of their associations with delightful siestas or exciting tournaments. They drape prettily and with a few sheafs of wheat, fan-palms or handsome grasses, convert a blank expanse of wall into a beauty spot.

CHAPTER XLI.

DESIGN FOR TATTING AND METHOD OF MAKING.

ATTING still retains its popularity as a decoration, sometimes entire panels of it appearing on skirts, and collars and cuffs of it on the bodies of cotton dresses. As an edging or insertion it forms a neat and desirable trimming for underwear and also for children's clothing. Pillow-shams and tidies are made of it, and when underlaid with some bright colored silk, satin, Silesia, or sateen are decidedly pretty.

Cotton or linen may be used, but the cotton is usually preferred on account of its wearing qualities. Of course there are many pretty designs but the stitch in all cases is the same.

A very neat edging is pictured at Figure No. 1 and the method of making it is here accurately described.

First insert the thread in the hole at the center of the shuttle, and tie it around the part of the shuttle in which the hole is made. Wind the thread around this part until it is filled even with the outside of the shuttle, taking care to wind it evenly, so that the thread will run easily. Figure No. 2 illustrates the position of the hand and thread. Hold the shuttle in the right hand, take the end of the thread between the thumb and forefinger of the left hand, pass the thread around the remaining fingers of this hand below the first joints; slip it between the thumb and forefinger and pass it loosely back of the fingers, again below the second joints, holding the fingers slightly apart as shown at this figure; now slip the shuttle from the front of the hand between the threads at the back of the hand, as illustrated at Figure No. 3, drawing the thread from the shuttle tightly, as shown at Figure No. 4 and allowing the *thread around the fingers* to form a loop on this thread as illustrated.

Figure No. 5 shows this loop after it has been drawn tight enough, and also illustrates the position of the thread for the next loop or the remainder of the stitch. For this loop the shuttle thread is passed in front of the fingers, and the shuttle is slipped between it and the thread at the back of the fingers as shown at Figure No. 6. The shuttle thread is then drawn tightly, the thread back of the fingers allowed to form a loop on it, and this loop together with the one already made form one stitch.

Great care must be taken to have the thread that is first passed around the hand, form the loops on the thread from the shuttle, or this thread cannot be drawn. Figure No. 7 shows a number of stitches and illustrates clearly the position the thread should be in. In order to by the maker. In the pattern illustrated at Figure No. 1, three stitches are first made, then about one-fourth of an inch allowed

FIGURE NO. 1.—TATTING EDGING.

FIGURE NO. 2.—POSITION OF THE HAND AND THREAD.

FIGURE NO. 3.—SLIPPING THE SHUTTLE.

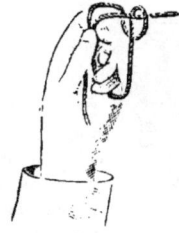

FIGURE NO. 4.—DRAWING THE THREAD.

FIGURE NO. 5.—DRAWING THE FIRST PART OF STITCH.

FIGURE NO. 6.—DRAWING THE NEXT LOOP, OR THE REMAINDER OF THE STITCH.

connect the parts loops must be formed as shown at Figure No. 8. The number of stitches between the loops must be decided between this stitch and the fourth as shown at Figure No. 8, and the stitches then drawn up close together.

Five loops of this kind are made, allowing three stitches between every two loops, and three stitches after the last loop, and then the

FIGURE NO. 7.—SHOWING A NUMBER OF STITCHES, AND ILLUSTRATING THE POSITION OF THE THREAD.

wheel is complete. Enough thread is allowed between the wheel and the next to equal the distance between two loops; and the thread is not broken but passed around the hand, as before directed. Make three stitches, draw the thread around the left hand through the nearest loop in the first wheel with a pin.

bringing the fingers on this hand close together, slip the shuttle through the loop thus formed and spread the fingers again to draw

FIGURE NO. 8.—SHOWING THE METHOD OF MAKING THE LOOPS.

the thread tight enough, taking care to have the shuttle thread run easily through the stitches. This forms the first part of a stitch, and the second part is made as shown at Figures Nos. 5 and 6; then proceed as in the first wheel.

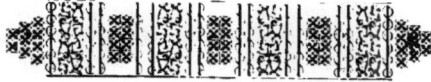

CHAPTER XLII.

DRAWN-WORK.

Drawn-Work.

IN this chapter three illustrations of drawn-work are given, two of them being somewhat elaborate in effect, while the other is extremely simple and exemplifies a method often followed for finishing the hems of handkerchiefs, pillow cases and other articles requiring an ornamental, but not elaborate completion.

Hem-Stitching.

FIGURE No. 1.—The simplest style of drawn-work is illustrated at this figure, and the method of execution is as follows: As many threads are drawn out of the article to be finished as will provide a ravelled space of the width desired for the drawn-work, the distance from the edge being calculated so as to leave whatever width is desired for a hem. The threads remaining in the frayed portions are divided by the following process into groups containing eight, ten, twelve or fourteen threads: A needle threaded with fine cotton is passed to the under side, back of the first group and brought to the upper side in *front* of this group, which is drawn tightly at its center by passing the thread over the needle, as for a button-hole stitch. The needle is passed *back* of the second group to the under side, brought to the upper side again, and the button-hole stitch repeated as before. This process is repeated until the groups have all been divided and securely fastened by the button-hole stitching. The hem is then turned, and the first stitch in it is made by bringing the needle, from underneath, through the middle of the first group and passing it through the turned-under edge. For the next stitch the needle is passed under the remaining threads in this group and brought through the hem between the groups. The third stitch is made half way of the next group, the same as the first, and so on until the hem is completed. Eight threads are as many as will usually be grouped when the article to be hem-stitched is a handkerchief, a tie, etc., and if the number be increased, as it often will be for towels, and larger articles, it must be by adding enough to always keep the number even, as nine, eleven, thirteen, etc., would not permit of dividing each group evenly along the hemmed edge.

Fancy Drawn-Work.

FIGURE No. 2.—This engraving shows a very effective, but not difficult specimen of drawn-work. When it is to be executed upon linen of medium fineness, the width illustrated may be achieved by drawing out thirty-five threads for each of the wide rows and twenty for each of the narrower ones, leaving a space equal to ten threads for each solid strip between the drawn portions. The needle is then threaded and brought from underneath through the first solid space, passed *back* of the first group of six threads in the again, and passed through *back* of the *third* cluster of six threads in the ravelled portion below the solid strip. This process forms a sort of herring-bone stitching, over and under every *second* group of *six* threads above and below the solid strip, and after one row has been worked all the way across a second row is made, beginning with the *first* group of

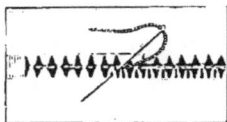

FIGURE NO. 1.—HEM-STITCHING.

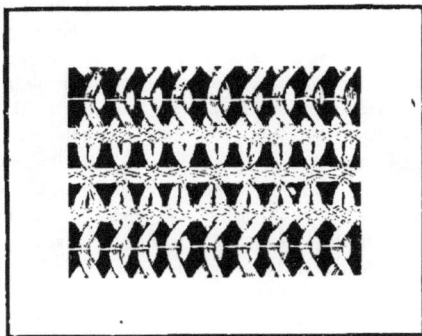

FIGURE NO. 2.—FANCY DRAWN-WORK.

ravelled portion above and brought out again in *front* of this group; it is then carried downward across the solid strip and passed back of the *second* group of six threads in the ravelled portion *below*, brought out in *front* of this group, carried upward across the solid strip and passed back of the *third* cluster of six threads in the upper row. It is then carried downward diagonally over the solid strip threads omitted above the solid strip and including *every alternating group* not taken up by the first row. The execution of the second row develops a double herring-bone effect.

Upon the second solid strip the process is repeated with a slight variation. The needle is brought up from underneath and passed *back* of the *first* group of *twelve* threads, carried diagonally downward across the solid strip, passed under the *second* group of *twelve* at the lower edge of the strip, brought out in *front* of this group and carried upward across the solid strip to the *third* group of *twelve*, passed through *back* of this group and brought out in *front* of it, the process being repeated all the way across. This omits every alternating group of *twelve* threads and these are taken up by the second row which begins with the *first* one omitted by the first row. When the double herring-bone is perfected it differs only from the double row first worked by being more open.

process is given in detail so as to be of the utmost possible help to those who are not acquainted with the detail of drawn-work; and by studying it in connection with the engraving, even a beginner will find it easier than it seems.

Drawn-Work in Block Pattern.

FIGURE No. 3.—This is the most delicate and cobwebby of the three styles of drawn-work illustrated, and extremely careful handling is requisite to its successful execution. Upon the material to be drawn squares of *fifteen* threads are first marked with tiny dots,

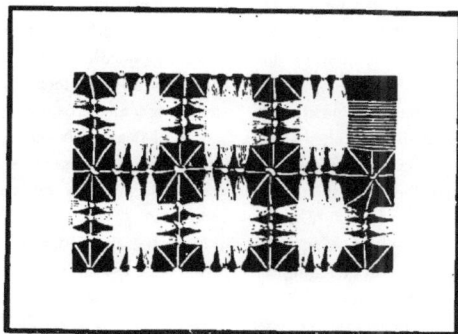

FIGURE No. 3.—DRAWN-WORK IN BLOCK PATTERN.

On the *third* solid strip the double herring-bone is worked exactly as on the *first*, and then the ravelled threads in each of the wide strips, which by the process described are divided into groups of six, are drawn over and under each other by running a needle (threaded) *under* the *first six*, bringing this group forward *under* the second, and slipping the needle and thread *between* them so as to hold them in their reversed positions at their center in the manner illustrated by the engraving.

Although the description is quite wordy the

and then every second square is cut out with sharp, short-bladed and pointed scissors. For the first row: pull out the *crosswise* threads from the *first* square, leaving the *next square* *solid* and repeat all the way across. For the second row: The first square being already cut out, leaves an opening beneath the first drawn square in the first row; from the square nearest this opening pull out the *lengthwise* threads and repeat through all the solid squares in this row: For the third row proceed as for the first. For the fourth as for the second, and so on, through whatever number of rows are desired. For the net-work or lace stitches thread a needle with fine cotton. Divide the first square from which the *crosswise* threads were drawn in beginning the work into *three* clusters of *five* threads each. Then pass the needle *under* the first cluster and bring it up between the first and the second clusters, passing the thread over the needle as for a button-hole stitch. Repeat this process for the second and third clusters and carry the thread across the open space to the next square from which the *crosswise* threads were drawn in the beginning, dividing the *lengthwise* threads in this square into clusters of five each and repeating the button-hole stitch as described for the first square. Repeat this process until all the squares from which the *crosswise* threads were first drawn have been divided and button-hole stitched. Then insert the needle at the first open space in the second row, and carry it diagonally to the opposite corner of the first solid square in the row below, securing it invisibly at this corner, and passing the needle diagonally *under* the solid square and also fastening the thread firmly at the opposite corner of this square : repeat this diagonal arrangement across all the open spaces.

Continue the net-work by inserting the needle at the *lower outer corner* of the left hand open square in the last row and carry it diagonally across this open space to the opposite corner of the solid square, fastening it securely and passing it *beneath* the solid square. Repeat this process until all the openings are crossed diagonally *upward* in the same manner as they were previously crossed diagonally *downward*.

Insert the needle at the center of the outside edge of the first open square and carry it to where the diagonal threads and also the straight thread (the one used in dividing the clusters), meet at the center of the squares, fastening all three threads together securely at their centers by a button-hole stitch. Now carry the needle to the middle of the adjacent square from which the *lengthwise* threads were drawn at the beginning, dividing them in groups of five and fastening each group with a button-hole stitch in the same way previously described, and so on until the design is completed.

From the knowledge gained in the development of these three specimens many variations in drawn-work may be thought out by anybody who is interested in this pretty process of elaborating the original warp and woof of a plain fabric.

CHAPTER XLIII.

APPLIQUÉ WORK.

PPLIQUE work is one of the most fashionable as well as fascinating varieties of fancy work, and it possesses the added advantage of being well adapted to the decoration of articles to which it is desired to give an elaborate effect with a small outlay of time and money. Of course care and attention to details are essential to a good effect in the development of any kind of needlework, and they cannot be ignored in this variety; but after a little practice the worker finds herself able to progress rapidly. Very handsome effects are obtainable by using satin, or ribbed silk for a background to felt, billiard-cloth, chamois or velvet. Felt or cloth in two shades may also be arranged to produce a very attractive result.

Cover, Decorated with Appliqué Work.

FIGURE No. 1.—This engraving illustrates a cover suitable for a table, or any piece of furniture upon which such an article is usually placed. It is made of felt in two shades, the darker shade being placed underneath so as to show beyond the edge and through the openings of the lighter shade.

The detail of the appliqué work is fully illustrated at Diagram A on page 316 ; and a simple process of reproducing the outline is as follows : The lower or extreme outer lines are traced on thin paper and then cut out and this paper serves as a pattern which may be duplicated on stiff paper or card-board and the edges of the under portion shaped by them. The second unbroken line in the diagram indicates the edge of the upper or lighter felt portion, and this, as well as the outlines which indicate the open spaces, may be traced upon thin paper, cut out and then used as patterns for shaping stiff paper or card-board to cut the felt by. The felt should be laid smoothly upon a table or board, and the outlines of the patterns marked upon them with red ink, a colored pencil or any implement which will leave a clear impression upon the fabric. With small, sharp-pointed scissors the outlines and openings are then cut, and the egg-shaped openings couched all around with filoselle. The upper and under portions of the cover are tacked together, invisibly between the curves of their outer edges and, if expedient, through the couching also. In cutting the oval corner openings the tiny space between the crossed portions must of course be delicately managed. As what appears to be two sections really consists of only one and as the shape is easily reproduced

however, to refrain from cutting more than it is probable can be finished within a short

FIGURE NO. 1.—COVER, DECORATED WITH APPLIQUE WORK.

FIGURE NO. 2.—CUSHION DECORATED WITH APPLIQUE WORK.

by the method described, not the slightest difficulty need be feared. It is a wise precaution.

time after cutting, because much handling is apt to fray or stretch the edges.

Filoselle is one of the best materials for couching. As many strands as are desired may be used and the stitches which hold them in place may be rendered invisible by proceeding in the following manner: Hold the strands in position with the left hand and with a needle threaded with silk or a strand of filoselle make a stitch through half of the strands to hold them along the edge they are to finish. Then carry the needle along the under side of the goods for a short distance before bringing it to the outside again. Pass the next stitch over the strands that were left loose by the preceding stitch, taking care to keep all the strands smooth. The next stitch should cover the same half as was held down by the first stitch, and so on, until the edge is entirely couched. Contrasting colors or graduated shades may be introduced in couching, with good effect. The openings inside the edges may also be couched, or all the edges may be finished with button-hole stitching or any kind of fancy stitching in keeping with the material selected. Of course the under portion should be cut enough larger than the upper to allow for the projection of its edges. The colors chosen for this cover are écru and seal, and the combination is very effective.

Cushion Decorated with Appliqué Work.

FIGURE No. 2.—This cushion is made of billiard-cloth and plush, the latter material consisting of pieces which are laid underneath the openings in the billiard-cloth. The exact shape and sizes of the openings are illustrated by Diagram B, on page 317. A few stitches are made along the edges of the openings to hold the plush in position and then all the edges are button-hole stitched with heavy Dargarran cotton. The diagram is one-fourth the size of the cushion, as much margin being allowable as is requisite to the dimensions

desired. The edges may be couched, if desired, and the plush under-portion may be in one piece; but as every lady who does fancy-work is apt to accumulate pieces that can be utilized for this purpose an opportunity to use them will not be overlooked. The outlines for the openings in the billiard-cloth may be marked on thin paper and then cut out as described at Figure No. 1; or they may be traced upon tracing paper, which may be perforated to permit of reproducing the outline upon the material with powder or tracing ink, according to the preference of the worker. This method of applying the smooth material upon the plush is more satisfactory and more easily developed than the opposite one of applying plush on a smooth fabric. Any materials suitable for appliqué work may be selected for a cushion of this style.

Diagrams C and D.—These two engravings show the detail of two very attractive styles of appliqué work. Both are especially pretty as borders for mantel-boards or for finishing scarfs or covers. Each design permits of either of two methods in its development. The outlines illustrated may be reproduced in whatever contrasting material is chosen for the purpose and applied upon the material proper with button-hole or couching stitch, or with any other variety or combination of stitches preferred. The outer lines represent the edges of an underlying material in each instance, and the lines next to them the edges of the outer material. The enclosed oblong spaces which come next in each and the smaller circles in Diagram C, as well as the tiny circles and the petal-shaped sections in Diagram D, may be cut out to permit the material underneath to show through; or the outlines above the lower two rows may be duplicated in contrasting material and set upon the outside. The large circles in Diagram C and the very small ones

DIAGRAM A.—SHOWING DETAIL OF COVER DECORATION.

(which are the only ones) in Diagram D may be worked in a back-stitch with floss, filoselle

When Bolton sheeting is selected for borderings, cushions or covers a beautiful effect is

DIAGRAM B.—SHOWING DETAIL OF APPLIQUÉ DESIGN FOR CUSHION.

or crewel instead of having the spaces they enclose covered with appliquéed work.

obtained by duplicating the outlines of any of the various designs given in this chapter and working over them with purlette and button-hole stitching done in the manner material may be treated upon its reverse side with a sizing of gum-arabic or white glue and

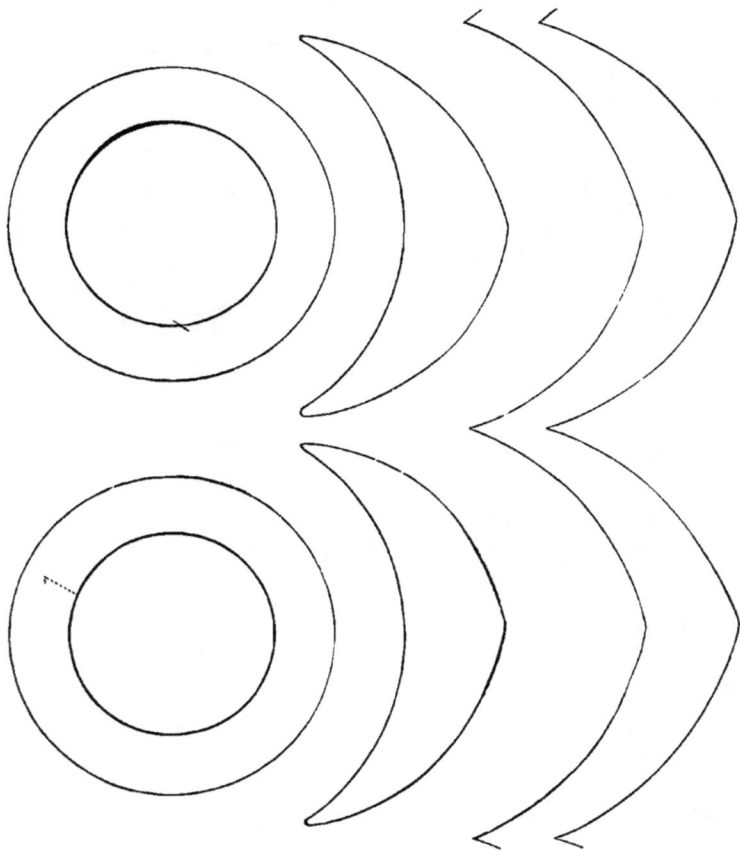

DIAGRAM C.—SHOWING DETAIL OF BORDER FOR APPLIQUÉ WORK.

described on another page of this book. When satin is used for the background the outer the satin pasted smoothly upon it to dispense with sewing.

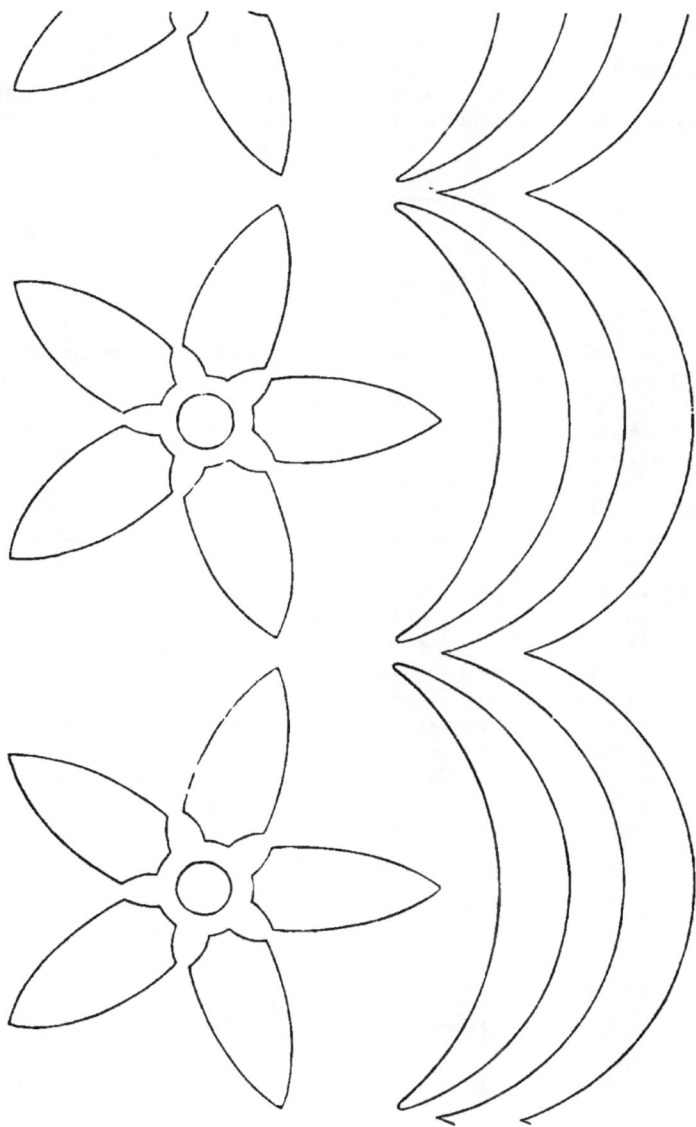

DIAGRAM D.—SHOWING DETAIL OF BORDER FOR APPLIQUÉ WORK.

A very artistic example of this class of work is a table-scarf of olivé cloth, having its ends cut out in an open pattern and underlaid with crimson satin. The latter is visible through a net-work of tinsel cord held in place with invisible stitches. The tinsel is such as is bought by the ball for a trifling sum, and the work is easily done and very attractive.

Tying the Curtains Back.

WHAT to use for tying back the curtains at doors and windows is often hard to decide, unless one be content to follow the lead of those who are satisfied to do as others do. Ribbon harmonizes with lace, but it is preferable to let lace curtains fall in unbroken lines, unless they are to remain permanently in the folds in which they are draped. If there are inner curtains of silk or any fancy fabric they may be draped back with good effect. Cord, ribbon, metal chains, strings of imitation antique coins, etc., are used for the purpose, and in addition there is a fancy for using scarfs of contrasting material. Those of thin Japanese or Chinese white cotton crape, enriched at their ends with silken and metallic embroidery, are especially admired. They tie more softly than ribbon, and their beauty is very apparent in such a disposal. A portière between two rooms may be draped with these scarfs, or with those of pongee or India silk, decorated with metallic cord or lustra painting. Where the arrangement of the hanging suggests the use of wide bands, which shall support without too closely confining its folds, wide velvet ribbon may be used with rich effect. Black is the best color, because it permits of the development of an elaborate embroidery pattern in a variety of metallic hues. The metal cord may be purchased at a slight expense, and easily sewed to position. Common ticking, in the familiar blue and white stripe, may also be utilized to make curtain straps. Of course it serves only as a foundation, the white stripe being overwrought with fancy stitches in a variety of colors, and the blue ones with tinsel cord or braid.

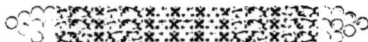

www.ingramcontent.com/pod-product-compliance
Lightning Source LLC
Chambersburg PA
CBHW031358270326
41929CB00010BA/1230